Designing the 21st Century

Design des 21. Jahrhunderts   Le design du 21ᵉ siècle

Right page/rechte Seite/page de droite:
Shin + Tomoko Azumi, **Wireframe** chair and stool/
Stuhl und Hocker/chaise et tabouret (self-production), 1998

To stay informed about upcoming TASCHEN titles, please request our
magazine at www.taschen.com or write to TASCHEN, Hohenzollernring 53,
D-50672 Cologne, Germany, Fax: +49-221-254919. We will be happy to
send you a free copy of our magazine which is filled with information about
all of our books.

Design: UNA (London) designers
Cover design: Sense/Net, Andy Disl and Birgit Reber, Cologne
Production: Ute Wachendorf, Cologne
German translation: Karin Haag, Vienna
French translation: Philippe Safavi, Paris

Printed in China
ISBN 3–8228–4802–6

Designing the 21st Century

Design des 21. Jahrhunderts Le design du 21ᵉ siècle

Edited by Charlotte and Peter Fiell

TASCHEN

Dumoffice, Whoosh lamp (prototype)/
Lampe (Prototyp)/lampe (prototype), 2000

With the unrelenting globalization of the free-market economy, so design has become a truly global phenomenon. Throughout the industrialized world, manufacturers of all types are increasingly recognizing and implementing design as an essential means of reaching new international audiences and of gaining competitive advantage. More than ever before, the products of design are shaping a worldwide material culture and impacting on the quality of our environment and daily lives. The importance of design, therefore, cannot be understated. For not only has design come to encompass an extraordinary range of functions, techniques, attitudes, ideas and values, all of them influencing our experience and perception of the world around us, but the choices we make today about the future direction of design will have a significant and possibly enduring effect on the quality of our lives and the environment in the years to come.

This book is first and foremost about the future of design. It focuses on those individuals who generally have the greatest input in the conception and planning of new products – designers. These are the creative thinkers able to identify and respond to the real needs and concerns of society, and whose decision-making can have a critical influence upon the nature and success of new products, manufacturing strategies and trends in the marketplace. What they think about the future really matters – thus *Designing the 21st Century* features the future vision statements and latest, most progressive work of 100 contemporary designers and design

Mit der fortschreitenden Globalisierung der freien Marktwirtschaft ist auch Design zu einem wahrhaft globalen Phänomen geworden. Überall in den Industriestaaten wird Design von den Produzenten sämtlicher Fertigungsbereiche zunehmend als ein wesentliches Instrument erkannt und eingesetzt, um neue, internationale Käuferschichten zu erreichen und um Wettbewerbsvorteile zu erlangen. Mehr als je zuvor prägen Designprodukte heute weltweit unsere Konsumkultur und beeinflussen die Qualität unserer Umwelt und unseres Alltagslebens. Die Bedeutung von Design darf daher nicht unterschätzt werden. Design umfasst inzwischen eine enorme Bandbreite an Funktionen, Techniken, Einstellungen, Ideen und Werten, die alle unser Erleben und unsere Wahrnehmung der Welt beeinflussen, und unsere jetzigen Entscheidungen im Bereich des Designs werden sich in den kommenden Jahren tiefgreifend auf unsere Lebensqualität und unsere Umwelt auswirken.

In diesem Buch geht es in erster Linie um die Zukunft des Designs. Dabei stehen diejenigen im Mittelpunkt, die im allgemeinen den größten Anteil an der Konzeption und Planung neuer Produkte haben – die Designer.

Als kreative Denker erkennen sie die wirklichen Bedürfnisse der Gesellschaft und gehen auf deren Anliegen ein. Ihre Entscheidungen können für Entwicklung und Erfolg neuer Produkte, Herstellungsstrategien und Markttendenzen ausschlaggebend sein. Weil es deshalb von großer Bedeutung ist, was Designer über die Zukunft denken, präsentiert *Design im 21. Jahrhundert* die Zukunftsvisionen

Avec la mondialisation acharnée de l'économie de libre marché, le design est véritablement devenu un phénomène planétaire. Partout dans le monde industrialisé, de plus en plus de fabricants de tout poil reconnaissent sa valeur. Ils s'en servent comme d'un outil primordial pour toucher un nouveau public international et se démarquer de la concurrence. Plus que jamais, les produits du design façonnent une culture matérielle à l'échelle mondiale et influent sur notre milieu ambiant et notre quotidien. L'importance du design ne doit donc pas être sous-estimée. Non seulement il concerne désormais une extraordinaire variété de fonctions, techniques, attitudes, idées et valeurs, toutes influençant notre expérience et notre perception du monde autour de nous, mais les décisions que nous prenons aujourd'hui sur la future orientation du design auront un effet significatif et sans doute durable sur la qualité de nos vies et de notre environnement dans les années à venir.

Ce livre traite avant tout de l'avenir du design. Il est centré sur ces individus qui jouent généralement le premier rôle dans la conception et la planification de nouveaux produits, à savoir les designers.

Ces penseurs et créateurs sont souvent les mieux à même d'identifier et de répondre aux vrais besoins et préoccupations de la société. Leurs choix peuvent avoir une influence déterminante sur la nature et le succès de nouveaux produits, sur les stratégies de fabrication et les tendances du marché.

La manière dont ils envisagent l'avenir est donc particulièrement pertinente.

groups, drawn from a wide range of disciplines – product design, transportation, furniture, ceramics, glassware and textiles – and many different parts of the world, from Europe to America, Australia, Brazil and Japan. Well-known figures such as Philippe Starck, Ron Arad, Ross Lovegrove and Marc Newson are joined by other, less familiar names who represent the equally important up-and-coming generation of designers. Also included are in-house designers who work for large corporations such as Apple Computer, Audi, Ford and Sony, and who often have a tremendous understanding of brand issues and the commercial imperatives of design. *Designing the 21st Century* is thereby not intended as a "chart-topping one hundred". Rather, the aim has been to bring together a highly representative cross-section of the international contemporary design community, so as

Sam Hecht, NTT Docomo phone/Telefon/téléphone for Electrotextiles, 2000

und aktuellen Arbeiten von 100 zeitgenössischen Designern und Designgruppen aus unterschiedlichsten Tätigkeitsfeldern – Produktdesign, Fahrzeugdesign, Möbel, Keramik, Glaswaren und Textilien – und verschiedensten Teilen der Erde von Europa bis Amerika, Australien, Brasilien und Japan. Berühmten Gestaltern wie Philippe Starck, Ron Arad, Ross Lovegrove und Marc Newson sind bislang noch weniger bekannte Namen zur Seite gestellt, welche die gleichermaßen bedeutende aufstrebende Generation junger Designer repräsentieren. Berücksichtigt werden darüber hinaus Designer, die bei großen Unternehmen wie Apple Computer, Audi, Ford und Sony arbeiten und häufig über außerordentliche Kenntnisse im Hinblick auf vermarktungstechnische Fragen und kommerzielle Notwendigkeiten von Design verfügen.

Design im 21. Jahrhundert ist folglich nicht als eine »Hitliste der hundert Besten« gedacht, sondern bietet einen repräsentativen Querschnitt der international aktuellen Designszene und damit eine detaillierte, aussagekräftige und zum Nachdenken anregende Sammlung von Statements zu jenen Kernfragen, die das Design und dessen mögliche Entwicklung in näherer Zukunft bestimmen werden.

Aus den Aussagen der in diesem Buch vorgestellten Designer lässt sich folgern, dass praktisch alle das Hauptziel von Design darin sehen, das Leben der Menschen zu verbessern. Es scheint ein allgemeiner Konsens darin zu bestehen, dass Designprojekte auf technische, funktionale und kulturelle Bedürfnisse reagieren und weiterhin innovative Lösungen schaffen sollten, die Sinn und Gefühl vermitteln und im Idealfall über die Grenzen ihrer jeweiligen Form, Konstruktion und Herstellungsweise hinausgehen. Abgesehen von dieser Gemeinsamkeit sind die auf den folgenden Seiten wiedergegebenen Antworten der Designer auf die Frage »Was ist Ihre Vision vom Design der Zukunft?« jedoch ausgesprochen vielfältig. Unter den vielen verschiedenen Anliegen,

Emmanuel Dietrich, Nutcracker (prototype)/ Nussknacker (Prototyp)/casse-noisettes (prototype) for Carl Mertens, 1998

C'est pourquoi *Le Design du 21e siècle* présente la vision du futur ainsi que les travaux les plus récents et innovateurs de 100 designers et groupes de design contemporains venant des horizons les plus variés – conception de produits, transport, mobilier, céramique, verrerie et textile – et travaillant aux quatre coins du monde, de l'Europe aux Etats-Unis en passant par l'Australie, le Brésil et le Japon. Aux grands maîtres du design tels que Philippe Starck, Ron Arad, Ross Lovegrove et Marc Newson se joignent des noms moins familiers qui représentent la nouvelle génération montante. Les créateurs indépendants sont associés à des designers travaillant au sein de grandes entreprises telles que Apple Computer, Audi, Ford et Sony et qui ont souvent une profonde compréhension des problèmes liés aux marques et des impératifs commerciaux du design.

Le Design du 21e siècle n'est donc pas un annuaire des « cent meilleurs » mais vise plutôt à réunir un échantillon très représentatif de la communauté internationale des designers afin d'offrir un ensemble de prévisions approfondies, pertinentes et inspirantes sur les questions clefs qui affecteront le design et sa trajectoire éventuelle dans un avenir prévisible.

to present an in-depth, relevant and thought-provoking collection of projections on the key issues that will affect design and its possible course for the foreseeable future.

Of the designers included in this survey, it can be reasonably deduced that virtually all believe the primary goal of design is to make peoples' lives better. Design practice should respond – it seems to be agreed – to technical, functional and cultural needs and go on to create innovative solutions which communicate meaning and emotion and which ideally transcend their appropriate form, structure and manufacture. Given this commonality of purpose, however, when posed the question "What is your vision for the future of design?", their responses – outlined on the following pages – are remarkably varied. Among the many different concerns, issues and predictions which are articulated, however, several recurring themes come to the fore: the potential offered by new materials; the effect of new technology (computing, communications and industrial processes); the need for simplification; emotionalism (the psychological aspects of design); and the tendency towards either individualistic or universal solutions.

The increasing availability of new synthetic materials is broadly identified as one of the key motivational forces behind the emergence of new products – a trend that is forecast to continue well into the future. The culture of continuous development within the field of material science has led to a plethora of advanced materials that challenge our preconceived notions of how plastics, metals, glass and ceramics should behave under accustomed conditions. With the recent introduction of flexible ceramics, foamed metals, conductive light-emitting plastics and shape-memory alloys, for example, the most basic properties of materials are being turned on their head.
In parallel with this, there is also a distinct trend towards the development

Problemen und Zukunftsvorstellungen, die geäußert wurden, kristallisieren sich aber mehrere Themenschwerpunkte heraus: das in neu entwickelten Materialien enthaltene Potential, die Auswirkungen neuer Technologien (Datentechnik, Kommunikationswesen und industrielle Produktionsabläufe), das Bedürfnis nach Vereinfachung, Emotionalität (die psychologischen Aspekte von Design) sowie die Tendenz zu entweder individualistischen oder universellen Lösungen.

Die zunehmende Verfügbarkeit neuer synthetischer Werkstoffe wird allgemein als eine der Hauptantriebskräfte hinter der Einführung neuer Produkte identifiziert – ein Trend, der sich voraussichtlich bis weit in die Zukunft fortsetzen wird. Die kontinuierliche Weiterentwicklung auf dem Gebiet der Werkstoffkunde hat zu einer Fülle von verbesserten Materialien geführt, die unsere Vorstellungen davon, wie sich Kunststoff, Metall, Glas und Keramik - unter üblichen Bedingungen verhalten sollten, infrage stellen. So werden beispielsweise mit der jüngsten Einführung von flexibler Keramik, Schaummetall, leitfähigen lichtemittierenden Kunststoffen und formstabilen Legierungen die grundlegendsten Materialeigenschaften auf den Kopf gestellt. Parallel dazu lässt sich außerdem ein eindeutiger Trend zur Entwicklung

Philippe Starck, TeddyBearBand toy/Kuscheltier/nounours (Catalogue GOOD GOODS–La Redoute) for Moulin Roty, 1998

On peut raisonnablement supposer que les designers inclus dans ce panorama sont pratiquement tous convaincus que l'objectif premier du design est d'améliorer la vie des gens. Sa pratique devrait d'abord répondre à des besoins techniques, fonctionnels et culturels (tout le monde semble être d'accord sur ce point). Ensuite, il devrait proposer des solutions innovantes qui communiquent un sens et une émotion et qui, idéalement, transcendent leurs formes, leur structure et leur mode de fabrication. Toutefois, en dépit de cet objectif commun, lorsqu'on pose la question « Quelle est votre vision de l'avenir du design », les réponses – brièvement synthétisées plus loin – sont remarquablement variées. Parmi les nombreuses préoccupations, questions et prédictions avancées, on observe néanmoins plusieurs thèmes récurrents : le potentiel offert par les nouveaux matériaux; l'effet des nouvelles technologies (l'informatisation, les outils de communication et les procédés industriels) ; le besoin de simplification ; l'émotivité (les aspects psychologiques du design) ; et l'opposition entre les solutions tendant vers l'individualisme ou l'universalité.

La disponibilité croissante de nouvelles matières synthétiques est généralement interprétée comme l'une des principales forces de motivation derrière l'émergence de nouveaux produits, une tendance dont on prévoit qu'elle perdurera. La culture du développement perpétuel au sein du domaine de la science matérielle a donné le jour à une myriade de matériaux très sophistiqués qui remettent en question nos idées préconçues sur la manière dont les matières plastiques, les métaux et les céramiques devraient se comporter dans des conditions habituelles. Avec l'introduction récente des céramiques flexibles, des mousses métalliques, des plastiques conducteurs et émetteurs de lumière ou des alliages capables de mémoriser des formes, entre autres, les propriétés les plus élémentaires des

and application of lightweight yet high tensile strength materials – from carbon-fibre to "floating" concrete – which are predicted to lead to either more expressive or essentialist forms. Synthetic polymers, which are increasingly able to mimic the properties of natural materials while also often possessing remarkable tactile qualities, have been shown in particular to be radically altering the formal potential of new products. Many of the designers included in this book are pioneering remarkable applications for materials such as these, as the product designs illustrated here demonstrate. But while most designers predict that the integration of highly technological materials and processes will widen and become more accessible, others have voiced concern that synthetics can sometimes be difficult to work with and are not always developed for their capacity to wear well.

New technologies – computers, communications and industrial processes – have in the last five years assisted enormously in the research and implementation of design, and are widely predicted to lead to increasingly miniaturized, multifunctional and better-performing products. More sophisticated CAD/CAM (computer-aided design/computer-aided manufacture) systems, RP (rapid prototyping) and aligned processes such as 3D stereolithography have considerably expedited the manufacture of smaller runs of products which are tailored more to meet individual needs. At the same time, these types of technologies are helping to streamline the design process from initial concept to working prototype.

Today, computer-generated designs can be sent via ISDN lines directly to RP facilities and to manufacturers at the touch of a button. By ultimately accelerating the design process, these technologies are not only reducing front-end costs for manufacturers but are also providing designers with greater freedom for experimentation. CAD/CAM and its related technologies have already had a profound effect on product develop-

und Anwendung leichtgewichtiger und dennoch hoch-elastischer Materialien ausmachen – von Kohlenstoff-Fasern (C-Fasern) bis zu »schwimmendem« Beton –, was in Zukunft entweder zu expressiveren oder essentielleren Formen führen wird. Insbesondere synthetische Polymerstoffe, die in immer stärkerem Maß die Eigenschaften natürlicher Materialien nachahmen können und häufig auch beachtliche taktile Qualitäten besitzen, haben das Potential neuer Produkte radikal verändert. Wie die in diesem Buch gezeigten Beispiele für Produktdesign verdeutlichen, haben viele der vorgestellten Designer bahnbrechende Arbeit in der Anwendung solcher Materialien geleistet. Aber während die meisten Designer prognostizieren, dass sich die Einbeziehung hochtechnischer Materialien und Fertigungsprozesse ausweiten und leichter zugänglicher werden wird, äußern andere ihre Bedenken, dass synthetische Stoffe schwierig in der Verarbeitung sein können und nicht immer im Hinblick auf bessere Nutzbarkeit entwickelt werden.

In den letzten fünf Jahren haben neue Technologien auf den Gebieten Computertechnik, Kommunikationswesen und Produktionsprozesse die Entwicklung und Umsetzung von Design enorm gefördert, was laut Aussage vieler Gestalter zu einer wachsenden Zahl miniaturisierter, multifunktionaler und leistungsstarker Produkte führen wird. Ausgefeilte CAD/CAM-Systeme (computergestütztes Design/computergestützte Fertigung), RP (Rapid Prototyping) und damit zusammenhängende Prozesse wie etwa die 3D-Stereo-Lithographie haben die Herstellung kleinerer Mengen von Produkten begünstigt, die stärker auf individuelle Bedürfnisse zugeschnitten sind. Gleichzeitig tragen diese Technologien dazu bei, den gesamten Gestaltungsprozess von der Konzeption bis zur Ausarbeitung von Prototypen zu rationalisieren.

Heutzutage können computergenerierte Entwürfe per Knopfdruck über ISDN-Verbindungen an RP-Einrichtungen und Hersteller geschickt werden. Durch den

matériaux ont été complètement chamboulées.

Parallèlement, on observe une tendance distincte vers le développement et l'application de matériaux ultralégers mais néanmoins très résistants et extensibles – des fibres de carbone au béton « flottant » – qui, selon les prévisions, devraient conduire à des formes plus expressives ou essentialistes. Les polymères synthétiques, qui sont de plus en plus capables d'imiter les propriétés des matières naturelles tout en possédant souvent également de remarquables propriétés tactiles, ont démontré qu'ils pouvaient modifier radicalement le potentiel formel de nouveaux produits. Un grand nombre de designers présentés dans ce livre ont mis au point de remarquables applications pour ce genre de matériaux. Mais, si la plupart d'entre eux prédisent, que l'intégration de matériaux et de processus de pointe se répanda et ils deviendront plus accessibles, d'autres s'inquiètent du fait que les matières synthétiques soient parfois difficiles à travailler et pas toujours développées pour résister à l'épreuve du temps.

Au cours des cinq dernières années, les nouvelles technologies – les ordinateurs, les outils de communication et les procédés industriels – ont énormément aidé la recherche et la mise en application du design. La plupart s'accordent à dire qu'elles mènent vers des produits de plus en plus miniaturisés, polyvalents et performants. La sophistication croissante des systèmes de CAD/CAM (Design et fabrication assistés par ordinateur) et de PR (Prototypage rapide) et de procédés apparentés tels que la lithographie stéréo en 3D a considérablement facilité la fabrication de gammes plus petites de produits conçus pour satisfaire des besoins individuels. Parallèlement, ces types de technologie contribuent à affiner le processus du design, du concept initial au prototype de travail.

Aujourd'hui, d'un simple clic, des projets entièrement réalisés sur ordinateur peuvent être envoyés par les lignes ISDN

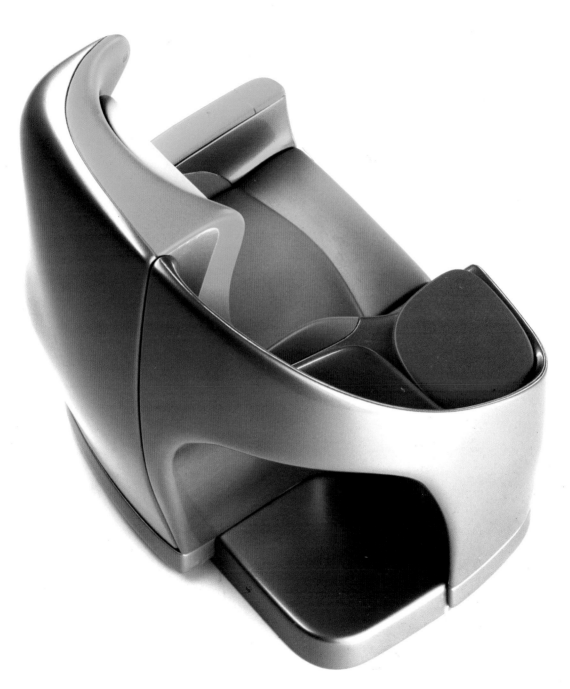

Ross Lovegrove, First class seating/Flugzeugsitz/
siège d'avion for Japan Airlines, 2000

ment, offering the designer the scope and flexibility to evolve exceptionally complex forms and to modify and customize products. Given the increasing potential for spawning a multiplicity of product variations, however, many of the featured designers agree with Jonathan Ive when he states that "our real challenge is to make relevant and extend technological capability."

Within the last five years, the Internet too has had a remarkable impact on the design process and has triggered, according to Lunar Design, "the move from mass production to mass customization". The freedom and ease of such communication technologies have also led to an ever-increasing transfer of design ideas and the cross-pollination of disciplines. This tendency towards integration is a result, too, of the increasing miniaturization of technology, which will undoubtedly continue unabated for the foreseeable future. Nano-technology has already led to the development of atomic-level mechanical components and will certainly play a significant role in the design of multi-functional "smart" products in the near to medium-term future. As the 21st century progresses, information technologies are widely expected to be incorporated into the design of products to such an extent that they will eventually be regarded as just another type of material – akin to glass or plastics – with which to develop innovative and better-performing solutions. Countering this vision of a brave new world of all-pervasive advanced technology, however, a few designers, such as Pia Wallén, are promoting the use of low-tech processes that not only have a minimal impact on the natural environment, but also reject the insatiable demand for ever more product variety and volume.

In response to the current and predicted technological complexity of the 21st century, simplification has clearly become a key objective in design. Many of the designers included here concur strongly with the words of Alberto

beschleunigten Gestaltungsprozess stellen solche Technologien nicht nur eine Kostenersparnis für die Hersteller dar, sondern sie verhelfen auch den Designern zu einer größeren Freiheit beim Experimentieren. CAD/CAM und deren verwandte Technologien haben die Produktentwicklung bereits stark beeinflusst, indem sie den Designern den Spielraum und die Flexibilität bieten, um außergewöhnlich komplexe Formen zu entwickeln und Produkte an den speziellen Kundenbedarf anzupassen. Angesichts des stetig wachsenden Potentials für eine Vielzahl von Produktvariationen stimmen jedoch viele der hier vorgestellten Designer Jonathan Ives These zu, dass »unsere wahre Herausforderung darin liegt, die technologischen Kapazitäten leichter anwendbar und zugänglich zu machen«.

Auch das Internet hatte während der letzten fünf Jahre deutliche Auswirkungen auf den Gestaltungsprozess und war, wie Lunar Design feststellt, der Auslöser für »den Aufbruch von der Massenproduktion zur Anpassung an Kundenwünsche«. Die Freiheit und Leichtigkeit in der Anwendung dieser Kommunikationstechniken haben außerdem einen stetig wachsenden Transfer von Designideen und eine gegenseitige Befruchtung unterschiedlicher Disziplinen mit sich gebracht. Diese Tendenz zur Integration ist auch ein Resultat der zunehmenden Miniaturisierung von Technologie, welche in absehbarerer Zukunft unvermindert anhalten wird. Die Nano-Technologie hat bereits zur Entwicklung mechanischer Bauteile in atomarer Größenordnung geführt und wird in naher bis mittlerer Zukunft mit Sicherheit eine bedeutende Rolle bei der Gestaltung multifunktionaler »intelligenter« Produkte spielen. Es wird erwartet, dass die Informationstechnologien in einem solchen Maß in die Produktgestaltung mit einbezogen werden, dass sie schließlich nur noch als ein weiterer Werkstoff betrachtet werden – so wie Glas oder Kunststoff –, mit dem sich innovative und funktional bessere Lösungen entwickeln lassen.

aux centres de PR et aux fabricants. En accélérant ces différentes étapes, ces technologies réduisent les frais initiaux des fabricants mais offrent également aux designers une plus grande liberté pour expérimenter. Les CAD/CAM et leurs technologies apparentées ont déjà profondément changé le développement des produits, apportant aux créateurs la portée et la souplesse nécessaires pour élaborer des formes d'une complexité exceptionnelle, ainsi que pour modifier et personnaliser leurs produits. Cependant, compte tenu du nombre croissant de possibilités pour générer une multitude de variantes d'un même produit, un grand nombre des designers présentés dans ce livre conviennent avec Jonathan Ive que « leur vraie mission est d'étendre les capacités technologiques et de les rendre pertinentes ».

Au cours des cinq dernières années, Internet a également eu un impact considérable sur le processus du design et a déclenché, selon Lunar Design, « la transition de la " production de masse " au " sur mesure de masse " ». La liberté et la facilité d'utilisation de ces technologies de la communication ont également entraîné un transfert toujours plus important d'idées de design et la pollinisation croisée des disciplines. Cette tendance à l'intégration est également le résultat de la miniaturisation croissante de la technologie, qui se poursuivra certainement à un rythme soutenu dans les années à venir. Les nano-technologies ont déjà entraîné le développement de composants mécaniques à l'échelle atomique et joueront certainement un rôle crucial dans le design de produits « intelligents » et polyvalents dans un futur proche et à moyen terme. Beaucoup s'attendent à ce que, au fil du 21e siècle, les technologies de l'information soient incorporées dans le design des produits au point qu'elles finiront par être considérées comme un matériau comme un autre – à l'instar du verre ou du plastique – avec lequel élaborer des solutions plus innovatrices. Néanmoins, prenant à contre-pied cette vision idéalisée d'une haute technologie

Meda: "Technology must be tamed in order to realize things that have the simplest possible relation with man – we must reject technologically driven industrial goods that have no regard for human needs and no communicative rationality." There can be little doubt that the future onus on designers will be to devise products that can be easily understood and used in an intuitive way. Similarly, the simplification of structural form – essentialism – will not only provide the means by which designers can gain the most from the least, but will also assist in the realization of forms that possess an inherent emotional purity. Simplification in design will thus both reduce the white noise of contemporary living and provide one of the best ways of enhancing the quality of products and, thereby, their durability.

The psychological aspects of design are also extensively addressed and given prominence as never before. There is a general consensus that products need to go beyond considerations of form and function if they are to become "objects of desire" in an increasingly competitive marketplace. To achieve this, products must make pleasurable

Im Gegensatz zu dieser Vision einer schönen neuen Welt, in der hochentwickelte Technologie allgegenwärtig ist, plädieren einige wenige Designer, wie etwa Pia Wallén, für den Einsatz von Low-tech-Verfahren, die nicht nur sehr viel weniger schädlich für die Umwelt sind, sondern die sich auch dem unersättlichen Verlangen nach immer größeren Produktmengen und -varianten widersetzen.

In Reaktion auf die bestehende und die prognostizierte technologische Komplexität des 21. Jahrhunderts ist Vereinfachung eindeutig zu einem der Hauptziele im Design geworden. Viele der hier vorgestellten Designer stimmen mit den Worten von Alberto Meda überein: »Die Technik muss gezähmt werden, damit man Objekte realisieren kann, die eine möglichst einfache Beziehung zum Menschen haben. Abzulehnen sind rein technisch orientierte Industrieerzeugnisse, die keine Rücksicht auf menschliche Bedürfnisse nehmen und keiner kommunikativen Logik folgen.« Deshalb liegt die zukünftige Verpflichtung für Designer darin, Produkte zu entwerfen, die leicht verständlich sind und auf intuitive Weise verwendet werden können. Gleichermaßen wird eine Vereinfachung der Konstruktionsform – Essentialismus – sich nicht nur als Instrument für Designer anbieten, um aus einem Minimum ein Maximum herausholen zu können, sondern sie wird auch zur Realisierung von Formen verhelfen, die eine emotionale Reinheit besitzen. Folglich wird sich Einfachheit im Design bereichernd und stabilisierend auf unser modernes Alltagsleben auswirken und einer der besten Wege sein, um die Qualität von Produkten und dadurch deren Lebensdauer zu verbessern.

Auch die psychologischen Aspekte des Designs werden ausführlich angesprochen, wobei ihre Bedeutung stärker in der Vordergrund gerückt wird als je zuvor. Wie übereinstimmend festgestellt wird, müssen Produkte über die Erwägungen von Form und Funktion hinausgehen, wenn sie in der zunehmend

omnipräsente, quelques designers tels que Pia Wallén défendent l'utilisation de processus plus naturels qui, outre le fait de ne pas nuire à l'environnement, rejettent la demande insatiable pour des produits toujours plus variés et nombreux.

En réaction à la complexité technologique actuelle et annoncée pour le 21e siècle, la simplification est clairement devenue un objectif clef du design. Un grand nombre de designers présents dans cet ouvrage conviennent avec Alberto Meda quand il dit : « La technologie doit être apprivoisée afin de réaliser des objets qui aient avec l'homme la relation la plus simple possible. Nous devons rejeter les produits industriels qui ne prennent pas en compte les besoins humains, qui n'ont aucune rationalité communicative ». Il ne fait aucun doute que les créateurs auront à l'avenir l'obligation de concevoir des produits faciles à comprendre et utilisables de manière intuitive. De même, la simplification de la forme structurelle – l'essentialisme – fournira les moyens par lesquels les designers obtiendront le plus par le moins, mais favorisera également la réalisation de formes pourvues d'une pureté émotionnelle inhérente. La simplification du design réduira donc à la fois le brouhaha du monde contemporain tout en fournissant l'un des meilleurs moyens de mettre en valeur la qualité des produits et, donc, leur durabilité.

Les aspects psychologiques du design sont également très souvent mentionnés et on leur accorde une importance plus grande que jamais. Le consensus général veut que, pour devenir des « objets de désir » sur un marché de plus en plus compétitif, les produits aient besoin d'aller au-delà des considérations sur la forme et la fonction. Pour atteindre cet objectif, ils doivent établir avec leurs utilisateurs des liens émotionnels associés au plaisir par la joie qu'ils auront à les manipuler ou la beauté de leur forme. L'émotivité est considérée par un grand nombre de

emotional connections with their end-users through the joy of their use and/or the beauty of their form. Emotionalism is considered by many of the designers included here not only as a powerful and essential way of facilitating better and more meaningful connections between products and their users, but as an effective means of differentiating their solutions from those of their competitors. To this end, many designers, such as Ross Lovegrove, promote the use of soft, sensual, organic forms in an effort to provide their products with an emotionally seductive appeal. The innate tactility of such forms is deeply persuasive, even at a subconscious level. Cognitive of the fact that the emotional content of a design can determine its ultimate success, the general view among the majority of participating designers is that it is now as important to fulfil the consumer's desire for tools for loving as that for tools for living.

Of all the themes to emerge from the vision statements gathered here, the tendency towards either individualistic or universal solutions potentially holds the farthest-reaching consequences for the future direction of design. While some designers promote individualism in design as a channel for personal creative expression or to cater to consumer demand for individualistic products, others advocate universal solutions, which are generally more environmentally sound and whose emphasis upon greater functional and aesthetic durability offers better value for money. Individualism in design can be regarded as a reaction against the uniformity of mass production and, ultimately, the increasing homogenization of global culture. But with the objective of providing more expressive content, individualistic design solutions can often lead to higher costs and accelerated stylistic obsolescence. Given this, it is not surprising that, as an approach to design, individualism has hitherto generally remained in the realms of one-off and batch-manufactured products, rather than making

schärfer werdenden Marktkonkurrenz zu einem »Objekt der Begierde« werden sollen. Aus diesem Grund sollten Produkte durch die Freude bei ihrem Gebrauch und/oder die Schönheit ihrer Form eine positive emotionale Verbindung zu ihren Benutzern herstellen. Emotionalität wird von vielen der hier zu Wort kommenden Designer nicht nur als ein wirksames und wichtiges Instrument angesehen, um Produkte und deren Käufer stärker aneinander zu binden, sondern sie betrachten Emotionalität auch als ein erfolgreiches Mittel, um ihre eigenen Entwürfe von denen ihrer Konkurrenten abzuheben. Zu diesem Zweck propagieren etliche Designer, wie etwa Ross Lovegrove, den Einsatz weicher, sinnlicher, organischer Formen mit dem Ziel, ihren Produkten eine emotional verführerische Ausstrahlung zu verleihen. Formen, die in solchem Maße zum Berühren einladen, wirken unbewusst zutiefst überzeugend. Da der emotionale Gehalt eines Designs letztendlich für dessen Erfolg ausschlaggebend sein kann, verfolgt die Mehrzahl der beteiligten Designer die Absicht, die emotionalen und funktionalen Bedürfnisse der Konsumenten zu erfüllen.

Zwei entgegengesetzte Trends werden an den hier zusammengetragenen Zukunftsvisionen deutlich: Während einige Designer gestalterischen Individualismus propagieren, sei es, um darüber den persönlich-kreativen Ausdruck zu transportieren, oder um das Verlangen der Konsumenten nach individualistischen Produkten zu bedienen, empfehlen andere universelle Lösungen, die im allgemeinen ökologisch verträglicher sind und funktional sowie ästhetisch einen höheren Gebrauchswert bieten. Die Individualisierungstendenzen im Design lassen sich als Reaktion auf die Uniformität der Massenproduktion und auf die wachsende Homogenisierung der globalen Kultur verstehen. Individuelle, eigenwillige Designlösungen führen jedoch oftmals zu höheren Produktionskosten und veralten (stilistisch) schneller. Insofern blieb ein individuelleres Gestaltungsprinzip bislang hauptsächlich

designers comme un outil puissant et essentiel pour faciliter des relations meilleures et plus significatives entre les produits et leurs utilisateurs, mais également un moyen efficace de différencier leurs solutions de celle de leurs concurrents. A cette fin, de nombreux créateurs, tels que Ross Lovegrove, défendent le recours à des formes douces, sensuelles et organiques afin de donner aux produits un attrait séduisant et émouvant. Le caractère tactile inné de ces formes est profondément convaincant, même à un niveau subconscient. Sachant que le contenu émotionnel d'un design peut déterminer sa réussite sur le marché, la majorité des designers présentés dans cet ouvrage considèrent qu'il est désormais aussi important de satisfaire le désir du consommateur d'outils à aimer que d'outils pour vivre.

De tous les thèmes qui émergent des visions du futur exprimées dans ce livre, la tendance vers des solutions tantôt individualistes tantôt universelles est celle qui pourrait avoir les conséquences les plus considérables sur l'orientation future du design. Si certains défendent l'individualisme comme vecteur de la créativité personnelle ou pour satisfaire la demande du consommateur pour des produits individualistes, d'autres prônent la recherche de solutions universelles, qui sont généralement plus écologiquement saines et dont l'accent sur une durabilité fonctionnelle et esthétique plus grande permet une meilleure rentabilité.
En design, l'individualisme peut être considéré comme une réaction contre l'uniformité de la production de masse et, au bout du compte, de l'homogénéisation croissante de la culture planétaire. Mais, en cherchant à apporter un contenu plus expressif, les solutions individualistes se traduisent souvent par des coûts plus élevés et une obsolescence stylistique accélérée. Il n'est donc pas étonnant que, en tant que démarche de design, l'individualisme soit jusqu'à présent resté cantonné au domaine de l'exemplaire unique et des produits fabriqués par lots, et qu'il n'ait

serious in-roads into large-scale industrial production. Although the individualism versus universality debate has raged since the earliest beginnings of Modern design practice, a fundamental paradox remains: while the nature of universal design solutions can sometimes be alienating, individualistic design solutions often remain the preserve of the wealthy élite. As has been discussed, however, new technologies are becoming widely available that would appear to be offering the means by which these two camps can be finally reconciled. The future of design may thus lie in the creation of universal solutions that can be efficiently adapted to meet individualistic needs.

The deliberation among the included designers on the appropriateness of individualistic versus universal solutions may well account for the relative absence of hypotheses on a unifying theory or new moral-philosophic basis of design. While many discuss the desirability of catering to the perceived need for greater individualism in design, for example, few comment on the future sustainability of such an approach, with its implications for increased waste

auf solche Produkte beschränkt, die in Einzelfertigung oder in kleinen Mengen produziert wurden, in der industriellen Großproduktion spielte es dagegen keine Rolle. Obwohl die Debatte um Individualismus kontra Universalität seit den frühen Anfängen des modernen Designs anhält, bleibt es bei einem grundlegenden Widerspruch: Während die Wirklichkeit universeller Designkonzepte manchmal entfremdend sein kann, bleiben individualistische Designlösungen häufig einer wohlhabenden Elite vorbehalten. Mit der beschriebenen Verbreitung neuer Technologien scheint sich aber eine Möglichkeit anzudeuten, die beiden Lager endlich miteinander zu versöhnen. Die Zukunft des Designs könnte deshalb in der Gestaltung universeller Lösungen liegen, die in ihrer Anwendung individuellen Bedürfnissen angepasst sind.

Ob sie eher individualistische oder universelle Lösungskonzepte bevorzugen, darüber äußern sich die beteiligten Designer sehr zurückhaltend, ebenso bleiben Aussagen über eine einheitliche Theorie oder eine neue moralisch-philosophische Basis für Design weitgehend aus. Während es viele von ihnen zwar

pas encore fait d'incursions sérieuses dans le secteur de la production industrielle à grande échelle. Bien que le débat entre individualisme et universalisme fasse rage depuis les début du design moderniste, un paradoxe fondamental demeure: si la nature des solutions de design universel peuvent parfois être aliénantes, les solutions de design individualiste restent souvent l'apanage d'une élite fortunée. Néanmoins, comme on l'a vu plus haut, les nouvelles technologies devenant de plus en plus accessibles, elles offriront peut-être le moyen de réconcilier enfin ces deux camps. L'avenir du design réside donc peut-être dans la création de solutions universelles qui puissent être adaptées avec efficacité pour répondre à des besoins individualistes.
Le débat des designers sur l'à-propos de l'opposition entre solutions individualistes et universalistes explique peut-être l'absence relative d'hypothèses sur une théorie unificatrice ou sur une nouvelle base philosophique et morale du design. Si beaucoup discutent de l'attrait qu'il pourrait y avoir à satisfaire le besoin d'un plus grand individualisme en design, par exemple, peu commentent la viabilité future d'une

J Mays, **24.7 PickUp** concept vehicle/Konzept-Fahrzeug/
concept de véhicule for Ford Motor Company, 2000

production. Some designers, however, take an holistic view of current and longer-term concerns, and are in accord with Stephen Peart when he states: "By creating something, you are personally approving its existence and directing the fate of many resources."
Certainly, there is a growing need for designers to view themselves as stakeholders in their product solutions and to develop them within an understanding of the environmental impact of every aspect of their manufacture, use and eventual disposal – from cradle to grave. But there is also a pressing requirement to connect consumers in more meaningful ways with technologically increasingly complicated products. To this end, it would seem that a more considered human-centric approach to

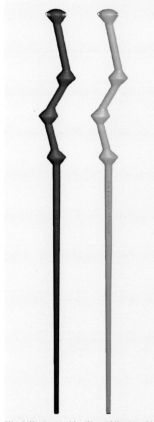

Björn Dahlström, **Joystick** walking stick/Spazierstock/
canne for Magis, 2000

für wünschenswert halten, das von den Konsumenten wahrgenommene Bedürfnis nach einem größeren Maß an Individualität zu befriedigen, äußern sich nur wenige über die zukünftigen Auswirkungen eines solchen Ansatzes und die damit verbundene wachsende Abfallproduktion. Allerdings betrachten einige Designer diese aktuellen und längerfristigen Fragen aus einer ganzheitlichen Perspektive. So äußert sich Stephen Peart zum Beispiel: »Indem wir etwas herstellen, billigen wir persönlich dessen Existenz und beeinflussen das Schicksal zahlreicher Ressourcen.«
Es lässt sich eindeutig feststellen, dass es für Designer eine wachsende Notwendigkeit gibt, sich als die Verantwortlichen für ihre Produktentwicklungen zu sehen. Das bedeutet, dass sie von Anfang bis Ende des gestalterischen Prozesses die Umwelteinflüsse zu jedem Aspekt der Produktion, Anwendung und schließlich Entsorgung ihrer Produkte mitbedenken müssen. Gleichzeitig aber ist es notwendig, die Konsumenten auf sinnvollere Weise mit technisch immer komplexer werdenden Produkten zusammenzubringen. Deshalb scheint ein Ansatz, der den Menschen noch bewusster als das Zentrum von Design auffasst, die beste Methode zu bieten, um gleichermaßen funktionale wie psychologische Bedürfnisse zu befriedigen.

Designer spielen eine entscheidende Rolle im Hinblick auf die Erwartungen und das Kaufverhalten der Konsumenten. Infolgedessen stellt sich ihnen immer wieder die Aufgabe, neue Wege im Bereich des Designs und der Produktentwicklung zu beschreiten, und zwar Wege, die zu dauerhaften Lösungen führen und nachhaltig den Anforderungen des Alltags entsprechen.
Indem sich Designer moderne Materialien und neue Technologien zunutze machen und Lösungen finden, die für Konsumenten verständlich und emotional leicht zugänglich sind, schaffen sie jene ethischen und sinnvollen Produkte, die zukünftig in hohem Maße benötigt werden. Da die Qualität der Kultur und des Lebens von unseren Handlungen und Ent-

telle approche, avec ses implications quant à l'augmentation de la production de déchets. Toutefois, certains créateurs adoptent une vision holistique des préoccupations actuelles ou à plus long termes, approuvent Stephen Peart quand il déclare : « En créant quelque chose, on approuve son existence et on influe sur le sort de nombreuses ressources ».
En effet, les designers éprouvent un besoin croissant de se sentir impliqués dans leurs solutions de produits et de les développer en connaissant à l'avance l'impact écologique de tous les aspects de leur fabrication, de leur utilisation et, enfin, de leur élimination, autrement dit du berceau à la tombe. Mais il est également urgent de rapprocher de manière plus sensée les consommateurs des produits qui reposent sur une technologie de plus en plus complexe. A cette fin, il semblerait qu'une démarche réfléchie et davantage centrée sur l'homme offrirait le meilleur moyen de satisfaire à la fois des besoins fonctionnels et psychologiques.

Les créateurs jouant clairement un rôle déterminant dans le choix de la nature des produits manufacturés, il ne fait aucun doute qu'ils peuvent exercer une influence exceptionnelle sur les attentes et les habitudes d'achat des consommateurs. Par conséquent, il leur incombe moralement d'élaborer une nouvelle et meilleure orientation pour le design, une qui soit centrée sur le développement de solutions humanistes, viables et basées sur de vrais besoins.
En exploitant les matériaux et les technologies de pointe identifiés ici tout en s'efforçant d'apporter des solutions de design simplifiées avec des liens émotionnels plus aisés pour le consommateur, ils devraient être capables de créer les types de produits éthiques et pertinents dont nous aurons besoin à l'avenir. La qualité de notre culture matérielle planétaire de demain sera déterminée par les actes et les choix que nous faisons aujourd'hui. Il est donc juste que chaque individu – créateur, fabricant, consommateur – reconnaisse

design would provide the best means of satisfying both functional and psychological needs.

As designers clearly play a key role in determining the nature of manufactured products, there is little doubt that they can have an exceptional influence on the expectations and buying habits of consumers. There is consequently a growing moral imperative for them to chart a new and better direction in design, namely one which focuses on the development of real-need based, humanistic and sustainable solutions. By harnessing the advanced materials and technologies identified here while striving to provide simplified design solutions with an easier emotional connection for the consumer, designers should be able to create the types of ethical and relevant products that are needed for the future. The quality of our global material culture is being determined by the actions and choices we take now, and so it must be right that every individual – creator, maker and consumer – should acknowledge the need for a responsibility-based culture and should share in the collective goal of forging a better tomorrow.

CHARLOTTE AND PETER FIELL

Editors' note: We would like to express our immense gratitude to all those designers and design groups who have contributed to the successful realization of this unique project.

scheidungen geprägt wird, sollte jede und jeder Einzelne – sei es als Gestalter, Hersteller oder Konsument – die Notwendigkeit einer auf Verantwortlichkeit beruhenden Gesellschaft anerkennen und zu dem kollektiven Ziel beitragen, ein besseres Morgen zu gestalten.

CHARLOTTE UND PETER FIELL

Anmerkung der Herausgeber: Wir möchten uns ganz besonders bei allen in diesem Buch vorgestellten Designern und Designergruppen bedanken, die zum erfolgreichen Abschluss dieses Projektes beigetragen haben.

Sydney 612, LightBox lamp/Lampe/lampe (self-production), 2000, design: Tonka Andjelkovic and Tina Gounios

le besoin d'une culture basée sur la responsabilité et participe à l'objectif collectif de forger un avenir meilleur.

CHARLOTTE ET PETER FIELL

Note des auteurs: Nous aimerions exprimer notre immense gratitude à tous les designers et groupes de design qui ont contribué à la réalisation de ce projet exceptionnel.

büro für form., Liquid Light
lamps/Lampen/lampes (self-production), 2000

"Exciting, visionary and innovative
design has always been the product
of new materials and technology."

Werner Aisslinger

Werner Aisslinger, Studio Aisslinger, Oranienplatz 4, 10 999 Berlin, Germany
T +49 30 31 505 400 F +49 30 31 505 401 aisslinger@snafu.de www.aisslinger.de

*»Aufregendes, visionäres und innovatives
Design war immer schon das Produkt
neuer Materialien und Technologien.«*

« Le design innovateur, excitant et
visionnaire a toujours été amené par de
nouvelles technologies et matières. »

1. **Plus Unit** trolley/Rollwagen/chariot for Magis, 2000
2. ↓ **Juli** chair/Stuhl/chaise for Cappellini, 1998-2000

« Au début du 21ᵉ siècle, le design surmontera le minimalisme branché de la décennie précédente dont la nouveauté résidait essentiellement dans les formes. Nous reviendrons aux paramètres qui ont toujours constitué la base des nouvelles époques et dimensions : une utilisation sophistiquée des technologies et des matériaux nouveaux. Les créations visionnaires et avant-gardistes qui ont marqué leur temps ont toujours reposé sur la transformation de matériaux et de technologies replacés dans un nouveau contexte. Aujourd'hui, des progrès technologiques fulgurants ont entraîné l'apparition de fibres de verre, de gels, de mousse d'aluminium, de textiles et de Néoprène tridimensionnels avec lesquels on peut créer des produits radicalement différents. Sur le plan esthétique, leurs lignes seront utilitaires, organiques, réduites, douces, épurées, modulaires et nomades. Les produits du futur associeront des aspects pratiques à des fonctions intégrées. Au bout du compte, le contact quotidien avec ces produits dépassera toutes considération technique et fonctionnelle, si bien que les designers devront être plus réceptifs que jamais au dialogue entre les émotions et la technologie. Le système de distribution sera lui aussi radicalement modifié, chaque objet étant équipé d'une petite puce qui permettra de le commander directement. Dans ce scénario futuriste, la pureté du design sera un facteur primordial de décision pour les consommateurs du commerce électronique. »
WERNER AISSLINGER

3. ← **Juli** chairs/Stühle/chaises for Cappellini, 1998-2000 (permanent collection MoMA, New York, and Vitra Design Museum, Weil am Rhein)
4. **Linn** tables/Tische for Jonas & Jonas, 2000

"Design at the beginning of the 21st century will overcome the stylish minimalism of the last decade, with its innovation based purely on shape. Instead, there will be a return to parameters that have always been the basis of new epochs and dimensions in design: the sophisticated use of new materials and technologies. Historically, exciting, visionary and pioneering designs have always rested on the transformation of materials and technology into a new context. Today's lightning-speed technological advancements have led to the appearance of three-dimensional fibreglass, gels, aluminium foam, three-dimensional textiles and neoprenes from which entirely new products can be created. Aesthetically, the design of these future products will be utilitarian, organic, reduced, soft, puristic, poetic, modular and nomadic.
The products of the future will combine functional aspects with certain built-in event facilities. Eventually the act of experiencing products will become more important than functional or technical considerations and designers will have to be ever more sensitive to the dialogue between emotions and technology.
The distribution of products will also alter radically, with every object possessing a small chip that will allow you to order it directly. In this kind of future scenario, pure design quality will be a major decision factor for e-commerce consumers." WERNER AISSLINGER

»Design am Beginn des 21. Jahrhunderts wird den modischen Minimalismus der letzten Dekade mit seinen ausschließlich auf Form basierenden Innovationen überwinden. Stattdessen wird es eine Rückkehr zu Parametern geben, welche immer schon die Basis neuer Epochen und Dimensionen im Design waren: die intelligente Nutzung neuer Materialien und Technologien. Historisch gesehen beruhte aufregendes, visionäres und bahnbrechendes Design stets auf der Übertragung von Werkstoffen und Technologien in einen neuen Kontext. Der rasante technische Fortschritt von heute hat zur Erfindung von Glasfasern, Gels, Aluminiumschaum, von dreidimensionalen Textilien und Neopren geführt – Materialien, aus denen vollkommen neue Produkte kreiert werden können. In ästhetischer Hinsicht wird das Design dieser zukünftigen Produkte utilitaristisch, organisch, reduziert, weich, puristisch, poetisch, modulierbar und nomadisch sein. Die Produkte der Zukunft werden praktische Aspekte mit integrierten situationsspezifischen Funktionen verbinden. Letztendlich wird der Erlebnischarakter der Produkte wichtiger sein als funktionale oder technische Überlegungen, und die Designer müssen stets sensibel sein für den Dialog zwischen Emotionen und Technologie. Auch der Vertrieb der Produkte wird sich radikal verändern, wobei jedes Objekt einen kleinen Chip enthalten wird, der dem Käufer ermöglicht, es direkt zu bestellen. In dieser Art von Zukunftsszenario wird die makellose Qualität des Designs zu einem wichtigen Entscheidungsfaktor für die Konsumenten im elektronischen Handel.«
WERNER AISSLINGER

8

9

10

5.-6. **Soft** chaises longues/Liegen for Zanotta, 2000
7. **Soft Cell** chair and stool/Stuhl und Hocker/chaise et tabouret (studio project – limited edition), 2000
8. **Cell-System** shelf/Regal/bibliothèque for Zeritalia, 2000
9. **Endless Plastic** shelves/Regale/bibliothèque for Porro, 1997-98 (permanent collection Die Neue Sammlung, Munich)
10. **Endless Plastic** panel/Wandpaneel/panneau for Porro, 1997-98

WERNER AISSLINGER		CLIENTS

BORN	1964	Nördlingen, Germany
STUDIED	1986	History of Art and Communication Sciences at Munich University
	1987-91	diploma in design at Hochschule der Künste, Berlin
PRACTICE	1989-92	design offices of Jasper Morrison, Ron Arad, London and Michele de Lucchi, Milan
	1993	founded Aisslinger Corporate Design
	1993-	teacher at Hochschule der Künste, Berlin and the Lahti Design Institute, Finland
	1998-	professor of product design, Hochschule für Gestaltung, Karlsruhe
AWARDS	1992	Design Plus Award, Frankfurt/Main
	1994	Wogg Design Award, Zurich; Design Selection Award, Design Zentrum Nordrhein-Westfalen, Essen
	1995	Compasso d'Oro selection, Milan
	1996	Bundespreis Produktdesign, Frankfurt/Main
	2000	Design Selection Award, Design Zentrum Nordrhein-Westfalen, Essen
EXHIBITIONS	1994	Design Innovationen, Design Zentrum Nordrhein-Westfalen, Essen
	1995	*Die Kunst und das schöne Ding*, Neues Museum Weserburg, Bremen; Compasso d'Oro exhibition, Milan
	1996	Bundespreis Produktdesign, Frankfurt/Main
	1998	Design Yearbook collection, Museum für Angewandte Kunst, Cologne; BIO 16 Biennial of Industrial Design, Ljubliana; *bewußt, einfach*, Vitra Design Museum, Weil am Rhein
	1999	*Identity Crisis – The 90s Defined*, The Lighthouse, Glasgow
	2000	*soft cell-down light*, Galerie Fiedler, Cologne; *vetro*, Museo Correr, Venice

CLIENTS

Arflex
Bertelsmann
Cappellini
DaimlerChrysler
E-Plus
Interlübke
Lufthansa
Magis
Porro
Rolf Benz
Stilwerk
Zanotta
Zeritalia
ZDF

11

12

13

14

11. **Plateau-System** trolley/Rollwagen/chariot (studio project), 1997
12. **Juli** table/Tisch for Cappellini, 2000
13. **Global Board** cupboard & shelf system/Schrank & Regalsystem/bibliothèque avec placard (studio project – limited edition), 1997
14. ↑ **Linn** table/Tisch for Jonas & Jonas, 2000

"Boredom is the mother of creativity."

Ron Arad

Ron Arad, Ron Arad Associates, 62, Chalk Farm Road, London NW1 8AN, England
T +44 20 7284 4963 F +44 20 7379 0499 info@ronarad.com www.ronarad.com

»Langeweile ist die Mutter der Kreativität.«

« L'ennui engendre la créativité. »

1. **RTW** shelves/Regale/bibliothèque
by Ron Arad Associates, 1996
2. ↓ **BOOP** coffee table/Couchtisch/table basse by
Ron Arad Associates for Gallery Mourmans, 1998

« Lors d'un communiqué de presse légèrement ironique pour " Non fabriqué à la main, non fabriqué en Chine ", une exposition d'objets réalisés par stéréo-lithographie et découpage sélectif au laser (Milan 2000), j'ai déclaré que, jusqu'à récemment, il n'y avait eu que quatre moyens de faire les choses. Tout processus de fabrication peut être décomposé en une ou plusieurs des étapes suivantes : ELIMINER (tailler, graver, tourner, moudre, buriner – soit enlever la matière en excès) ; MOULER (mouler par injection, par rotation, couler dans un moule, extruder – soit verser un matériau liquide qui, en durcissant, prend la forme de son contenant) ; MODELER (courber, presser, marteler, plier, façonner sous vide – soit donner une forme à une feuille de matériau) ; ASSEMBLER (visser, coller, riveter, clouer, souder, soit joindre des parties par un moyen ou un autre). Puis j'ajoutai qu'il existait désormais un quatrième moyen : DEVELOPPER, un objet peut croître dans un bac, couche après couche, à l'aide de rayons laser contrôlés par ordinateur.

Tout ceci peut encore être réduit : un objet peut-être fabriqué PAR ADDITION ou SOUS-TRACTION. Les ordinateurs, avec leur ZEROS et leurs UNS, adorent ça. Avec le CNC (Contrôle numérique informatisé), le RP (Prototypage rapide), les matériaux GM et un petit ↓

3. ← **Tom-vac** stacking chairs/Stapelstühle/chaises encastrables for Vitra, 1997
4. **Bouncing** vase/Vase, **Not made by Hand, Not made in China** series by/Serie von/séries de Ron Arad Associates for Gallery Mourmans, 2000

"In a slightly tongue-in-cheek press release for 'Not Made By Hand, Not Made in China', an exhibition of objects made by stereolithography and selective laser sintering (Milan 2000), I claimed that until recently there had been only four ways of making things. The process of making any object could be broken down into one or more of the following steps: WASTE (chip, carve, turn, mill, chisel – i. e. removal of excess material), MOULD (injection moulding, casting, rotation moulding, extruding etc. – i. e. pouring liquid material to take the form of its vessel when hardened); FORM (bending, pressing, hammering, folding, vacuum forming etc. – i. e. forcing sheet material into a shape), ASSEMBLE (bolting, gluing, riveting, soldering, welding etc. – i. e. joining parts together by any means), and, I went on to claim, there is now a fifth way – GROW, an object can be grown in a tank, layer by layer, by computer controlled laser beams. Now I think all this can be reduced further – an object can be made by either ADDING or SUBTRACTING. Computers, with their ZEROS & ONES, love it. With CNC (Computer Numeric Control), RP (Rapid Prototyping), GM materials, and a little help from robotic friends, virtual can easily become actual; an image on screen rapidly transforms to a ↓

»In einer leicht ironischen Pressemitteilung für ›Not Made By Hand, Not Made in China‹, eine Ausstellung von Objekten, die durch Stereolithographie und selektive Laser-Sinterung hergestellt wurden (Mailand 2000), habe ich behauptet, dass es bis vor kurzem nur vier Arten gegeben habe, Dinge anzufertigen. Jeder Produktionsprozess lasse sich nämlich einem oder mehreren der folgenden Verarbeitungsschritte zuordnen: ENTFERNEN (abraspeln, schnitzen, drehen, fräsen, meißeln – d. h. Entfernen von überflüssigem Material), MODELLIEREN (Spritzgießen, in Formen gießen, Rotationsschmelzen, Strangpressen etc. – d. h. flüssiges Material in eine Form gießen), FORMEN (biegen, pressen, hämmern, falten, Vakuumformen – d. h. einer Materialplatte eine Form geben), ZUSAMMENSETZEN (schrauben, kleben, nieten, löten, falzen – d. h. einzelne Teile zusammenfügen). Dann fuhr ich fort, dass es nun eine fünfte Art gebe: ZÜCHTEN – d. h. man kann ein Objekt Schicht um Schicht durch computergesteuerte Laserstrahlen in einem Tank wachsen lassen.

Inzwischen glaube ich, dass man das Ganze noch weiter reduzieren kann: Objekte lassen sich entweder durch HINZUFÜGEN oder ENTFERNEN produzieren. Computer mit ihren NULLEN & EINSEN lieben das. Mittels CNC (Computer Numeric Control), RP (Rapid Prototyping), GM-Materialien und ein wenig Hilfe von unseren Roboter-Freunden kann das Virtuelle leicht zum Reellen werden. Ein Bild auf ↓

		RON ARAD	CLIENTS
BORN	1951	Tel Aviv, Israel	Alessi
STUDIED	1971-73	Academy of Art, Jerusalem	Allia
	1974-79	Architectural Association, London	Artemide
PRACTICE	1981	co-founded One Off Ltd., London with Caroline Thorman	Bigelli Marmi
	1989	co-founded Ron Arad Associates with Caroline Thorman	Draenert
	1994	established Ron Arad Studio, Como (production facility)	Driade
	1994-97	Professor of Product Design, Hochschule für angewandte Kunst, Vienna	Fiam
	1997	Professor of Furniture Design, Royal College of Art, London	Hidden
	1998	Professor of Industrial Design and Furniture, Royal College of Art, London	Kartell
	1999-	Professor of Product Design, Royal College of Art, London	Lippert Wilkins
AWARDS	1994	Designer of the Year, Salon du Meuble, Paris	Martell
	1999	Design Plus Award, Frankfurt/Main; Internationaler Designpreis Baden-Württemberg, Design Center Stuttgart	Moroso
			Noto
	2001	co-winner of Perrier-Jouët Selfridges Design Prize, London	Poltronova
EXHIBITIONS	1986	*Intellectual Interiors*, Tokyo (with Philippe Starck, Rei Kawakubo, Shiro Kuramata)	Vitra
	1987	*Nouvelles Tendances*, Centre Georges Pompidou, Paris	also self-production
	1990	*Ron Arad Recent Works*, Museum of Art, Tel Aviv	
	1990-95	*Sticks and Stones*, touring exhibition, Vitra Design Museum, Weil am Rhein	
	1993	*One Off and Short Runs*, Centre for Contemporary Arts (Warsaw, Krakow, Prague)	
	1994	*L'Esprit du Nomade*, Fondation Cartier, Paris	
	1995	*Ron Arad and Ingo Maurer*, Triennale, Milan; *The Work of Ron Arad*, Museum of Applied Arts, Helsinki	
	1999	*Not Made by Hand, Not Made in China*, Milan	
	2000	*Before and After Now*, Victoria & Albert Museum, London	

coup de main de la part de nos amis de la robotique, le virtuel peut facilement devenir réel : une image sur un écran peut rapidement se transformer en une masse solide. Tout peut être dessiné, modelé et fabriqué. (Qui sont ces gens qui créent les logiciels capables de satisfaire nos moindres caprices ? Comment ont-ils pu prévoir, depuis leur vallée, qu'un designer de Chalk Farm (à Londres) voudrait construire, par exemple, une balle en spirale au diamètre toujours changeant, la faire rebondir, enregistrer avec précision ses distorsions en une série de modèles puis les développer en objets solides dans un réservoir de résine époxy ?) Il n'y a virtuellement plus de limites. Les matières intelligentes, les outils de pointe, une production digne de la science-fiction, tout est déjà là. Aujourd'hui. Le présent est trop fascinant pour s'appesantir trop longuement sur le futur. En examinant attentivement le présent, on peut y lire l'avenir. » RON ARAD

5. **BOOP** small vases/kleine Vasen/petits vases by Ron Arad Associates for Gallery Mourmans, 1998
6.–8. **Ge-Off Sphere** lamp/Lampe/lampe, **Not Made by Hand, Not Made in China** series by/Serie von/séries de Ron Arad Associates for Gallery Mourmans, 2000

solid mass. Anything can be drawn, modelled and made. (Who are those people who write the software to cater for any eventual possible obscure whim we might come up with? How could they anticipate, from their valley, that some designer in Chalk Farm (London) would want to build, say, a spiral ball with an ever-changing section, to bounce it, accurately record the distortions in a series of virtual models and then grow them as solid objects in a tank of epoxy resin?). There are virtually no limits. Smart materials, sharp tools, sci-fi production, it's all here. Now. The present is too fascinating to stop and worry too much about the future. If you look at the present deeply enough, the future will become discernible." RON ARAD

dem Monitor lässt sich dann rasch in eine feste Masse transformieren. Alles Erdenkliche kann gezeichnet, modelliert und angefertigt werden. (Wer sind eigentlich diese Leute, die eine Software entwickeln, mit der sich jeder obskure Einfall, der uns vielleicht mal durch den Kopf geht, verwirklichen lässt? Wie können sie von Silicon Valley aus vorhersehen, dass irgendein Designer in Chalk Farm, London, beispielsweise einen spiralförmigen Ball mit einem flexiblen Teil basteln möchte, der die Verformungen, die entstehen, wenn man den Ball aufspringen lässt, in einer Serie virtueller Modelle genauestens festhält und diese dann als feste Objekte in einem mit Epoxidharz gefüllten Tank entwickelt?) Es gibt praktisch keine Grenzen mehr. Intelligente Materialien und Werkzeuge, Produktionsmethoden wie aus der Sciencefiction-Welt – es ist alles da. Jetzt. Die Gegenwart ist viel zu faszinierend, um innezuhalten und sich allzu viele Gedanken über die Zukunft zu machen. Wenn man die Gegenwart aufmerksam genug betrachtet, wird darin die Zukunft erkennbar.« RON ARAD

9. **Victoria & Albert** armchair/Sessel/fauteuil for Moroso, 2000
10. ↓ **Victoria & Albert** chaise longue/Liege for Moroso, 2000

11. **Victoria & Albert** chairs/Stühle/
chaises for Moroso, 2000
12. ↓ **Victoria & Albert** sofa/Sofa for Moroso, 2000

"Simplicity and surprise, materiality and immateriality, from object to space."

Shin + Tomoko Azumi

Shin + Tomoko Azumi, Unit 7, Haybridge House, 15 Mount Pleasant Hill, London E5 9NB, England
T +44 20 8880 0031 F +44 20 8880 0697 mail@azumi.co.uk www.azumi.co.uk

»Schlichtheit und Verblüffung, Materia-
lität und Immaterialität, vom Objekt zum
Raum.«

« Simplicité et surprise, matérialité et
immatérialité, de l'objet à l'espace ».

1. **Big Arm** armchair/Sessel/fauteuil for Brühl & Sippold, 2000
2. **Wireframe** chair and stool/Stuhl und Hocker/chaise et tabouret (self-production), 1998

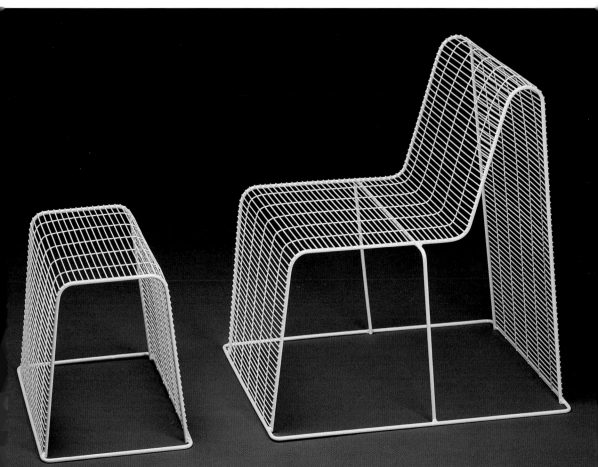

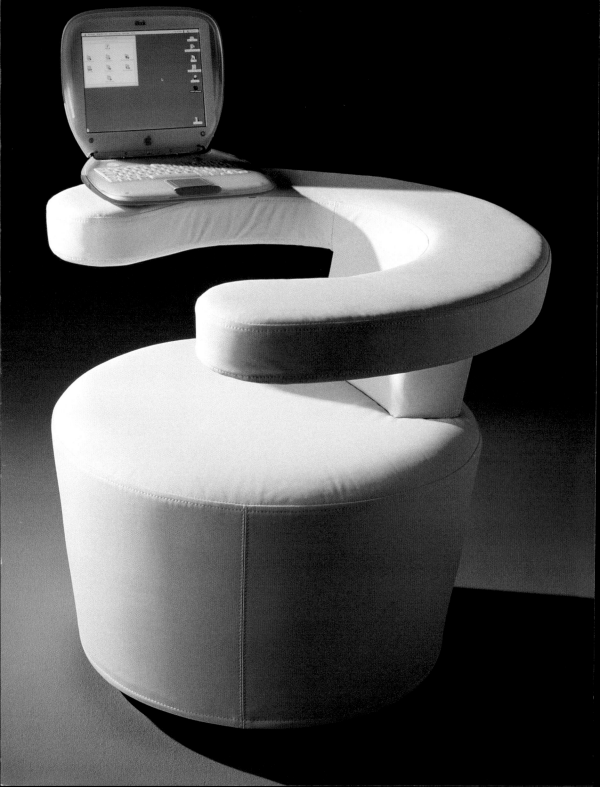

"In the future we hope that design will help us achieve a 'better life' rather than just 'better sales'. Between the 80's and early 90's, design became a tool for commercial marketing. That was not altogether a bad thing, but now we think it should be used to create a desirable environment and that greater emphasis should be placed on 'individuality' in the future. People will have more choice as quick communication and fast transportation make a wider range of designs from across the world accessible to them. In that situation, personal attachment will become a more important factor in design. Finally, for us, the future of design is an extended horizon of where we are and what we feel at the moment. It is not an entity in itself." SHIN + TOMOKO AZUMI

»Für die Zukunft erhoffen wir uns ein Design, das uns zu einem ›besseren Leben‹ statt bloß zu ›besseren Umsätzen‹ verhelfen wird. Das Design wurde während der achtziger und frühen neunziger Jahre zu einem Marketinginstrument. Das war nicht durchwegs schlecht, wir finden jedoch, dass Design nun dazu dienen sollte, eine erstrebenswerte Umwelt zu gestalten. Außerdem sollte in Zukunft mehr Nachdruck auf ›Individualität‹ gelegt werden. Die Menschen werden mehr Wahlmöglichkeiten haben, da ihnen durch schnellere Kommunikations- und Transportmittel eine größere Bandbreite an Designprodukten aus der ganzen Welt zugänglich gemacht wird. In diesem Zusammenhang wird der persönliche Bezug zu einem wichtigen Faktor für die Gestaltung von Design. Und schließlich sehen wir das Design der Zukunft als einen erweiterten Horizont dessen, was wir im Moment sind und fühlen. Es ist keine feste Größe an sich.«
SHIN + TOMOKO AZUMI

4

« Pour l'avenir, nous souhaitons un design au service d'une " meilleure vie " plutôt que de " meilleures ventes ". Des années 80 au début des années 90, il a servi d'outil de marketing. Ce n'était pas forcément un mal, mais nous préférerions qu'il serve à créer un environnement désirable et que l'accent soit mis davantage sur les besoins " individuels ". Les moyens de communication et les transports devenant toujours plus rapides et accessibles, l'offre de produits provenant des quatre coins du monde ne cessera de s'élargir. Dans ce contexte, le goût et les affinités de chacun deviendront un facteur important de la création. Enfin, l'avenir du design dépend de l'horizon élargi de ce que nous sommes et de ce que nous ressentons dans l'instant. Il n'existe pas en lui-même. » SHIN + TOMOKO AZUMI

3. ← **Big Arm** armchair/Sessel/fauteuil for Brühl & Sippold, 2000
4. **Snowman** salt and pepper shakers/Salz- und Pfefferstreuer/salière et poivrière for Authentics, 1999
5. **Upright** salt and pepper shakers/Salz- und Pfefferstreuer/salière et poivrière by Azumi, 1998

5

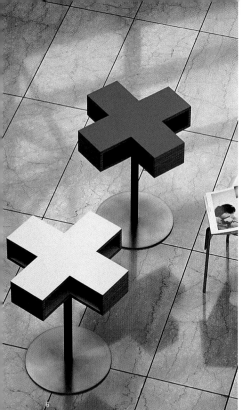

6. **Cross** tables/Tische for Trunk/Sumitomo Bakelite, 1999
7.-9. **Table=Chest**/Tisch=Truhe/table = coffre (self-production), 1995
10. **Keen Stand**/Ausstellungsstand/présentoir at *100% Design* exhibition, London 2000 (with animation by Yuko Hirosawa)
11. **Music Tube**/Musik-Röhre/tube musical at Resitr, Kobe 2000 (in collaboration with Noriyuki Ohtsuka)
12. **Stacking Chair**/Stapelstuhl/chaise encastrable by Azumi for Kettle's Yard Gallery, 1998
13.-14. **H3** speaker/Lautsprecher/haut-parleur and **HB-1** sub woofer/unterer Basstonlautsprecher/amplificateur de graves for TOA, 2000

9

12

13

14

SHIN + TOMOKO AZUMI

FOUNDED	1995	Azumi Design Studio, London by Shin (b. 1965 Kobe, Japan) and Tomoko Azumi (b. 1966 Hiroshima, Japan)
STUDIED		SHIN AZUMI
	1989	BA Product Design, Kyoto City University of Art, Japan
	1994	MA Industrial Design, Royal College of Art, London
		TOMOKO AZUMI
	1989	BA Environmental Design, Kyoto City University of Art, Japan
	1995	MA Furniture Design, Royal College of Art, London
PRACTICE		SHIN AZUMI
	1989-92	NEC Design Centre Co., Tokyo (Personal Computer Dept)
		TOMOKO AZUMI
	1989-90	Kazuhiro Ishii Architect & Associates, Japan
	1990-92	Toda Construction Corporation, Japan (Design Office)
AWARDS		SHIN AZUMI
	1989	Grand Prize, Seki Cutlery Design Competition, Japan
	1991	G-Mark/Good Design Award, JIDPO, Tokyo
	1992	G-Mark/Good Design Award, JIDPO, Tokyo
		TOMOKO AZUMI
	1989	Misawa Student Housing Design Award, Japan
	1993	ABSA/Arthur Andersen Trophy Design Award, London
	1995	FX-HNB Furniture Award, New Designers Exhibition, London
		JOINT
	1998 & 99	finalist *Blueprint*/100% Design Award, London; Peugeot Design Award, London
	2000	Product of the Year Award, FX International Interior Design Awards, London
EXHIBITIONS	1996	*Design of the Times – 100 Years of the Royal College of Art*, London
	1997	*Flexible Furniture*, Crafts Council, London
	1998	*Objects of Our Time*, American Craft Museum, New York
	1999	*Lost and Found*, Museum für Kunsthandwerk, Frankfurt/Main
	2000	room installation *Misty Lounge* in *Tectonic*, Crafts Council, London
	2001	*Home Sweet Home*, Kulturhuset, Stockholm

CLIENTS

Authentics
Brühl & Sippold
E&Y
Guzzini
Habitat
Hitch Mylis
Lapalma
TOA
Wire Works
also self-production

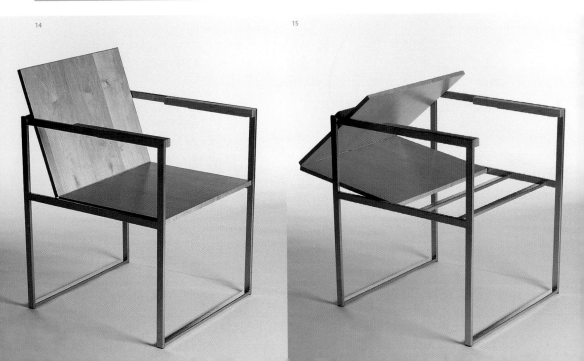

14.-16. **Armchair=Table**/Sessel=Tisch/fauteuil = table (self-production), 1998
17.-18. **Overture & Cabinet with Screens**/Overture & Kabinettschrank mit Wandschirmtüren/ouverture & cabinet avec paravent for Lapalma, 1998
19. **LEM** high stool/Barhocker/tabouret de bar for Lapalma, 2000

SHIN + TOMOKO AZUMI · 47

"We like to design friendl
obtrusive products, which
might always have been
place them."

Bartoli Design

Bartoli Design, Via Grigna 2, 20052 Monza, (MI), Italy
T +39 039 387 225 F +39 039 386 698 pbartoli@iname.com

»Wir gestalten gern freundliche, unauf-
dringliche Produkte, die den Eindruck
erwecken, als seien sie immer schon dort
gewesen, wo man sie hingestellt hat.«

« Nous aimons concevoir des produits
sympathiques et discrets qui, une fois
qu'on les a placés chez soi, semblent
avoir toujours été là. »

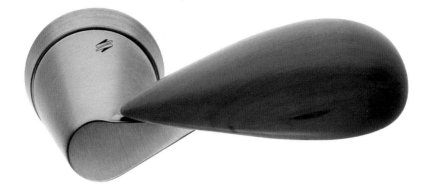

1. **Tacta** doorhandle/Türgriff/poignée de porte for
Colombo Design, 1992 – design: Carlo Bartoli
2. ↓ **Cloud** armchairs/Sessel/fauteuils for Segis, 1999 –
design: Carlo Bartoli

3. **Sha** sofas and ottomans/Sofas und Fußhocker/canapés
et repose-pieds for Rossi di Albizzate, 2000

»Ich weiß nicht, wie die Zukunft des Designs tatsächlich aussehen wird, aber ich weiß, wie sie aussehen sollte: Gebrauchsgüter sollten stets ein selbstverständlicher Teil der alltäglichen Umgebung des Benutzers sein. Aus diesem Grund sollte die Designsprache möglichst ungezwungen und normal sein. Das heißt nicht, dass Design banal, sondern mehr auf eine ausgewogene Balance ausgerichtet sein sollte. Und es sollte die in unserer Kultur geachteten Werte auf das Produkt übertragen – mit Respekt vor der menschlichen Würde von Tradition.« CARLO BARTOLI FÜR BARTOLI DESIGN

"I don't know what the future of design will be but I know what it should be: I think objects for widespread use should always become part of the user's daily landscape in a non-prevaricating way. For that reason the project language should be 'non-emerging', not far from normality. This does not mean banal, but rather oriented to a proper balance, transferring what is valued in culture to the product, with respect for the human dignity of tradition."
CARLO BARTOLI FOR BARTOLI DESIGN

« J'ignore ce que nous réserve l'avenir du design mais je sais ce qu'il devrait être : les objets usuels devraient toujours s'intégrer au paysage quotidien de leurs utilisateurs sans se faire remarquer. Pour cette raison le projet de langage devrait être " non émergeant ", proche de la normalité. Cela ne signifie pas " banal " mais plutôt orienté vers un juste équilibre, transférant au produit ce qui est précieux dans la culture, en respectant la dignité humaine de la tradition. »
CARLO BARTOLI POUR BARTOLI DESIGN

4. **Temper** heater/Heizung/radiateur for Deltacalor, 1998
5. **Maxima** cupboard/Anrichte/buffet for Laurameroni Design Collection, 2000
6. **Gallery** chair/Stuhl/fauteuil for Segis, 2000

		BARTOLI DESIGN		CLIENTS

		BARTOLI DESIGN	CLIENTS
FOUNDED	1963	by Carlo Bartoli	Arclinea
	1999	name adopted by a studio in Monza, Italy by Albertina Amadeo (b. 1932 Cadorago), Anna Bartoli (b. 1963 Milan), Carlo Bartoli (b. 1931 Milan), Paolo Bartoli (b. 1968 Milan), Paolo Cresenti (b. 1966 Rome) and Giulio Ripamonti (b. 1952 Lecco)	Arflex
			Colombo Design
			Confalonieri
STUDIED		ANNA BARTOLI	Delight
	1988	Architecture degree, Politecnico di Milano	Deltacalor
		CARLO BARTOLI	Kartell
	1957	Architecture degree, Politecnico di Milano	Kristalla
		PAOLO BARTOLI	Laurameroni Design Collection
	1994	Architecture degree, Politecnico di Milano	Matteograssi
		PAOLO CRESCENTI	Multipla 2000
	1990	Industrial Design degree ISIA (Istituto Superiore per le Industrie Artistiche), Rome	Rossi di Albizzate
		GIULIO RIPAMONTI	Segis
	1976	Architecture degree, Politecnico di Milano	Tisettanta
AWARDS		CARLO BARTOLI	Varenna-Poliform
	1991	Compasso d'Oro selection, Milan	Ycami
	1996	*I. D. Magazine Annual Design Review* Award, New York; Roter Punkt Award, Design Zentrum Nordrhein-Westfalen, Essen; IIDA Apex Product Design Award; iF Design Award, Hanover	
	1998	iF Design Award, Hanover	
EXHIBITIONS		CARLO BARTOLI	
	1968	*Plastics as Plastics*, Museum of Contemporary Crafts, New York	
	1970	*Modern Chairs 1918-1970*, Whitechapel Art Gallery, London	
	1972	*Design and Plastic*, Museum of Decorative Arts, Prague	
	1975	*The Plastic Chair*, Centrokappa, Noviglio (Milan)	
	1979	*Design & Design*, Milan; *Italian Office Design*, Milan; *Italian Design*, Hong Kong	
	1980	*Italian Design*, Athens	
	1981	*Italienisches Möbeldesign 1950-1980*, Museum für Angewandte Kunst, Cologne	
	1983	*From the Spoon to the City – Paths of 100 Designers*, Milan	
	1988	*Kitchens in the Shop Window*, Milan	
	1992	Biennial of Industrial Design, Ljubljana	
	1998	*Due Generazioni di Designer*, Udine	

5

6

"Life meets death in objects
as in the theatre of life."

Jonas Bohlin

Jonas Bohlin, Jonas Bohlin Design AB, Södermalmstorg 4, 11645 Stockholm, Sweden
T +46 8 615 2389 F +46 8 615 2398 info@jonasbohlindesign.se
www.scandinaviandesign.com/jonasbohlin

*»Das Leben trifft mit dem Tod zusam-
men, in Objekten ebenso wie im Theater
des Lebens.«*

« La vie rencontre la mort dans des
objets comme dans le théâtre de la
vie. »

1. **Liv-Collection** easy-chair/Stuhl/fauteuil
(self-production), 1997
2. ↓ **Liv-Collection** pendant lamps and stools/
Hängelampen und Hocker/lustres et tabourets
(self-production), 1997

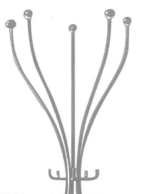

»Zur Zeit arbeite ich an einem Objekt mit dem Titel ›Theater‹. Dabei handelt es sich um einen bettähnlichen Tisch aus schwarz gestrichenem Stahl und weiß gestrichenem Holz mit einem handgemalten Kissen, einem ledernen Polster und einem aus seiner Rinde geschälten Zweig. Es wird ein Objekt sein, mit dem man leben und interagieren kann. Ich will, dass meine Möbel berühren und erfreuen, dass sie mit Zeit und Raum kommunizieren, mit der Hand und dem Herzen gemacht und achtsam gegenüber Mensch und Natur sind. Möbel sind zum Gebrauch bestimmt, können jedoch auch Stärke und Seelenruhe vermitteln. In ihnen trifft das Funktionale mit dem Dekorativen zusammen, das Kommerzielle mit dem Künstlerischen und das Unendliche mit dem Endlichen.«
JONAS BOHLIN

"Right now I am working on a piece entitled 'Theatre'. The idea is to create a bed-like table of black painted steel and white painted wood with a hand-painted pillow, a leather-upholstered cushion and a branch stripped of its bark. It will be a piece to live with and to interact with. I want my furniture to touch and please, to communicate with time and space, to be made by hand and heart, and to be considerate of mankind and nature. Furniture is meant to be used yet it can also provide strength and peace. Functional meets decorative. Commercial meets artistic. Infinite meets finite." JONAS BOHLIN

« En ce moment, je travaille sur une pièce intitulée " Théâtre ". C'est une table qui rappelle un lit, en acier noir et en bois blanc, avec un oreiller peint à la main, un coussin en cuir et une branche écorcée. Ce sera une pièce avec laquelle vivre et interagir. Je voudrais que mes meubles émeuvent et plaisent, qu'ils communiquent avec le temps et l'espace, qu'ils soient faits à la main et avec le cœur, et qu'ils respectent l'homme et la nature. Les meubles sont faits pour être utilisés mais cela ne doit pas les empêcher de conférer un sentiment de force et de paix, d'être fonctionnels et décoratifs, commerciaux et artistiques, infinis et finis. » JONAS BOHLIN

3. **Spira** coat-stand/Kleiderständer/portemanteau (self-production), 1999
4. **Formula 2000** sofa/Sofa (self-production), 1999
5. **Liv-Collection** table/Tisch (self-production), 1997
6. **Liv-Collection** chair/Stuhl/chaise (self-production), 1999

		JONAS BOHLIN	CLIENTS
BORN	1953	Stockholm, Sweden	Asplund
STUDIED	1976-81	Interior Architecture, Konstfackskolan (National College of Arts, Crafts and Design), Stockholm	Jonas Bohlin Design
PRACTICE	1983	established own architectural office	Källemo
	1985-87	founded "Stockholm Mobile" art/design gallery, Stockholm	Kasthall
	1988-	professor, Beckman's School of Design, Stockholm	Lammhults
	1991-93	Chairman of SIR (The National Association of Swedish Interior Architects)	Reimyre
	1998	established Bohlin Design in Stockholm	Rörstrand
AWARDS	1981	Konstfackskolan scholarship, National College of Arts, Crafts and Design, Stockholm	
	1981	Svensk Form scholarship, Swedish Society of Crafts and Design, Stockholm	
	1983 & 92	honorary mention, Excellent Swedish Design Award, Stockholm	
	1984	Swedish State Cultural Grant	
	1985	Grant, Estrid Ericson Foundation	
	1986	Grant, Swedish Board of Fine Arts	
	1988	The Georg Jensen Prize, Copenhagen	
	1989	Best Interior of the Year, *Forum* magazine	
	1994	Project grant, Swedish State Fund for the Arts	
	1997	Major grant, Swedish State Fund for the Arts	
EXHIBITIONS	1985	*Art & Craft 100 Years*, National Art Gallery, Stockholm	
	1986	*Nordic Furniture Design*, Design Center, Malmö	
	1987	*A Way of Life*, touring exhibition, Japan	
	1988	*Excellent Swedish Design*, touring exhibition, USA	
	1991-92	*Swedish Design*, touring exhibition, India	
	1993	*Four Furniture Designers: Mathsson/Chambert/Kandell/Bohlin*, National Art Gallery, Stockholm	
	1994	*Nordic Profiles*, National Art Gallery, touring exhibition, Stockholm & Scandinavia	
	1997	*Nordic Touch*, Kalmar Art Museum, Kalmar	
	1998	*Sven Lundh's Eye*, Färgfabriken gallery, Stockholm	
	1999	*Sweden Builds*, Museum of Architecture, Stockholm	
	2000	*Angles Suedois*, European travelling exhibition; *Designers for Their Time*, Rörstrand	

4

5

6

"Our work finds its characteristic in a diversity of approaches, from industry to craft, from the micro to the macro."

R. & E. Bouroullec

Ronan & Erwan Bouroullec, 51 Rue des Ursulines, 93200 Saint Denis, France
T/F +33 1 4820 3660 bouroullec@wanadoo.fr

»Unsere Arbeit ist gekennzeichnet durch eine Mannigfaltigkeit der Herangehensweisen: von der Industrie zum Handwerk, vom Mikro- zum Makro-Bereich.«

« Notre travail se caractérise par la diversité des approches, de l'industrie à l'artisanat, du micro au macro. »

1. **Square** vase/Vase for Cappellini, 1999
2. ↓ **Lis Clos** bed/Bett/lit for Cappellini, 2000

« Le futur du design tend pour nous vers un déplacement des domaines d'interventions, moins lié a la seule question de l'objet ou de la propriété, il repose sur une harmonie des situations, un écosystème personnel équilibré. La production s'établira, dans le futur, autour des propriétés/capacités qu'auront les objets/ les hommes/le savoir, à reguler les tensions engendrées par une vie en mouvement. Se dégageant ainsi d'une notion d'objet, le design alors engendré par un système complexe, sera une intelligence des situations, une liberté permanente de mouvement. Des objets/matériaux/ustensiles sensibles (thermorégulation, du léger au lourd, etc.) pourront déjà accompagner le corps de l'homme d'une manière réactive, mais, par-delà la notion de sensations/facilités/conforts, la question sera surtout celle d'une intelligence des dialogues entre l'objet, les différentes dimensions de sa production et celui qui en jouit; où les efforts consentis par chacun concrétisent cet écosystème serein et conscient de son développement/histoire. » RONAN & ERWAN BOUROULLEC

3. ← **Torique** ceramic collection/Keramikwaren/ligne de céramiques for Vallauris (limited edition), 1999
4. **Torique** ceramic stools/Keramikstühle/tabourets en céramique for Vallauris (limited edition), 1999

"We believe the future of design will tend towards a displacement of the fields of intervention. It will no longer rest solely on the question of the object or property, but rather on a harmony of situations, on a balanced personal ecosystem. In the future, production will be established around the properties/ capacities of objects/people/the management of the tensions generated by a constant movement in life.
Liberated from the concept of the object, design will be generated by a more complex system which will involve an understanding of situations and a permanent freedom of movement. Objects/materials/ sensitive devices (thermoregulated, lighter instead of heavier, etc.) are already able to accompany the human body in a responsive way. But, beyond the concept of emotions/ease of operation/comfort, it will be a question above all of a knowledge of the dialogues between an object, the various dimensions of its production and the user; where the individual efforts that have gone into its realization reflect a well-balanced ecosystem and an awareness of its development/history."
RONAN & ERWAN BOUROULLEC

»Wir glauben, dass die Zukunft des Designs zu einer Verlagerung der Interventionsebenen tendieren wird. Es wird nicht länger ausschließlich um die Frage von Objekt oder Besitz gehen, sondern mehr um eine Harmonie der Situationen, um ein ausgeglichenes persönliches Ökosystem. In Zukunft wird sich die Produktion von Design ansiedeln um Eigenschaften/Fähigkeiten von Objekten/Menschen/Wissen, wie sich die von einem sich kontinuierlich verändernden Leben erzeugten Spannungen in Grenzen halten lassen. Befreit vom Konzept des Objekts wird Design durch ein komplexeres System hervorgebracht werden und ein Verständnis für Situationen sowie eine dauerhafte Bewegungsfreiheit umfassen. Objekte/Materialien/sensitive Vorrichtungen (wärmeguliert, leichter statt schwerer etc.) sind bereits heute imstande, den menschlichen Körper auf stabilisierende Weise zu begleiten. Über das Konzept der Gefühle/des Bedienungskomforts hinaus aber geht es besonders um eine Kenntnis der kommunikativen Verbindungen zwischen einem Objekt, den verschiedenen Dimensionen seiner Fertigung und dem Anwender. An diesem Punkt reflektieren die individuellen Bemühungen, die in die Realisierung des Objekts eingeflossen sind, ein wohl ausbalanciertes Ökosystem und ein Bewusstsein seiner Entwicklung/ Geschichte.« RONAN & ERWAN BOUROULLEC

	RONAN & ERWAN BOUROULLEC		CLIENTS
BORN	RONAN BOUROULLEC		Ardi
1971	Quimper, France		Authentics
	ERWAN BOUROULLEC		Boffi
1976	Quimper, France		Cappellini
STUDIED	RONAN BOUROULLEC		Domeau & Perès
1991	Industrial Design diploma, École Nationale Supérieure des Arts Appliqués et des Métiers d'Arts, Paris		Evans and Wong
			Habitat
1995	post-graduate diploma, École Nationale Supérieure des Arts Décoratifs, Paris		Iittala
	ERWAN BOUROULLEC		Issey Miyake
1999	diploma, École Nationale d'Arts, Cergy		La Monnaie de Paris
PRACTICE	RONAN BOUROULLEC		Ligne Roset
1995	began work as freelance designer		Magis
1997	taught at the École Nationale des Beaux Arts, Nancy		Ricard
1998	taught at the École Nationale des Beaux Arts, Saint-Étienne		Rosenthal
1999	established partnership with his brother Erwan		Smack Iceland
2000	taught at the École Cantonale d'Art, Lausanne, and at the École Nissim de Camondo, Paris		Sommer
	ERWAN BOUROULLEC		Units
1998	began assisting his brother Ronan on numerous projects		
1999	established partnership with Ronan		
AWARDS	RONAN BOUROULLEC		
1998	First Prize, Biennale du Design, Saint-Étienne; grand prize Salon du Meuble, Paris		
1999	New Designer Award, International Contemporary Furniture Fair, New York		
EXHIBITIONS 1997	*Homo Domus*, French Cultural Centre, Milan; *Made in France*, Centre Georges Pompidou, Paris		
1998	*La vie en rose*, Fondation Cartier, Paris		
1999-2000	*A Grand Design*, Victoria & Albert Museum, London; *Joint-Venture*, Neuilly		
2000	solo exhibition, Galerie Peyroulet & Cie, Paris; *Byob*, Galerie Néotu, Paris		

5

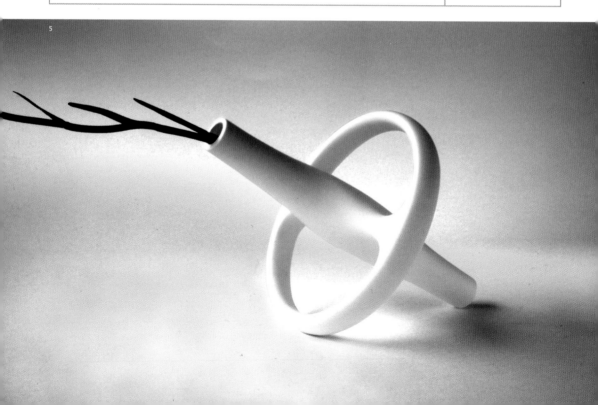

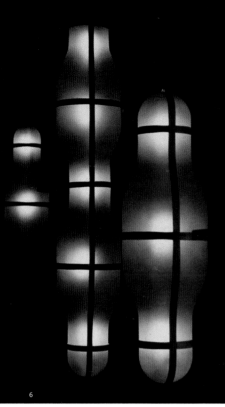

6

7

5. **Sans Titre** vase/Vase for Cappellini, 1998
6. **Hole** lamps/Lampen/lampes for Cappellini, 1999
7. **Vases Combinatoires Collection** polyurethane vase/
Vase aus Polyurethan/vase polyuréthane for Galerie
Néotu, 1997
8. **Vases Combinatoires Collection**/Vasen/vases for
Galerie Néotu, 1997
9. **Safe Rest** day-bed/Liege/lit de repos for Domeau &
Pérès, 1999

8

9

"Products need more than perfect
function and ergonomics, they need
some poetry."

 büro für form.

Benjamin Hopf & Constantin Wortmann, Büro für Form, Hans-Sachs-Str. 12, 80 469 Munich, Germany
T +49 89 26 949 000 F +49 89 26 949 002 buerofuerform@metronet.de www.buerofuerform.de

»Produkte brauchen mehr als perfekte
Funktion und Ergonomie, sie brauchen
Poesie.«

« Il faut aux produits plus qu'une fonctionnalité et une ergonomie parfaites,
ils ont besoin de poésie. »

1. **Tria** modular hanging lamp/Hängelampe/
lustre for Habitat, 2000
2. ↓ **Eat & Lounge** chaise longue & thronelike chair
(prototype)/Liege & thronartiger Stuhl (Prototyp), 1999

»Unser Zeitalter der rapiden technologischen Veränderung und des wachsenden Konsums hat das Design verändert: Jedes Jahr werden noch mehr neue Produkte mit noch kürzerer Lebensdauer entwickelt. Während hierbei die Faktoren Zeit, Kosten, Daten und Funktion bestimmend sind, stellen sie gleichzeitig Gebote dar, die wiederum ein Bedürfnis nach Träumen und Gefühlen erzeugen. Die Qualität der Dinge, mit denen wir uns umgeben, können bei der Erfüllung dieses Bedürfnisses eine wichtige Rolle spielen. Bei Design geht es um mehr als nur um das Objekt selbst. Und es geht auch nicht bloß darum, ein Produkt durch einen neuen Stil aufzupolieren. Produkte korrespondieren mit unseren Bedürfnissen und Wünschen und haben einen direkten Einfluss auf unsere Lebensqualität. Je besser ein Produkt ist, desto länger wird man es behalten. Das ist gut für die Umwelt. Das Design der Zukunft wird diesen ökologischen Aspekt berücksichtigen müssen, während es gleichzeitig auf neue und sinnvolle Art eine Verbindung zwischen Funktionalität und Emotionalität – also zwischen der physischen und der psychologischen Verwendung eines Produkts – herstellt.« BÜRO FÜR FORM.

"Our age of rapid technological change and increasing consumption has changed design – each year even more new products are developed with an even shorter lifespan. While time, costs, facts and function are the determining factors in this, they are dictates that create the need for dreams and emotion. The quality of the things with which we surround ourselves can play an important part in fulfilling this need. Design is about more than just the object. Nor is it simply about revamping a product in a new style. Products correspond with our needs and desires and impact directly on the quality of our lives. The better a product is the longer it will be kept. This is good for the environment. Design in the future will have to take this into consideration while combining functionality and emotion – the physical and psychological use of a product – in new and more meaningful ways." BÜRO FÜR FORM.

« Notre époque de transformations technologiques rapides et de consommation accrue a modifié le design : chaque année, on développe toujours plus de produits à la durée de vie réduite. Si le temps, le coût, les faits et la fonction sont des facteurs déterminants dans ce phénomène, ce sont autant de diktats qui créent un besoin de rêves et d'émotions. La qualité des objets dont nous nous entourons peut jouer un rôle important dans la satisfaction de ce besoin. Le design, c'est plus que l'objet lui-même. Il ne s'agit pas uniquement de re-dessiner un produit pour l'adapter à un nouveau style. Celui-ci doit correspondre à nos besoins et à nos désirs et influencer directement notre qualité de vie. Mieux un produit est conçu, plus on le gardera longtemps. C'est bon pour l'environnement. A l'avenir, le design devra en tenir compte tout en conjuguant fonctionnalité et émotion – l'utilisation physique et psychologique d'un produit – de manières nouvelles et plus censées. » BÜRO FÜR FORM.

3. **Fingermax** paint brush/Malerpinsel/pinceau for Fingermax GBR, 1998-99
4. **Flat** chair/Stuhl/chaise for Habitat, 2000
5. **Dio** modular hanging lamp/Hängelampe/lustre for Habitat, 2000
6. **Il Crollo** chair/Stuhl/chaise for Kundalini, 2000

BÜRO FÜR FORM.			CLIENTS
FOUNDED	1998	Munich, Germany by Benjamin Hopf (b. 1971 Hamburg) and Constantin Wortmann (b. 1970 Munich)	Fingermax
STUDIED		BENJAMIN HOPF	Habitat
	1998	MA Industrial Design, University of Design, Munich	Kundalini
		CONSTANTIN WORTMANN	Next
	1998	MA Industrial Design, University of Design, Munich	
AWARDS	1997	Hewi Innovation Award (special award); Hoesch Design Award (special award)	
	1998	Nachlux (special award); Designale Third Prize	
	1999	Bonaldo Design Contest (Third Prize); Design Award Neunkirchen (Second Prize)	
	2000	Best of Category, iF Design Award, Hanover; Design for Europe, Kortrijk	
EXHIBITIONS	1999	*Light & Lounge*, Büro für Form, Munich	
	2000	*Light & Lounge*, International Furniture Fair, Cologne; *Urban Gravity*, International Furniture Fair, Milan; *Liquid Light*, Munich; *Form 2000*, International Furniture Fair, Cologne	
	2001	*Charlie's Angels*, International Furniture Fair, Milan	

"It is the relationship between the object and its use, together with a capacity for ageing while increasing in value, that will deem an object classical."

Antonio Citterio

Antonio Citterio, Antonio Citterio & Partners, Via Cerva 4, 20 122 Milan, Italy
T +39 02 763 8801 F +39 02 763 88080 citterio@mdsnet.it

»Was ein Objekt zu einem Klassiker macht, ist der Bezug zu seiner Verwendung zusammen mit seiner Fähigkeit, zu altern und dabei an Wert zu gewinnen.«

« Ce qui fait d'un objet un classique, c'est sa relation avec son utilisation ainsi que sa capacité à vieillir tout en prenant de la valeur. »

1. **Citterio 2000** cutlery/Besteck/couverts for Hackman, 2000
2. ↓ **Web** armchairs/Sessel/fauteuils for B&B Italia, 1998

« Je n'emploie jamais le mot " moderne ". Le concept de modernité implique de comprendre ce qui est ancien. Cela peut paraître paradoxal mais c'est ainsi. Pour décrire la recherche de " l'esprit du temps " qui sous-tend mon travail, je préfère le terme " contemporain ". La contemporanéité d'un projet de design inclut et nourrit un profond désir d'anticipation. L'interaction constante entre l'anticipation du projet et la contemporanéité du produit fini constitue l'essence même de ma démarche. J'essaie toujours de concevoir des objets qui soient absolument contemporains, précisément parce qu'ils coïncident parfaitement avec leur temps. Ces dernières années, l'évolution sociale qui a accompagné l'émergence de nouvelles technologies et de nouveaux codes de communication a incité de nombreux designers à intégrer ces éléments dans leur propres conceptions, d'une manière directe mais inexpliquée, au sein des paramètres proposés par l'informatisation du design. Toutefois, je ne pense pas que ce genre de design, qui ne nécessite pas un effort formel pur, puisse aboutir à des résultats substantiels. Pour moi, la pertinence du sujet (sans réveiller le vieux débat sur la forme et la fonction) dépend avant tout de la capacité à créer des objets clairs et compréhensibles, puis de celle à susciter le plaisir et le désir de les posséder. Je travaille comme un connaisseur hypothétique du design. Je cherche moins à être surpris ou amusé par un objet qu'à travailler sur sa précision, résultat d'une ↓

"I never use the word 'modern'. The concept of modernity implies an understanding of ancient things. I know this sounds like a paradox, but so it is. When expressing the tension found in my work, which is about the search for the 'spirit of the time', I use the word 'contemporary'. The contemporaneity of a design project includes and feeds the deep desire of anticipation. There is a perpetual shift between the anticipation of the project and the contemporaneity of the final product, which is the essence of my approach to design. I always try to design objects that are absolutely contemporary, exactly because they coincide perfectly with their time. The past years have seen a social evolution with the emergence of new technologies and new codes of communication, which have driven many designers to combine these elements in their own design, in a direct but unexplained way, within the stylistic parameters suggested by the computerization of design. I do not think, however, that this kind of design, which involves no pure formal effort, can lead to any substantial result. For me, the pertinence of the subject (without raising old questions of form and function) relies firstly on the ability to create clear and understandable objects and secondly on the ability to excite pleasure and the desire for ownership. I work like a hypothetical connoisseur of design, a man not so much interested in being surprised and deriving fun from an object but pursuing an interest in the precision of an object that is the result of an appropriate use of construction and detailing. I am fascinated by the intrinsic qualities of materials and the way in which ↓

»Ich verwende niemals das Wort ›modern‹. Das Konzept von Modernität impliziert ein Verständnis für alte Dinge. Ich weiß, das klingt paradox, aber es ist so. Wenn ich die in meiner Arbeit enthaltene Spannung, bei der es um die Suche nach dem ›Zeitgeist‹ geht, beschreiben soll, verwende ich das Wort ›zeitgemäß‹. Die Aktualität eines Designprojekts beinhaltet und nährt den tiefen Wunsch nach gedanklicher Vorwegnahme. Der fortwährende Wechsel zwischen der Antizipation des Projekts und der Aktualität des Endprodukts ist die Essenz meiner Herangehensweise. Ich bin immer bestrebt, Objekte zu entwerfen, die absolut zeitgemäß sind, gerade weil sie sich in vollkommener Übereinstimmung mit ihrer Zeit befinden. Während der vergangenen Jahre fand eine soziale Evolution statt, die mit dem Aufkommen neuer Technologien und Kommunikationssysteme einherging. Viele Designer reagierten auf diese Entwicklung, indem sie die neuen Techniken mittels stilistischer Parameter, die sich durch die Computerisierung des Designs ergeben, auf direkte, aber unausgesprochene Weise in ihre Entwürfe einbezogen. Ich glaube jedoch nicht, dass diese Art von Design, die kein rein formales Bemühen erfordert, zu irgendwelchen nennenswerten Ergebnissen führen wird. Für mich beruht die Relevanz von Design (ohne die alte Debatte über Form und Funktion wieder aufwärmen zu wollen) auf der Fähigkeit, Objekte zu entwerfen, die erstens leicht verständlich sind und zweitens Freude hervorrufen, sowie den Wunsch, das Objekt zu besitzen. Ich arbeite wie ein hypothetischer Connaisseur von Design. Mir liegt weniger an der Verblüffung durch ein Objekt und dem Spaß daran, als an der Präzision eines Objekts, welche das Resultat eines ausgewogenen Verhältnisses zwischen Gestaltung und Ausführung ist. Ich bin fasziniert von den inneren Eigenschaften der unterschiedlichen Materialien und von der Art, wie sie ein Projekt durchdringen. Meiner Meinung nach erlaubt nur eine profunde Kenntnis von Werkstoffen und Techniken, dass ein Projekt glatt und ohne allzu große Abweichung vom ursprünglichen Konzept verläuft. Abgesehen von meinen Prinzipien ↓

3. **Freetime** sofa/Sofa/canapé for B&B Italia, 1999
4. **Freetime** chaise longue & sofa/Liege & Sofa/chaise longue & canapé for B&B Italia, 1999
5. **Beam** lighting system/Beleuchtungssystem/système d'éclairage for Flos, 2000

ANTONIO CITTERIO			CLIENTS
BORN	1950	Meda, Italy	Ansorg
STUDIED	1972	graduated in architecture at the Milan Polytechnic	Arclinea
PRACTICE	1973-81	partnership with Paolo Nava	B&B Italia
	1987-96	partnership with Terry Dwan	Boffi Cucine
	1999	founded Antonio Citterio and Partners with Patricia Viel	Flexform
AWARDS	1987	Compasso d'Oro, Milan	Flos
	1995	Compasso d'Oro, Milan	Fusital
EXHIBITIONS	1988	*I segni dell'Habitat*, Paris	Hackman
	1992	*Objets et Projets* (concept and layout), Paris	Hansgrohe
	1994	*Antonio Citterio & Terry Dwan* (design), AXIS Gallery, Tokyo	Inda
	1999	*Antonio Citterio and Partners. Progetti di architettura 4 case e 4 uffici* (concept and layout), Galleria Aam, Milan	JCDecaux
			Kartell
	2000	*Design 4:3 – Fünfzig Jahre italienisches und deutsches Design*, Kunst- und Ausstellungshalle der Bundesrepublik Deutschland, Bonn; *Esercizi di Stile*, Ace Gallery, New York – ICE	MaxData
			Pozzi & Ginori
			Tisettanta
			Vitra

6

7

utilisation adéquate de la construction et du détail. Je suis fasciné par les qualités intrinsèques des matériaux et par la manière dont elles influent sur un projet. A mon avis, seule une profonde connaissance des matières et des techniques peut permettre à un projet d'aboutir sans trop dévier de son concept initial. Outre mes principes sur " la pertinence du sujet " et la " précision ", je crois aussi que le design devrait s'appuyer sur une éthique qui ne s'aventure pas dans d'improbables transformations technologiques mais, plutôt, recherche un résultat univoque basé sur la relation entre les techniques de production, la forme et la fonctionnalité. » ANTONIO CITTERIO

they inform a project. In my opinion, only a profound understanding of materials and techniques will allow a project to run smoothly without deviating too far from the initial concept. Apart from my principles regarding 'the pertinence of the subject' and 'precision', I also believe that design should rely on a kind of 'ethic' that does not venture into improbable technological transformations but instead searches for an unequivocal result based on the relationship between production techniques, form and functionality." ANTONIO CITTERIO

bezüglich ›Relevanz‹ und ›Präzision‹ bin ich der Ansicht, dass sich Design auf eine Art ›Ethik‹ stützen sollte, die sich nicht in abgehobenen technologischen Transformationen erschöpft, sondern nach dem bestmöglichen Ergebnis sucht, das auf einem ausgeglichen Verhältnis zwischen Fertigungstechniken, Form und Funktionalität beruht.«
ANTONIO CITTERIO

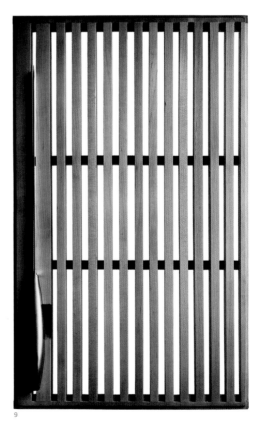

6. **Dado** sofa/Sofa/canapé for B&B Italia, 2000
7. **Cross** shelving/Regale/bibliothèque for B&B Italia, 1999
8. **H-Beam** lighting/Beleuchtungskörper/plafonnier for Flos, 2000
9. **Citterio Collective Tools 2000** bread knife and cutting board/Brotmesser und Schneidebrett/couteau à pain et planche à découper for Hackman, 2000

9

"Design is about how something works, not how it looks. It's what's inside that counts. The best designs are the result of someone's questioning everything around them."

James Dyson

James Dyson, Dyson Appliances Ltd., Tetbury Hill, Malmesbury, Wiltshire SN16 0RP, England
T +44 1666 827 200 F +44 1666 827 299 dyson.@dyson.com www.dyson.com

»Beim Design kommt es darauf an, wie etwas funktioniert und nicht, wie es aussieht. Was zählt, ist der Inhalt. Die besten Entwürfe entstehen, wenn jemand alles in Frage stellt.«

« Ce qui compte en design, c'est la manière dont un objet fonctionne, pas son aspect. L'important, c'est ce qui est à l'intérieur. Les meilleurs créations sont conçues par des designers qui remettent tout en question. »

1. **DC05** dual cyclone cleaner/Dual-Zyklon-Bodenstaub-
sauger/nettoyeur double cyclone for Dyson, 1998
2. ↓ **DC06** dual cyclone robotic cleaner/Dual-Roboter-
Zyklon-Bodenstaubsauger/robot nettoyeur double cyclone
for Dyson, 1999

« Autrefois, on pensait qu'au 21ᵉ siècle l'homme aurait davantage de temps libre alors qu'en fait, il travaille de plus en plus. Dans les foyers, je pense qu'on utilisera de plus en plus de nouvelles technologies recourant à l'intelligence artificielle, libérant hommes et femmes des corvées domestiques. Quand j'étais petit, on lavait le linge avec une essoreuse à rouleaux. Aujourd'hui, 93 % des foyers sont équipés de machines à laver. Cela laisse plus de temps pour les loisirs. On peut lire un livre ou regarder un film pendant que des machines font le ménage. D'un autre côté, la nouvelle technologie risque de devenir de plus en plus compliquée et je crois que le rôle du design sera de la rendre plus simple à utiliser, notamment grâce à la reconnaissance vocale, surtout pour des systèmes tels le chauffage central. Pour le moment, ils sont assez difficiles à programmer à cause du jargon absurde des modes d'emploi. A mon avis, les innovations futures et le bon design rendront la technologie moderne plus accessible à tous. L'avenir du design et de l'industrie dépend des jeunes qu'on forme actuellement dans les écoles, les collèges et les universités. Nous devons nous assurer que ce secteur d'activité reste créatif, passionné par les produits qu'il fabrique et les gens qui les utilisent. Pour ça, il faut s'y intéresser dès son plus ↓

3. ← **CR01** Contrarotator two-drum washing machine/Waschmaschine mit Doppeltragwalze/machine à laver à double tambour for Dyson, 1996–2000
4. **DC04** Absolute dual cyclone cleaner/Absolut-Dual-Zyklon-Bürststaubsauger/nettoyeur double cyclone for Dyson, 1999

"We once thought that the 21st century would mean increased leisure time for all, but in fact more people are working, and working longer hours. I believe that in the home we will increasingly see new technology using artificial intelligence, liberating men and women from household chores. When I was born we washed our clothes using a mangle, now 93 % of homes have automatic washing machines. It allows more time for leisure, we can read a book or watch a film while machines help with the housework. Yet new technology is in danger of becoming increasingly complicated, and I think it is the role of design to make it simpler to use, for example through voice recognition, especially for things such as central heating systems. At the moment these are rather difficult to program because of the ridiculous vernacular used in instruction manuals. I think that in the future innovation and good design will make complex modern technology more available and accessible to everyone. The future of design and the manufacturing industry ultimately rests with the young people being educated in schools, colleges and universities today. We need to make sure that it is a creative industry ↓

»Wir dachten einmal, das 21. Jahrhundert würde mehr Freizeit für alle bedeuten. Aber faktisch arbeiten mehr Menschen, und sie arbeiten immer länger. Ich glaube, dass neue Technologien auf der Basis von künstlicher Intelligenz verstärkt Einzug in unser Zuhause halten werden, was Männer und Frauen im Haushalt entlasten wird. Als ich geboren wurde, haben wir unsere Wäsche noch mit der Hand gewaschen, heute besitzen 93 Prozent der Haushalte eine Waschmaschine. Das verschafft uns mehr Freizeit. Wir können ein Buch lesen oder uns einen Film ansehen, während die Maschinen bei der Hausarbeit helfen. Es besteht jedoch die Gefahr, dass die neuen Technologien immer komplizierter werden. Deshalb sehe ich die Aufgabe von Design darin, Gebrauchsgegenstände in der Anwendung einfacher zu machen, beispielsweise durch Spracherkennung. Das gilt besonders für Dinge wie Zentralheizungsanlagen, die gegenwärtig wegen der unverständlichen Ausdrucksweise in den Bedienungsanleitungen schwierig zu programmieren sind. Ich denke, dass die komplexen modernen Technologien in Zukunft durch Innovation und gutes Design für jeden einzelnen leichter verfügbar und nutzbar gemacht werden können.
Die Zukunft des Designs und der weiterverarbeitenden Industrie liegt letzten Endes bei den jungen Menschen, die heute in Schulen, Akademien und Universitäten ausgebildet werden. Wir müssen dafür Sorge tragen, dass sie Design als ein kreatives Gewerbe erlernen, das den Produkten, die es hervorbringt und den Menschen, die sie benutzen, leidenschaftlich zugetan ist. Und das muss meiner Meinung nach bereits in einem frühen Alter einsetzen. Der Akt des kreativen Gebrauchs der ↓

JAMES DYSON

BORN	1947	Norfolk, England
STUDIED	1965-66	Byam Shaw School, London
	1966-70	MA furniture and interior design, Royal College of Art, London
PRACTICE	1970-74	Rotork, Bath
	1974-79	developed *Ballbarrow*
	1979-84	developed *Dual Cyclone* vacuum cleaner
	1993	established Dyson Appliances, Chippenham, Wiltshire
AWARDS	1975	Duke of Edinburgh's special prize, England
	1977	Building Design Innovation Award, England
	1991	International Design Fair Prize, Japan
	1995	elected Fellow of the Chartered Society of Engineers
	1996	Gerald Frewer Memorial Trophy, Institute of Engineering Design, England; Grand Prix Trophy and Consumer Product Design Award, UK Design Council and Design in Business Awards (DBA)
	1997	Honorary Doctor of Science, Brookes University, Oxford; Honorary Doctor of Science, Huddersfield University Business School; Prince Philip Designers Prize
	1998	Honorary Doctor of Science, Bradford University
	1999	Honorary Doctor of Engineering, West of England University; Internationaler Designpreis Baden-Württemburg, Design Center Stuttgart; G-Mark/Good Design Award, JIDPO, Tokyo
	2000	Etoiles de l'Observeur du Design, Paris
EXHIBITIONS	1989	*British Design – New Traditions*, Rotterdam
	1996	Glasgow International Festival of Design; *Doing a Dyson*, Design Museum, London
	1997	Sonsbeek Design and Art Museum, Arnhem
	1999	*Designing in the Digital Age*, Victoria & Albert Museum, London

CLIENTS

Self-production

5

6

jeune âge. Apprendre à utiliser ses mains et son cerveau de manière créative représente un aspect vital de l'éducation et un défi immense. C'est une activité socialement inclusive et cohésive, dont tous les étudiants peuvent bénéficier quelles que soient leurs capacités académiques. Connaître et comprendre le processus du design ne peut qu'être utile à tous les adolescents. Pour que le design ait un avenir, nous devons tous comprendre la valeur de la créativité, de la technologie et de la fabrication. Ceci dit, au bout du compte, quels que soient les obstacles rencontrés, on continuera à inventer et à fabriquer de nouveaux produits : il est dans la nature humaine de créer, d'améliorer ses conditions de vie. » JAMES DYSON

5. **DC03 Clear** dual cyclone cleaner/Dual-Zyklon-Bürststaubsauger/nettoyeur double cyclone for Dyson, 1998
6. **DC02** dual cyclone cleaner/Dual-Zyklon-Bodenstaubsauger/nettoyeur double cyclone for Dyson, 1995
7. **CR01** washing machine, two-drum contrarotator/Waschmaschine mit Doppeltragwalze/machine à laver, double tambour for Dyson, 1996-2000

that cares passionately about the products it makes and the people who use them. I believe this needs to start at an early age. The act of creatively using your hands together with your brain is a vital part of education and an immensely challenging one. It is a socially inclusive and cohesive activity, which benefits all students whatever their academic abilities. It is helpful for everyone to grow up knowing and understanding the design process. People need to understand the value of creativity, technology and manufacturing for the future of design. In the end though, whatever obstacles are thrown in their way, people will continue to invent and make new products: it is part of the human drive to create, to improve our lot." JAMES DYSON

Hände zusammen mit dem Verstand ist ein wichtiger – und zudem ungeheuer herausfordernder – Bestandteil von Erziehung. Von dieser sozial integrativen und bindenden Aktivität profitieren alle Schüler, unabhängig von ihren akademischen Fähigkeiten. Es ist für jeden Heranwachsenden von Nutzen, den Prozess des Gestaltens zu kennen und zu verstehen. Damit das Design eine Zukunft hat, müssen die Menschen den Wert von Kreativität, Technologie und Produktion begreifen. Im Grunde werden die Menschen jedoch ständig neue Produkte erfinden und herstellen, gleichgültig welche Hindernisse ihnen dabei in den Weg gelegt werden, denn es gehört einfach zur menschlichen Natur, schöpferisch tätig zu sein und danach zu streben, unsere Lebenswelt zu verbessern.« JAMES DYSON

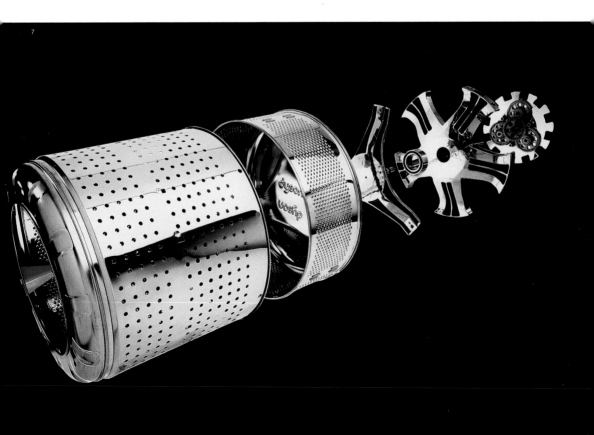

"Designing free of the constraints of mass production."

Elephant Design

Elephant Design, Nikko Akasaka Building 6F, 2-9-11 Akasaka Minato-ku, Tokyo 107-0052, Japan
T +81 3 5545 3061 F +81 3 5545 3062 www.elephant-design.com

»Ein Design, das frei ist von den Zwängen der Massenproduktion.«

« Créer, libéré des contraintes de la production de masse. »

1. **Nuigurumi-kun** remote control/Fernbedienung/
télécommande (self-production), 1999
2. ↓ **Washing machine**/Waschmaschine/machine à
laver (concept study, designed by Klein Dytham
architecture), 1999

« Ce qui manque au design industriel aujour-d'hui ? Il a perdu son rôle de symbole du futur. Partout autour de nous, on ne voit qu'un design assujetti aux tendances arrêtées pour l'année en cours. On rencontre rarement des créations qui soient excitantes en soi, comme c'était souvent le cas dans les années 60. D'un autre côté, on sent une puissante créativité chez les architectes et les stylistes de mode. Pourquoi cette différence ? Probablement parce que ces derniers peuvent travailler sans être soumis aux contraintes de la production de masse.

En relevant le défi de ce paradigme, nous avons trouvé une solution – grâce à l'Internet – en rassemblant les idées de créateurs sur notre site web puis en les peaufinant à l'aide du feed-back des consommateurs qui visitent notre site. Nous réunissons les amateurs qui approuvent ces projets de design puis nous nous mettons en quête d'un fabricant capable de les produire. Une fois que le nombre de commandes atteint le minimum requis pour la fabrication d'un lot, le consommateur obtient ce qu'il "voulait vraiment". Les créateurs peuvent ainsi offrir au public un design très original. L'avenir du design industriel peut être radieux, à condition de ne pas se sentir obligé d'obéir aux vieux diktats de la production de masse. » ELEPHANT DESIGN

3.-4. ← **Cigarro** personal computer/Personalcomputer/ ordinateur PC, (limited production of 100 units), 2000
5.-10. **Denki-Hataki** static electric duster/statischer Elektroentstauber/dépoussiéreur à électricité statique (self-production), 2000

"What is lacking in industrial design today? We could say it no longer provides a symbol of the future. Everywhere we look, we see designs that serve only to distinguish new models year by year. We rarely encounter a design that excites us just by looking at it, as was often the case in the sixties. On the other hand, the powerful imagination of architects and fashion designers is coming right across. What is the difference? The answer lies in whether or not one is allowed to design free of the constraints of mass production.

Taking up the challenge of this paradigm, we have found a solution in the Internet — gathering the ideas of artistic designers on our web site and then refining them through the opinion of consumers who visit the site. We bring people together who approve of certain design ideas and then begin looking for the right manufacturer. Once the number of orders reaches the volume required for a minimum lot, the consumer is then able to obtain what he or she 'really wanted'. In this way, artistic designers can present highly original designs to the public. The future could be bright for industrial design, as long as we don't feel the need to operate under the old dictates of mass production". ELEPHANT DESIGN

5

»Woran mangelt es dem heutigen Industriedesign? Man könnte sagen, es stellt kein in die Zukunft weisendes Symbol mehr dar. Überall um uns herum sehen wir eine Form von Design, die lediglich Jahr für Jahr die jeweils aktuellen Trends hervorhebt. Nur selten treffen wir auf ein Design, das uns durch seinen bloßen Anblick in Begeisterung versetzt, wie es in den 60er Jahren häufig der Fall war. Im Gegensatz dazu ist der Ideenreichtum heutiger Architekten und Modedesigner deutlich erkennbar. Was ist der Grund für diesen Unterschied? Das hängt davon ab, inwieweit es den Gestaltern erlaubt ist, frei von den Zwängen der Massenproduktion zu arbeiten. Wir haben die Herausforderung dieses Paradigmas angenommen und die Lösung im Internet gefunden: Auf unserer Website versammeln wir die Ideen von Gestaltern und überarbeiten diese dann in Absprache mit den Konsumenten, die unser Informationsangebot abrufen. Dadurch bringen wir Menschen zusammen, denen bestimmte Designideen gefallen, und suchen dann nach dem geeigneten Hersteller für die Objekte. Hat die Anzahl der Bestellungen die erforderliche Mindestabnahmesumme erreicht, kann der Kunde das Objekt kaufen, das er oder sie ›wirklich haben wollte‹. Auf diese Weise können Designkünstler höchst originelle Ideen in die Öffentlichkeit bringen. Das Industriedesign kann einer freundlichen Zukunft entgegensehen, sofern wir uns nicht dem alten Diktat der Massenproduktion unterwerfen.« ELEPHANT DESIGN

6-10

	ELEPHANT DESIGN	CLIENTS
FOUNDED	1997 by Kohei Nishiyama (b. 1970 Hyogo, Japan) and Yosuke Masumoto (b. 1970 Okayama, Japan)	Self-production
STUDIED	KOHEI NISHIYAMA	
1991-93	Industrial Design, Kuwasawa Design School, Tokyo	
	YOSUKE MASUMOTO	
1991-93	Industrial Design, Kuwasawa	
AWARDS	2000 G-Mark/Good Design Award, JIDPO, Tokyo; Gold Prize, *Digital Design of the Year*, *Popeye* magazine	
EXHIBITIONS	1997 *Venture Fair Japan*, Tokyo	
	1999 first *cuusoo.kaden* (imaginary home electrical appliances) exhibition, AXIS Gallery, Tokyo	
	2000 First *cuusoo.com* exhibition, Daikanyama, Tokyo	
	2001 second *cuusoo.com* exhibiton, Living Design Center OZONE, Tokyo	

11   12   13

11.-12. **Patapata** memory-stick MP3 player/MP3-Player/
lecteur de MP3, (self-production), 1999
13. **PaqPaq** shockproof cell-phone case – first consumer-
participation product to be launched/stoßfestes
Handy-Gehäuse – erstes unter Konsumentenbeteiligung
gestaltetes Produkt, das auf den Markt gebracht werden
soll/boitier incassable de téléphone portable – premier
produit lancé avec la participation des consommateurs,
1997
14. **TPF** compact fax machine/Kompakt-Faxgerät/
télécopieur compact, 1999
15. **Insipid** rice cooker/Reiskocher/riseuse
(self-production), 1999
16. **Armadillo** cell-phone and information terminal/Mobil-
telefon und Informationsterminal/téléphone et récepteur
de données portable (self-production), 2000

"A design that is not intentional, that has the freedom to offer a variety of appeals, can be discovered over the course of time spent with the object."

Naoto Fukasawa

Naoto Fukasawa, c/o IDEO Japan, AXIS Bldg. 4F, 5-17-1 Roppongi, Minato-ku, Tokyo 106-0032, Japan
T +81 3 5 570 2664 F +81 3 5 570 2669 naoto@ideojapan.co.jp www.ideo.com

»Ein Design, das nicht zweckbestimmt ist, sondern auf vielfältige Weise Anreize gibt, kann im Laufe der Zeit entdeckt werden, die man mit dem Objekt verbringt.«

« Un design non intentionnel, assez libre pour présenter une variété d'attraits, se découvre au fil du temps que l'on passe avec l'objet. »

1. **Kinetic** watch/Armbanduhr/montre for Seiko, 1997
2. ↓ **Message Watch**/Nachrichten-Armbanduhr/montre
for Seiko, 1997

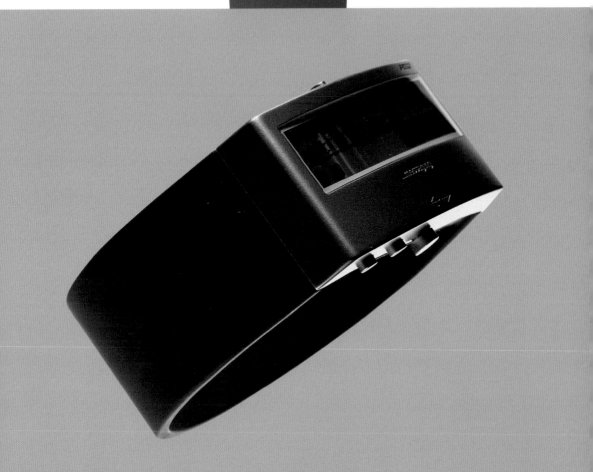

« L'environnement est un tout qui incarne le tout, mais il tend à être perçu comme existant à l'extérieur de soi. De même, on dessine parfois un objet en présumant qu'il ne sera vu que de face. On considère souvent un objet ou l'environnement comme ayant une fonction limitée, une seule raison d'être, mais ni l'environnement ni l'objet ne devraient jamais perdre leur immense potentiel de diversité. Se gratter le front avec son stylo ou empiler des documents sur une chaise sont également d'autres moyens d'utiliser ces objets. Le design peut être perçu comme un processus qui, non seulement répond à la fonction première de l'objet, mais facilite également ses fonctions alternatives que l'on découvre dans l'environnement actif de cet objet. »
NAOTO FUKASAWA

3. ← **Without Thought** cd player/CD-Player/lecteur de cd for DMN, as part of **Without Thought** project, 1990 manufactured and distributed by Muji
4. **Computer monitor**/Monitor/écran d'ordinateur for NEC, 1998

"Environment means the whole embodying the whole, but it tends to be perceived as if it exists outside of the self. Similarly, design is sometimes given an expression that assumes it will only be seen from the front. People often view an object or the environment as having a limited function, a single reason for being, but neither the environment nor the object should ever lose their immense potential for diversity. Scratching your forehead with a pencil or stacking documents on a chair are also ways of using these objects. Design can be seen as a process that not only accommodates the primary function of the object but also facilitates alternative functions that can be discovered within the object's active environment." NAOTO FUKASAWA

»Umwelt bedeutet die vollständige Verkörperung des Ganzen, aber sie wird meist als etwas wahrgenommen, das außerhalb des Selbst existiert. Auf ähnliche Weise wird Design manchmal als etwas dargestellt, vom dem man nur die Außenseite sieht. Die Leute betrachten ein Objekt oder ihre Umwelt häufig so, als hätten diese lediglich eine begrenzte Funktion, als gebe es nur einen einzigen Grund für ihre Existenz. Aber weder die Umwelt noch das Objekt sollten jemals ihr immenses Potential für Mannigfaltigkeit verlieren. Wenn man sich mit einem Bleistift am Kopf kratzt oder Schriftstücke auf einem Stuhl stapelt, sind auch das Möglichkeiten, diese Objekte zu benutzen. Design kann als ein Prozess betrachtet werden, der sich nicht nur in der primären Funktion des Objekts erfüllt, sondern darüber hinaus alternative Funktionen ermöglicht, die in der aktiven Umgebung des Objekts entdeckt werden können.« NAOTO FUKASAWA

NAOTO FUKASAWA		CLIENTS
BORN	1956	Kofu, Japan	Acuson
STUDIED	1976-80	Industrial Design, Tama Art University, Tokyo	Apple
PRACTICE	1989-	IDEO, ID Two, San Francisco	Alps
	1996	Director IDEO, Japan	Avocet
AWARDS	1991	IDSA/IDEA Gold Award	Baxter
	1994	Roter Punkt Award, Design Zentrum Nordrhein-Westfalen, Essen	Details
	1995	G-Mark/Good Design Award, JIDPO, Tokyo	Epson
	1996	iF Design Award, Hanover; IDSA/IDEA Gold Award; G-Mark/Good Design Award, JIDPO, Tokyo	Hitachi
	1997	iF Design Award, Hanover; Roter Punkt Award, Design Zentrum Nordrhein-Westfalen, Essen; G-Mark/Good Design Award, JIDPO, Tokyo	INAX
			Matsuhita
	1998	iF Design Award, Hanover; Roter Punkt Award, Design Zentrum Nordrhein-Westfalen, Essen; G-Mark/Good Design Award, JIDPO, Tokyo	Muji
			NEC
	1999	iF Design Award, Hanover	Nike
	2000	IDSA/IDEA Gold Award	NMV
EXHIBITIONS	1995	*Mutant Materials in Contemporary Design*, Museum of Modern Art, New York	Seiko
	1999	*International Design*, Berlin; Ozone Gallery, Tokyo	Sharp
	2000	*Spiral*, Tokyo	Steelcase
	2001	Workspheres, Museum of Modern Art, New York	Toshiba

off **on**

8

5. **Visio** concept packaging/Verpackungskonzept/concept de packaging for Noevir, 1998
6. **Whitebox** central processing unit (CPU)/Zentralprozessor/unité centrale d'ordinateur for NEC, 1997
7.-8. **Tile** light/Lampe/luminaire for INAX, 1998
9. **Printables** printer/Drucker/imprimante for Epson, 1998
10. **New Domestic Cooking Tools** kettle/Kessel/bouilloire for Matsushita, 1998

9

10

National

"Moving to an emotional supermarket."

Stefano Giovannoni

Stefano Giovannoni, Giovannoni Design srl, Via Gulli 4, 20 147 Milan, Italy
T +39 02 487 03495 F +39 02 487 01141 studio@stefanogiovannoni.com www.stefanogiovannoni.com

»Aufbruch zu einem emotionalen Super-
markt.«

« Vers un supermarché des émotions. »

1. **Big Bubbles** soap dish/Seifenschale/porte-savon for
Alessi, 1999
2. ↓ **Big Switch** lamp/Lampe/lampe for Segno, 1996

« Les objets ne sont ni beaux ni laids, mais adaptés ou pas à leur époque. Par leur image et la technologie utilisée pour les produire, ils communiquent des valeurs particulières qui s'intègrent à notre culture. Communiquer à travers des objets signifie raconter une histoire qui parle de la vie au travers d'un attrait sensoriel et chaleureux lié à notre mémoire et à notre monde imaginaire.
Le designer est toujours plus impliqué dans la technologie et les concepts de marketing. Il ne se contente plus de concevoir des objets mais doit adapter ses objectifs à des stratégies de design. Son champ d'action n'est plus l'objet en soi mais une hypothèse de développement global pour un produit et/ou une marque. Cela signifie de placer au cœur de son travail des stratégies liées à la communication, au marketing et à la technologie. Les besoins et les désirs du public évoluant rapidement, il doit constamment tenir compte de ces transformations tout en exprimant haut et fort sa vision personnelle du monde.
Je me suis souvent demandé si nous avions vraiment besoin de nouveaux produits. Dans la société moderne, chacun possède des objets satisfaisant à tous ses besoins fonctionnels. Mais, pour créer la richesse, les compagnies doivent produire en quantités toujours plus grandes. D'un côté, nous n'avons pas besoin de nouveaux produits, de l'autre, nous devons développer un nouveau système virtuel afin d'anticiper l'architecture fictive et toujours plus sophistiquée de nos désirs. Les produits de cette nouvelle réalité virtuelle sont de plus en plus éloignés de toute véritable fonction. Notre réalité se construit étape par étape, en annexant de nouveaux paysages virtuels qui élargissent les frontières de notre pays des merveilles. »
STEFANO GIOVANNONI

3. ← **Magicbunny** toothpick holder/Zahnstocherhalter/porte cure-dents for Alessi, 1998
4. **Molly** weighing scale/Küchenwaage/balance for Alessi, 1995
5. **Mago'** broom/Besen/balai for Magis, 1998
6. **Alibaba** vacuum jug/Thermoskanne/cruche Thermos for Alessi, 1998

4

"Objects are not beautiful or ugly but are either suited or not to their time. Through their image and the technology used to produce them they communicate particular values that become part of our culture. To communicate through objects means telling a story of something that relates to life through a warm sensorial appeal connected with our memory and imaginary world.
The designer is increasingly involved in marketing concepts and technology. He cannot simply 'design' objects but must now shift his goals towards design strategies. The field of action is no longer that of the object but a hypothesis of comprehensive development for the product/company. This means putting strategies linked to communication, marketing and technology at the core of one's work. The public's needs and desires evolve rapidly – so it is necessary to take in these transformations all the time, while delivering loud and clear your personal view of the world.
I have asked myself many times whether we really need new products. Everybody in a developed society is in possession of the objects that answer every functional need. But to create wealth, companies have to produce in larger and larger quantities – on the one hand we have no need for new products, but on the other hand we must develop a new virtual system in order to anticipate the new and increasingly sophisticated fictional architecture of our desires. Products belonging to this kind of virtual reality are further and further removed from real function. Our reality is built step by step by annexing new virtual landscapes which extend the borders of our wonderland."
STEFANO GIOVANNONI

6

»Die Frage ist nicht, ob Designobjekte schön oder hässlich sind, sondern ob sie zeitgemäß sind oder nicht. Durch ihr Image und durch die zu ihrer Herstellung eingesetzte Technik vermitteln sie bestimmte Werte, die zu einem Bestandteil unserer Kultur werden. Durch Objekte zu kommunizieren, bedeutet, eine Geschichte zu erzählen, die eine Beziehung zum Leben hat. Das gelingt mit Objekten, die eine warme, sinnliche Ausstrahlung haben, mit der sich unsere Erinnerungen und unsere Vorstellungswelt verbinden.
Designer sind zunehmend in die Bereiche Marketing und Technologie involviert. Sie können nicht mehr einfach nur Objekte gestalten, sondern müssen ihre Ziele nun darauf verlagern, Designstrategien zu entwerfen. Das Tätigkeitsfeld von Designern ist nicht länger auf das Objekt beschränkt, sondern es gehört jetzt auch eine Analyse der allgemeinen Entwicklung des Produkts oder des Unternehmens dazu. Das heißt, dass man die mit Kommunikation, Marketing und Technik verbundenen Strategien zum Kernpunkt seiner Arbeit macht. Da sich die in der Öffentlichkeit herrschenden Bedürfnisse und Wünsche mit großer Geschwindigkeit entwickeln, ist es notwendig, diese Wandlungen ständig zu reflektieren und gleichzeitig seine persönliche Weltsicht laut und deutlich kundzutun.
Ich habe mich schon oft gefragt, ob wir wirklich ständig neue Produkte brauchen. In unserer Industriegesellschaft besitzt jeder die Gebrauchsgegenstände, die zur Befriedigung sämtlicher funktionalen Bedürfnisse erforderlich sind. Um ihren Profit zu steigern, müssen die Untenehmen jedoch in immer größeren Mengen produzieren. Auf der einen Seite haben wir zwar keinen Bedarf an neuen Produkten, aber andererseits müssen wir ein virtuelles System entwickeln, um die neue und zunehmend differenzierte fiktive Struktur unserer Bedürfnisse vorauszusehen. Die Produkte dieser virtuellen Realität entfernen sich immer weiter von einer wirklichen Funktion. Unsere Realität entsteht Schritt für Schritt durch die Annexion neuer virtueller Landschaften, welche die Grenzen unserer Phantasiewelten ausdehnen.« STEFANO GIOVANNONI

5

7. **Bombo** chair/Stuhl/chaise for Magis, 1999

8. **Volcano** watch/Armbanduhr/montre for Alba-Seiko, 1998

STEFANO GIOVANNONI	CLIENTS
BORN 1954 La Spezia, Italy	Alessi
STUDIED 1978 graduated in Architecture, University of Florence	Asplund
1979- teaching and research, Faculty of Architecture, University of Florence, Domus Academy, Milan and the Institute of Design, Reggio Emilia	Cappellini
	Flos
AWARDS 1980 First Prize, *Shinchenchiku Residential Design Competition*, Tokyo; First Prize, *Competition for a square at Santa Croce sull'Arno*, Florence	Kankyo
	Magis
1985 Second Prize, *Shinchenchiku Residential Design Competition*, Tokyo	Pulsar
1989 First Prize (with Andrea Branzi and Remo Buti), *Competition for the restructuring of the historical centre at Casteldisangro-Aquila*	Saab
	Seiko
1994 Design Plus Award, Frankfurt/Main	
1996 Design Plus Award, Frankfurt/Main	
1999 if Design Award, Hanover	
EXHIBITIONS 1991 designed the Italian Pavilion at *Les Capitales Européennes du Nouveau Design*, Centre Georges Pompidou, Paris	

9. **Octopussy** watch/Armbanduhr/montre for Alba-Seiko, 1999
10. **Rimini** cutlery drainer/Abtropfgefäß für Besteck/égouttoir à couverts for Alessi, 1998
11. **Rigatone** spaghetti storage jar/Spaghettiglas/bocal à spaghettis for Alessi, 1998
12. **Bruce** table-lighter/Tischfeuerzeug/briquet de table for Alessi, 1999
13. **Big Clip** photo frame/Bilderrahmen/cadre de photo for Alessi, 1998
14. **Johnny the Diver** plunger/Saugnapf/ventouse for Alessi, 2000
15. **Bombo** revolving stool/Drehhocker/tabouret pivotant for Magis, 1998

"The less you see the designer's effort in the work, the better – effort should not be a visual commodity; it's simply a means to an end."

Sam Hecht

Sam Hecht, c/o Industrial Facility, Pegasus House, 2nd Floor, 116–120 Golden Lane, London EC1Y OTF, England, T +44 207 253 3234 F +44 207 490 4411
sam@industrialfacility.co.uk www.industrialfacility.co.uk

»Je weniger man einem Objekt die Mühe des Designers ansieht, desto besser. Die Mühe sollte keine visuelle Ware werden; sie ist einfach Mittel zum Zweck.«

« Moins l'on perçoit l'effort du designer dans son travail, mieux c'est. L'effort ne devrait pas constituer un produit mais uniquement le moyen d'arriver à une fin. »

1. **Rice cooker**/Reiskocher/riseuse for Matsushita, 1997
2. ↓ **Water faucet** and control/Wasserhahn und Regler/
robinetterie for INAX, 1998

« Le design continue d'être confronté à un dilemme : déterminer quelle part du produit devrait être développée afin qu'il soit choisi en boutique et quelle part développer pour qu'il soit utilisable. Dans un modèle théorique, le design est conçu pour un usage spécifique et la popularité d'un produit se mesure à la réussite de cet objectif. Mais, dans la pratique, bien fonctionner ne suffit pas. Le produit doit être choisi et acheté sur un lieu de vente où il sera en concurrence avec de nombreux autres produits fonctionnant aussi bien. D'où une situation où les marchés saturés nécessitent que " l'attrait " prime sur la " fonction ". Les produits sont devenus l'incarnation de leur propre marque.

Si je veux créer un objet, dois-je renoncer à la fonction pour privilégier l'attrait ? Nous n'avons pas besoin de voir ce que nous faisons pour obtenir un résultat. La forme est un mécanisme plutôt qu'une esthétique (ou une surface sur laquelle intervient le choix). Elle doit être élaborée et non appliquée. La simplicité des outils illustre cette idée : leur simplification résulte d'une production culturelle complexe. La question " allons-nous concevoir un beau marteau ou un marteau tout court ? " n'a pas de sens. Pourquoi un ordinateur ou une télévision ne seraient-ils pas conçus de la même manière ? L'avenir deviendra simpliste. C'est indispensable si nous voulons consommer de la technologie. L'illustration de la complexité n'est pas importante, seul le résultat compte. La forme deviendra mécanique, puisant ses racines dans l'ordinaire. Les projets impliquant une complexité toujours croissante, la vérité doit être d'autant plus éclatante. » SAM HECHT

3. ← **Soft Wrist** phone/Telefon/téléphone for ElekSen (limited edition), 1999-2000
4. **XY** toaster/Toaster/grille-pain for Matsushita, 1999

"Design continues to face a dilemma when determining what portion of a product should be developed to be chosen in the shop, and what portion of it should be developed to be used. In an educational model, design is produced according to use, and a product's popularity is measured by how successfully it does its job. But in the shop model, working well is simply not enough. The product needs to be selected and purchased in an arena where many products, from different manufacturers, work just as well. This has led to a situation where saturated markets require the 'choosing' to be more important than the 'using'. Products have become their own embodiment of branding.

If I am to design, must I relinquish the using for the choosing? Like the phrase 'things become second nature', we do not need to see what we are doing to achieve a result. Form is a mechanism for use, rather than an aesthetic (or a surface upon which choice is played out). It is something that needs to be evolved and not applied. The simplicity of tools illustrates this idea: their simplification results from complex cultural production. The question 'shall we design a beautiful hammer or a plain hammer?' is absurd. And there is no reason why a computer or a television is not thought of in the same way. The future will become simplistic. It needs to be, if we are to consume technology, where the illustration of complexity is of no importance, but only the result. Form will become mechanical, with its roots in the ordinary. As projects involve an ever-greater complexity, the more resonant the truth needs to be." SAM HECHT

»Design steht weiterhin vor einem Dilemma, wenn es darum geht, zu entscheiden, welcher Aspekt eines Produkts für den Kaufanreiz und welcher für den Gebrauch entwickelt wird. Im theoretischen Modell wird Design im Hinblick auf seine Funktionalität produziert, und der Erfolg eines Produkts misst sich daran, wie gut es seine jeweilige Funktion erfüllt. In der Verkaufspraxis reicht es jedoch nicht, dass ein Produkt gut funktioniert. Denn es muss in einem Umfeld ausgewählt und gekauft werden, in dem es viele Produkte von anderen Herstellern gibt, die genauso gut funktionieren. Das hat zu einer Situation geführt, die gesättigte Märkte dazu zwingen, dem kommerziellen Aspekt Vorrang vor dem funktionalen Aspekt einzuräumen. Die Produkte sind damit zu ihrem eigenen Markenzeichen geworden. Muss ich als Designer zugunsten des Marktwerts auf den Gebrauchswert verzichten? Wie in dem Satz ›Dinge werden zur zweiten Natur‹ anklingt, brauchen wir nicht zu verstehen, was wir tun, um ein Ergebnis zu erzielen. Form ist mehr ein Mechanismus für den Gebrauch als ein ästhetisches Kriterium (oder eine Oberfläche, die den kommerziellen Aspekt ausspielt). Form ist etwas, das entwickelt und nicht angewendet werden muss. Diese Idee wird in der Einfachheit von Werkzeugen anschaulich, denn die Vereinfachung ist das Resultat eines komplexen kulturellen Produktionsprozesses. Absurd ist die Frage, ob man einen schönen oder einen schlichten Hammer entwerfen soll. Und es gibt keinen Grund, warum das nicht auch für die Gestaltung eines Computers oder eines Fernsehers gelten soll. Die Zukunft wird eine zunehmende Vereinfachung bringen. Und das muss auch so sein, wenn wir eine Technologie nutzen wollen, bei der nicht die Darstellung von Komplexität zählt, sondern nur das Ergebnis. Form wird mechanisch werden und ihre Wurzeln im Alltäglichen haben. Gerade weil Designprojekte immer komplexer werden, muss der Aspekt der Wahrhaftigkeit umso deutlicher zur Geltung kommen.« SAM HECHT

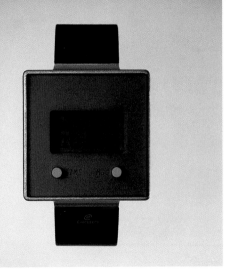

5. Desktop computer/Arbeitsplatzrechner/ordinateur
de bureau for NEC, 1998
6. **Airbus A380** window/Flugzeugfenster/hublot for Airbus
Industrie, 2000
7. **Post-It** e-mail watch/E-Mail-Armbanduhr/montre
for Seiko Communications, 1997
8. **Watercycle Pavilion**/Wasserkreislauf-Pavillon/Pavillon
du cycle de l'eau for Thames Water, 2000
9. **LG** dishwasher/Geschirrspüler/lave-vaisselle for LG
Electronics, 2000

"I see myself as a consultant who's thoughtful yet passionate, who aims to create benefits and magic for clients and consumers alike."

Geoff Hollington

Geoff Hollington, Hollington, 8th Floor, Newcombe House, 45 Notting Hill Gate, London W11 3LQ, England
T +44 20 7792 1865 F +44 20 7792 8145 geoff@hollington.co.uk www.hollington.com

»Ich sehe mich selbst als nachdenklichen und dennoch leidenschaftlichen Berater, der bestrebt ist, für Auftraggeber ebenso wie für Konsumenten Vorteile und Magie zu erzeugen.«

« Je me vois comme un consultant, à la fois prévenant et passionné, cherchant à apporter un plus et à faire rêver tant mes commanditaires que les consommateurs. »

1. **VuTable** home-office concept project/Entwurf für ein Heimbüro/projet de bureau intégré for Herman Miller, 2000
2. ↓ **Advantix T7000** advanced Photo System camera/APS-Kamera/appareil photo for Eastman Kodak Company, 2000

»Was ist Design? Man findet es in verschiedenen Formen. Ein großer Teil des Produktdesigns ist ›Mode‹. Dann gibt es das ernsthafte, ›problemlösungsorientierte‹ Design. Hier sind die Anforderungen komplex, und divergierende Faktoren wie Kosten, Leistung, Benutzerfreundlichkeit, Fabrikation und Nachhaltigkeit müssen miteinander in Einklang gebracht werden. Manches Design ist auch einfach (?) inspirierte ›Erfindung‹, eine brillante Idee, die ausgearbeitet und verwirklicht wurde.
Und dann gibt es die Art von Design, bei der es darauf ankommt, die komplexen Neigungen und ›Leidenschaften‹, die Sehnsüchte und Wünsche anzusprechen, die für individuelle Benutzer und Konsumenten kennzeichnend sind. Meiner Ansicht nach ist dieser Bereich der härteste, und der, in dem der Produktdesigner allein operiert. Um Produkte zu entwerfen, die von Menschen begehrt und geschätzt werden, muss man sich ernsthaft mit all den Formen von Design auseinandersetzen, die ich erwähnt habe. Ansonsten wird das Produkt mit Sicherheit auf die eine oder andere Weise am Wesentlichen vorbeigehen. Aber das menschliche Wesen, das im Zentrum des Unternehmens steht, der Konsument oder Anwender, braucht oft viel mehr als eine vernünftige Lösung: Er oder sie braucht etwas, das ein wenig Leidenschaft entfacht. Und man kann keine Leidenschaft hervorrufen, ohne sie selbst zu geben. Das bedeutet, dass ich als Designer leidenschaftlich sein muss. Gegenwärtig hat das Produktdesign gewaltige soziale und kommerzielle Konsequenzen. Aber Designer werden immer noch häufig als etwas naive Kunsthandwerker betrachtet, von denen man nicht erwartet, dass sie ihre Arbeit in einem globalen Zusammenhang sehen. Diese Perspektive wird dem Management vorbehalten, und das ist schade. Ich als Produktdesigner habe mehr Erfahrungen in unterschiedlichen Wirtschaftszweigen und Märkten als die meisten meiner Klienten. Etliche von ihnen schätzen das und profitieren von unserer Erfahrung und unserem Wissen. Zu Beginn dieses neuen Jahrhunderts sollten wir dem Produktdesign jenen Rang einräumen, der ihm gebührt.« GEOFF HOLLINGTON

"What is design? It certainly comes in several flavours. A lot of product design is 'fashion'. There's serious 'problem-solving' design, where the brief is complex and issues of cost, performance, usability, manufacture and sustainability must be reconciled. Some design is simply (?) inspired 'invention', a brilliant idea worked out and made real.
And then you have the kind of design that's about addressing the complex drives and 'passions', desires and needs that characterize individual users and consumers. That's the really tough arena so far as I can see and the place where the product designer operates alone. To create products that people will desire and then enjoy, you have to deal seriously with all the kinds of design I've described or the product is sure to miss the point in some fatal way. But the human being at the focus of the enterprise, the consumer, the user, often needs a lot more than a sensible solution; she or he needs something to feel a little bit passionate about. And you can't engender passion without giving of it so, as a designer, I have to be passionate.
Product design is now of enormous social and commercial consequence. Designers, however, are still often regarded as somewhat naïve artisans who are not expected to see their contribution in terms of the big picture; that place belongs to management, which is unfortunate. As a product designer, I have experience of more business in more categories and more markets than most of my clients and some of them value that and make use of our experience and insights. As the new century unrolls, let's give to product design the status it deserves."
GEOFF HOLLINGTON

« Qu'est-ce que le design ? On le trouve sous différentes formes. Une grande partie de la production relève de la " mode ". Il y a ensuite le design sérieux qui " résout des problèmes ", où les directives sont complexes et les questions de coût, de performance, de fonctionnalité, de fabrication et de rentabilité doivent être prises en compte. Certaines créations sont simplement (?) des " inventions " inspirées, une idée brillante élaborée et concrétisée.
Puis il y a le design qui traite des pulsions complexes et des " passions ", des désirs et des besoins des utilisateurs et des consommateurs individuels. A mon avis, c'est la branche la plus difficile, celle où le designer opère seul. Pour créer des objets que les gens désireront et apprécieront, il faut traiter sérieusement tous les types de design que je viens de décrire, autrement le produit est sûr de rater sa cible d'une manière ou d'une autre. Mais l'être humain que vise l'entreprise, le consommateur, l'utilisateur, a souvent besoin de bien plus que d'une solution astucieuse : il lui faut quelque chose qui le passionne. Or, on ne peut susciter de la passion sans en ressentir soi-même. Donc, en tant que designer, je dois être passionné.
Le design de produits a aujourd'hui une énorme portée sociale et commerciale. Pourtant, les designers sont encore souvent considérés comme des artisans un peu naïfs dont on attend rarement qu'ils sachent situer leur travail dans un contexte plus grand. En tant que designer de produits, j'ai pourtant plus d'expérience dans de nombreux domaines et sur de nombreux marchés que la plupart de mes commanditaires, ce que certains d'entre eux apprécient et savent exploiter. En ce début de millénaire, donnons au design de produits le statut qu'il mérite. »
GEOFF HOLLINGTON

3.-4. **Alu-1** sunglasses/Sonnenbrillen/lunettes de soleil (studio concept project), 1999
5. **Fit ... for Life** fan, torch and radio/Ventilator, Taschenlampe und Radio/ventilateur, lampe torche et radio for New Pacific Industrial, 2001

GEOFF HOLLINGTON		CLIENTS
BORN	1949	Essex, England
STUDIED	1971	BA Industrial Design (Engineering), Central St Martin's College of Art and Design, London
	1974	MA Environmental Design, Royal College of Art, London
PRACTICE	1976-78	member of design team for new town of Milton Keynes – responsible for landscaping and street furniture
	1978	formed a consulting partnership with architect Michael Glickman
	1980	founded Hollington Associates, London
AWARDS	1988	Gold Award, Institute of Business Designers, USA
	1989	Silver and Bronze Awards, Institute of Business Designers, USA
	1991 & 92	Silver Award, Institute of Business Designers, USA; Gold IDEA Award, IDSA
	1993	Best of Category, iF Design Award, Hanover
	1996	Good Design Award, Chicago Athenaeum
	1998	Merit Award, One Club, One Show Interactive, New York
	2001	iF Design Award, Hanover

CLIENTS

Artifort
Cable & Wireless
Caradon Group
Eastman Kodak
Ericsson
Filofax
Gillette
Herman Miller
Hille
Matsushita
NEC
New Pacific Industrial
Parker Pen
Science Museum, London

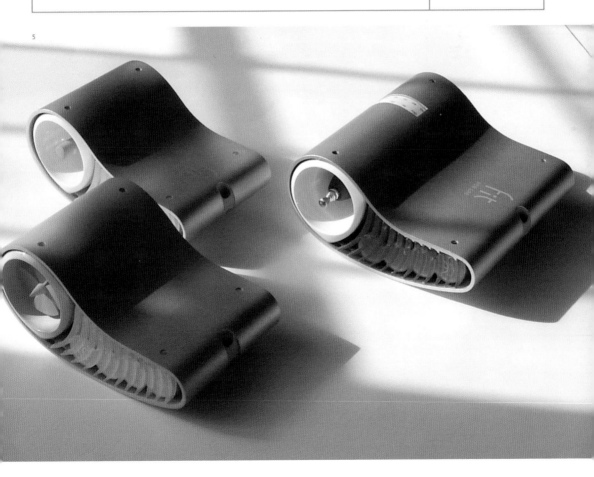

"Design is about creatively exploiting constraint."

Inflate

Inflate, 11, Northburgh Street, London EC1V 0AN, England
T +44 20 7251 5453 F +44 20 7250 0311 info@inflate.co.uk www.inflate.co.uk

»Beim Design geht es um die kreative Ausnutzung von Beschränkungen.«

« Le design, c'est exploiter les contraintes de manière créative. »

1. **Egg cup**/Eierbecher/coquetier for Inflate,
1995 – designer: Michael Sodeau
2. ↓ **Lounge chair**/Klubsessel/transat for Inflate,
1997 – designer: Nick Crosbie

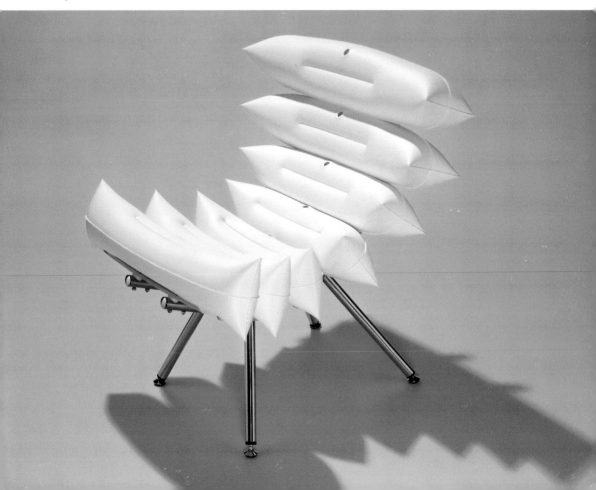

« Nous sommes spécialisés dans le développement de projets autour de processus de fabrication vieux et sous-exploités. A l'origine, toutes nos créations étaient gonflables et utilisaient des soudures à hautes fréquences. En 1997, nous avons ajouté à notre portfolio le moulage par immersion puis, en 2000, nous avons lancé nos premiers produits moulés par rotation. Nous utilisons nos propres produits de marque pour expérimenter commercialement des processus de fabrication et illustrer le potentiel de notre travail. Parallèlement, nous aimons surprendre nos clients avec des gadgets ingénieux allant des petites invitations publicitaires à l'architecture portable. Tout le monde veut laisser sa trace. Nous voulons marquer les esprits mais, pour cela, il nous faut nous démarquer des autres. Notre priorité est de présenter quelque chose de nouveau et non de capitaliser sur ce que nous avons déjà fait. Pour être reconnus en tant que source d'inspiration, nous devons aller de l'avant. C'est pourquoi nous avons monté "The Shed", une unité à part chargée de générer de nouvelles idées et des principes inédits qui nous permettront de continuer à vendre de la surprise sans frais supplémentaires. »
INFLATE

3. ← **Fruit bowl**/Fruchtschale/coupe à fruits for Inflate, 1995 – designer: Nick Crosbie
4. **Digital Grass** cd & letter & toast holder/CD- & Brief- & Toastgestell/porte cd, lettres et toasts for Inflate, 1997 – designer: Mark Garside

"We specialise in developing projects around old, under-exploited manufacturing processes. Initially all our designs were inflatable and used high-frequency welding processes. By 1997 we had added dip moulding to our portfolio, and in 2000 our first rotational moulded products were launched. We use our own branded products as a way of commercially experimenting with manufacturing processes and illustrating the potential of our work. Alongside our branded products, we like to surprise the client with ingenious gimmicks ranging from small promotional invitations to portable architecture.
Everyone wants to make history in some sort of way. We want to make an impact, but you won't if you do the same things as everyone else. Our priority is coming up with something new, not just capitalizing on what we've already done. To be known as a source of inspiration, we need to keep moving along, and for this we've set up 'The Shed' – a separate unit for the generation of new ideas and principles that will enable us to continue selling surprise at no extra cost." INFLATE

»Wir sind auf die Entwicklung von Projekten rund um alte, wenig genutzte Herstellungsverfahren spezialisiert. Ursprünglich waren alle unsere Designs aufblasbar und verwendeten Schweißverfahren mit Hochfrequenz. 1997 fügten wir unserer Palette das Heißtauchen hinzu, und im Jahr 2000 liefen unsere ersten rotationsgeformten Produkte vom Stapel. Wir verwenden unsere eigenen Markenprodukte für das kommerzielle Experimentieren mit verschiedenen Produktionsmethoden und zur Illustration unseres Arbeitspotentials. Neben unseren Markenprodukten überraschen wir unsere Kunden gerne mit geistreichen Spielereien, die von kleinen Werbegeschenken bis zu tragbarer Architektur reichen. Jeder möchte auf die eine oder andere Art Geschichte machen. Auch wir wollen eine beeinflussende Wirkung haben, aber das schafft man nicht, indem man das Gleiche tut wie alle anderen. Unser oberstes Ziel ist, etwas Neues zu präsentieren und nicht bloß Kapital aus dem zu schlagen, was wir bereits gemacht haben. Um als Inspirationsquelle anerkannt zu sein, müssen wir uns ständig weiter vorwärtsbewegen, und deshalb haben wir ›The Shed‹ gegründet – einen gesonderten Geschäftszweig für die Entwicklung neuer Ideen und Prinzipien, die uns ermöglichen werden, auch in Zukunft Design zu verkaufen, das verblüfft, aber keine Mehrkosten verursacht.«
INFLATE

INFLATE

FOUNDED	1995	by Nick Crosbie (b. 1971 – Art Director) and Mark Sodeau (b. 1970 – Production Manager) with Michael Sodeau (see separate entry)
STUDIED		NICK CROSBIE
	1990-93	BA Industrial Design, Central St Martin's College of Art and Design, London
	1993-95	MA Industrial Design, Royal College of Art, London
		MARK SODEAU
	1989-92	B-Eng Aeronautical Engineering, City University, London
AWARDS	1996	*Blueprint*/100 % Design Award
	1998	Talente Award
	1999	*Blueprint*/100 % Design Award
	2001	Peugeot Design Award
EXHIBITIONS	1996	100 % Design, London; *Plastic Fantastic*, Frankfurt/Main
	1998	British Council, Cologne; *Light & Design – The Best of the 20th Century*, Interieur Biennial, Kortrijk
	1998-99	*Swell*, Victoria & Albert Museum, London
	1999	*British Design – 9000 Miles from Home*, Taipei; *Happening*, Tokyo

CLIENTS

Boots the Chemist
Creation Records
Habitat
Imagination
L'Oreal
Paul Smith
Virgin
also self-manufacture

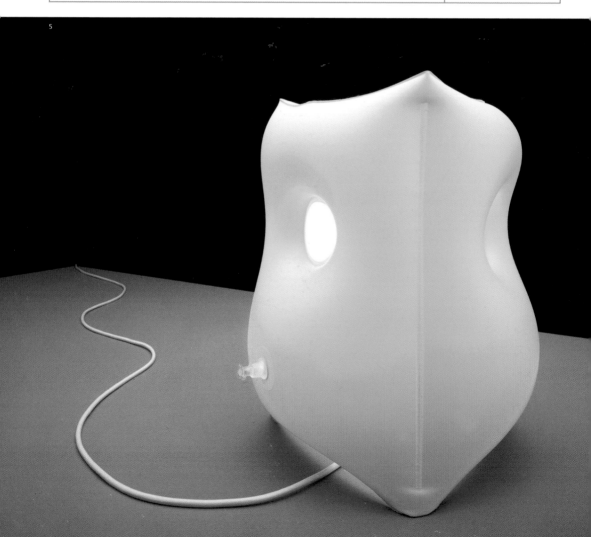

5

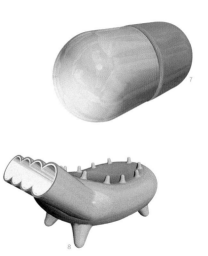

5. **Table light**/Tischlampe/lampe de table for Inflate,
1995 – designer: Nick Crosbie
6. **Mr & Mrs Prickly** salt and pepper shakers/Salz- und
Pfefferstreuer/salière et poivrière for Inflate, 1997 –
designer: Nick Crosbie
7. **Lozenge** storage capsule/Aufbewahrungskapsel/capsule
de rangement for Inflate, 2000 – designer: Inflate Studio
8. **Soap lounger** soap and toothbrush holder/Seifen- und
Zahnbürstenhalter/porte savou et brosse à dents for
Inflate, 2000 – designer: Inflate Studio
9. **MEMO** bean bag/Sitzsack/pouf for Inflate, 1999 –
designers: Inflate & Ron Arad

"The strength of design is that it provides a way of thinking in advance of the consequences of our actions on materials."

Massimo Iosa Ghini

Massimo Iosa Ghini, Iosa Ghini srl, Via Castiglione 6, 40 124 Bologna, Italy
T +39 051 236 563 F +39 051 237 712 info@iosaghini.it www.iosaghini.it

»Die Stärke von Design liegt darin, dass es vor die sichtbaren Folgen unserer Materialverarbeitung das Denken setzt.«

« La force du design est qu'il anticipe les conséquences de nos actes sur les matériaux. »

1. **Clone** armchair/Sessel/fauteuil from Biosphere
Collection for Bonaldo, 2000
2. ↓ **Metropolis 2000** sofa/Sofa/canapé for Roche Bobois,
2000

»In Zukunft wird es zwei Arten von Design geben: Die eine wird mit Interpretationen und neuen Ideen einhergehen, die in Zusammenarbeit mit der Großindustrie entwickelt werden. Dieser Ansatz wird immer Lösungen hervorbringen, die der Maßschneiderei gleichen, wo die äußeren Aspekte eines Objekts seine inneren Aspekte verbessern. Das Hauptziel dieser Art von Design wird die Verknüpfung von Computertechnologie mit dem eigentlichen Inhalt des Objekts sein, wodurch dieses eher die Funktion einer Schnittstelle erhält.

Die andere Art entspricht einer besonderen Eignung des Designs: Es ist die Adaptierung bereits bestehender Lösungen. Hierbei wird stets die Ressourcenknappheit mitbedacht, aus der sich die Themen Entwicklung und Innovation des materiellen Objekts ergeben, so dass es sich schließlich für die Massenproduktion eignet.

In beiden Kategorien werden jene die führenden Kräfte sein, die am ehesten imstande sind, zeitgemäße Ausdrucksformen zu finden. Die Herausforderung für alle Designer wird in der Darstellung dieser Entwicklung durch Ästhetik oder andere Kommunikationsmittel liegen.«
MASSIMO IOSA GHINI

"Design of the future will be of two kinds. One kind will involve interpretations and new ideas evolved in co-operation with large-scale industries. This approach will always produce solutions that look more like tailoring, where the outer aspects of an object can improve its internal aspects. The primary aim of this type of design will be the linking of computer technology with the body of the object, thereby allowing it to function more as an interface.

The other type will be that for which design is particularly well suited, i. e. the adaptation of existing solutions while bearing in mind the shortage of resources, from which the themes of development support and innovation of the material object will emerge, so that finally the object is suitable for mass production.

Within these two approaches, the leaders will be those who are best able to express contemporaneity. The challenge for all designers will be the presentation of this evolution through aesthetics or other means of communication."
MASSIMO IOSA GHINI

« A l'avenir, il y aura deux formes de design. L'une fera appel à des interprétations et de nouvelles idées élaborées en coopération avec des industries à grande échelle. Cette approche produira toujours des solutions proches de la confection, où les aspects extérieurs d'un objet améliorent ses aspects intérieurs. L'objectif principal de ce type de design sera de lier la technologie informatique au corps de l'objet, lui permettant de fonctionner davantage comme une interface.

La seconde forme est celle qui convient le plus au design : adapter des solutions existantes tout en tenant compte de la pénurie de ressources, faire ressortir les aspects de soutien au développement et de recherche de nouveaux matériaux afin que l'objet en question soit mieux adapté à la production de masse.

Dans ces deux approches, les leaders seront ceux qui sauront le mieux exprimer la contemporanéité. Pour tous les designers, le défi sera de présenter cette évolution à travers une esthétique ou d'autres moyens de communication. » MASSIMO IOSA GHINI

3. **Lithos** vase holder/Vasenhalterung/porte-vase from Biosphere Collection for Bonaldo, 2000
4. **Giorno** faucet/Wasserhahn/robinet for Dornbracht, 1999-2000
5. **DNA** shelves/Regale/bibliothèque from Biosphere Collection for Bonaldo, 2000
6. **T** espresso & cappuccino & chocolate maker/Espresso- & Cappuccino- & Kakaomaschine/machine à express, cappuccino et chocolat chaud for Massin Tuttoespresso, 1999
7. **H2O** table/Tisch from Biosphere Collection for Bonaldo, 2000
8. **Crio** cosmetics table/Kosmetiktisch/table cosmétique from Biosphere Collection for Bonaldo, 2000

MASSIMO IOSA GHINI		CLIENTS
BORN	1959 Borgo Tossignano, Bologna, Italy	Bonaldo
STUDIED	1983-87 Studied architecture in Florence	Cassina
	1987-89 Politecnico di Milano	Duravit
PRACTICE	1981 member of Zak-Ark group	Dornbracht
	1983 co-founded the Bolidismo movement with Pierangelo Caramia and others	Ferrari
	1985 member of Memphis design group; established Studio Iosa Ghini	Fiam
AWARDS	1987 *Young Design in Milan*	Flou
	1988 Roscoe Award, USA	Hoesch
	1990 *100 top Designers* by *Metropolitan Home*, USA	Massin Tuttoespresso
EXHIBITIONS	1986 Memphis *12 New* collection, Milan	Moroso
	1988 installation at the Centre Georges Pompidou, Paris	Roche Bobois
	1989 first solo exhibition of graphics and objects, Inspiration Gallery, AXIS Centre, Tokyo, *M. Iosa Ghini*, Design Gallery, Milan	Silhouette
		Suaidero
	1992 Design Show *M. Iosa Ghini*, Bologna	Üstra
	1995 *12 nach Memphis*, Museum für angewandte Kunst, Frankfurt/Main	Yamagiwa Lighting
	2000 train station for Expo 2000, Hanover, Essete Benessete, Milan Triennale	Zumtabel

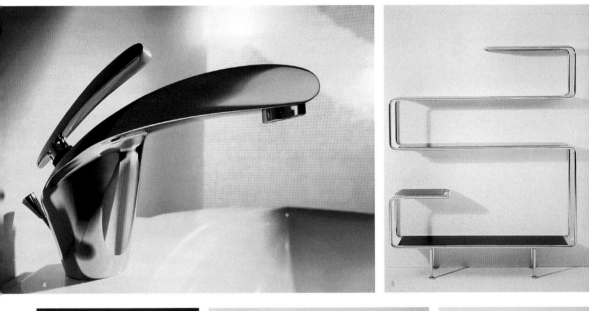

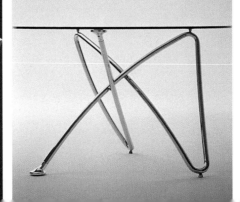

"Always question why you are doing something, unless you are being paid a ridiculous amount of money, then really question it."

James Irvine

James Irvine, Via Sirtori 4, 20 129 Milan, Italy
T +39 02 295 34532 F +39 02 295 34534 james@james-irvine.com www.james-irvine.com

»Man sollte sich immer fragen, warum man etwas tut – es sei denn, man bekommt eine absurde Summe Geld dafür bezahlt; dann sollte man es wirklich in Frage stellen.«

« Toujours remettre en question ce pour quoi on fait quelque chose, à moins d'être payé des sommes astronomiques pour le faire, auquel cas, il faut vraiment se poser des questions. »

1. **Soundwave** microwave & radio/Mikrowellenherd &
Radio/four à micro-ondes & radio for Whirlpool, 2000
2. ↓ **Üstra** city bus (Hanover)/Stadtbus(Hannover)/
autobus (Hanovre) for Mercedes Benz, 1999

« Le rôle classique du designer est destiné à évoluer dans un futur proche. Naturellement, la récente "guerre des styles" continuera et deviendra de plus en plus sophistiquée. Toutefois, les designers et les industriels prennent déjà conscience de sa futilité. Même les consommateurs s'en sont lassés. Ils commencent à remettre en question la nécessité fondamentale de tous ces biens : " Ai-je besoin de dépenser des milliers de livres dans une voiture pour rester bloqué dans des embouteillages ? Je peux peut-être m'en passer. Mais alors, par quoi vais-je la remplacer ? " J'ai l'impression que beaucoup de produits sont conçus étape par étape par des gens qui ne se parlent pas, des spécialistes aveuglés par leur propre spécialité. On se pose rarement les questions de base. Je suis sûr qu'une nouvelle race de penseurs verra le jour dans l'industrie. Ils ne seront pas designers mais des gens capables de relier différentes disciplines afin de donner un nouveau sens aux produits sur le plan écologique ou social. J'attends avec impatience le jour où l'industrie me demandera de participer à cette pensée. Naturellement, en attendant, je suis prêt à débattre de questions plus pointues telles que le diamètre du pied de ma prochaine chaise. » JAMES IRVINE

3. ← **Luigi** bottle opener & corkscrew/Flaschenöffner & Korkenzieher/ouvre-bouteilles et tire-bouchons for Alfi, 1998
4. **Flik** folding chairs/Klappstühle/chaises pliantes for Magis, 1998

"The classic role of designers is destined to change in the near future. The recent 'style wars' will of course carry on and become more and more sophisticated. However, industry and designers alike are becoming aware that it's all getting a bit pointless. Even consumers are starting to wise up. They are beginning to question the fundamental necessity of all these things: 'Do I need to spend thousands of pounds on a car then sit in a traffic jam? Perhaps I don't need a car. But the problem is how do I replace it?'
I have the feeling many products are designed in steps by people who don't talk to each other – specialists blinkered by their own speciality. Basic issues are rarely discussed. I am sure a new breed of thinkers will become relevant to industry. They will not be designers but people capable of connecting different disciplines to bring a new relevance to products whether ecological or social. I am looking forward to the day when my relationship with industry will be participating in such thinking. Of course in the meantime, I am quite willing to discuss the finer points of the radii on the leg of my next chair." JAMES IRVINE

»Die klassische Rolle von Designern wird sich in naher Zukunft zwangsläufig verändern. Der unlängst ausgebrochene ›Krieg der Stile‹ wird natürlich weitergehen und sogar immer subtilere Formen annehmen. Industrie und Designer selbst werden sich jedoch allmählich der Sinnlosigkeit dessen bewusst. Sogar die Konsumenten sind inzwischen schlauer geworden und beginnen, die grundsätzliche Notwendigkeit all dieser Dinge in Frage zu stellen: ›Muss ich wirklich Zehntausende Mark für ein neues Auto bezahlen, nur um dann damit im Stau zu stehen? Vielleicht brauche ich ja gar kein Auto. Das Problem ist nur: ›Was nehme ich stattdessen?‹
Ich habe den Eindruck, dass viele Produkte in einzelnen Arbeitsschritten von Leuten entworfen werden, die nicht miteinander reden – Spezialisten, die sich von ihrem eigenen Spezialistentum Scheuklappen anlegen lassen. Dabei werden grundlegende Probleme nur selten zur Sprache gebracht. Ich bin sicher, dass eine neue Generation von Denkern für die Industrie an Bedeutung gewinnt. Das werden allerdings keine Designer sein, sondern Menschen, die interdisziplinär vorgehen, um Produkten eine neue Relevanz zu verleihen – sei es auf ökologischer oder sozialer Ebene. Ich freue mich schon auf den Tag, an dem ich in meiner Zusammenarbeit mit der Industrie an dieser Denkweise teilhaben werde. Bis dahin bin ich natürlich gerne bereit, über die Feinheiten der Radiusberechnung für die Beine meines nächsten Stuhls zu diskutieren.«
JAMES IRVINE

5. **Earth** planters/Übertöpfe/pots de fleurs for Arabia, 2001

JAMES IRVINE			CLIENTS
BORN	1958	London, England	Alfi
STUDIED	1978-81	BA (Des.) Kingston Polytechnic Design School, London	Asplund
	1981-84	MA (Des.) Royal College of Art, London	B&B Italia
PRACTICE	1984-92	Olivetti design studio, Milan	BRF
	1987	Toshiba Design Centre, Tokyo	Cappellini
	1988	established own studio in Milan	CBI
	1992-98	partner of Sottsass Associati, Milan	Mabeg
AWARDS	2000	iF Product Design Award, Hanover	Magis
EXHIBITIONS	1993	solo exhibition, Royal College of Art, Stockholm	Mercedes Benz
	1999	retrospective exhibition, Asplund, Stockholm	Üstra
			Whirlpool
			WMF

6. **Tubo** low chair and sofa/Couchgarnitur/chaise et canapé bas for BRF, 1997
7. **Tubo** chairs/Stühle/chaises for BRF, 1997
8. **Spider** chair/Stuhl/chaise for Cappellini, 1996
9. **J1** sofa bed/Bettcouch/canapé-lit for CBI, 1996
10. **Lunar** sofa bed/Bettcouch/canapé-lit for B&B Italia, 1998

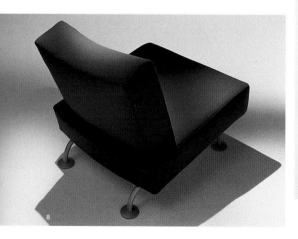

9

10

"Vision is not only a founding idea but necessarily the resolution to ensure its realization."

Jonathan Ive
AND THE DESIGN TEAM

Apple Computer Inc., Industrial Design,
20 730, Valley Green Drive, Cupertino, California, 95 014 USA
T + 408 996 1010 www.apple.com

»Eine Vision ist nicht nur die Grundidee, sondern notwendigerweise die Entschlossenheit, ihre Umsetzung zu realisieren.«

« La vision n'est pas seulement une idée fondatrice, elle contient nécessairement le moyen d'assurer sa réalisation. »

1. **iSub** subwoofer/Subwoofer/amplificateur
de graves for Harman Kardon, 1999
2. ↓ **Power Mac G4** computer/Computer/
ordinateur for Apple Computer, 1999

3.-4. **Apple Cinema Display** 22" flat panel/Flachbildschirm
(Vorder- und Seitenansicht)/écran plat for Apple Computer
(front and side views), 1999

»Ein Designobjekt existiert dort, wo Technologie und Mensch zusammentreffen. Wir als
Designer beeinflussen nicht nur die Art dieses
Zusammentreffens, sondern wir verfügen –
indem wir etwas Materielles schaffen – über
ein starkes und unmittelbares Medium zur
Übermittlung der Identität und Bedeutung
eines Objekts.
Die wirkliche Herausforderung besteht für
uns nicht darin, Gehäuse für anonyme, wenn
auch mächtige Denksysteme zu entwerfen,
sondern darin, die technologischen Kapazitäten leichter anwendbar und zugänglich zu
machen. Die Suche nach vollkommen neuen
Methoden der Gestaltung und Herstellung
von Produkten erfordert die Entwicklung
grundlegend neuer Materialien und Herstellungsverfahren.
Zukunftsweisende Lösungen ergeben sich
meistens dann, wenn neue Produktionstechni-
ken als Mittel zu einem guten Zweck genutzt
werden – damit meine ich die handwerkliche
Gestaltung von Objekten, die mehr den Menschen als produktionstechnischen oder funktionalen Geboten verpflichtet sind.«
JONATHAN IVE

"An object exists at the meeting of
technology and people. As designers
we not only influence the nature of
that meeting but by creating something physical we have a potent and
immediate means of communicat-
ing the identity and very meaning
of an object.
Far from designing enclosures
around anonymous albeit powerful logic boards, our real challenge
is to make relevant and extend technological capability. Searching for
wholly new approaches to product
configuration and manufacturing
requires the development of funda-
mentally new materials and processes.
Significant solutions tend to
emerge when new production technologies are exploited as a means
to a greater end; the crafting of
objects that stand testament to
people rather than manufacturing
or functional imperatives." JONATHAN IVE

« Un objet existe à la rencontre entre la technologie et les hommes. En tant que designers,
non seulement nous influons sur la nature de
cette rencontre mais, en créant quelque chose
de physique, nous disposons d'un moyen puissant et immédiat de communiquer l'identité
et le sens même d'un objet.
Notre vraie mission n'est pas de décrire des
cercles concentriques autour de projets lo-
giques anonymes mais néanmoins puissants,
mais d'étendre les capacités technologiques
et de les rendre pertinentes. La recherche
d'approches radicalement nouvelles dans la
configuration et la fabrication des produits
nécessite de développer des matériaux et
des procédés fondamentalement nouveaux.
Lorsque les nouvelles technologies de production sont exploitées à de meilleures fins, des
solutions importantes émergent. Il s'agit de
concevoir des objets qui rendent hommage
aux hommes et non à des impératifs de fabrication ou de fonction. » JONATHAN IVE

5. **Power Mac G4 Cube** computer/Computer/ordinateur
for Apple Computer, 2000
6. **17" Apple Studio Display (CRT)**/Monitor/écran
d'ordinateur for Apple Computer, 2000
7. **iBook** laptop computer/Laptop/ordinateur portable
for Apple Computer, launched 2001
8. **iMac** computer/Computer/ordinateur for Apple
Computer, 1998
9. **Apple Pro Mouse**/Maus/souris for Apple Computer,
2000

		JONATHAN IVE	CLIENTS
BORN	1967	London, England	In-house designer
STUDIED	1985-89	Newcastle Polytechnic	
PRACTICE	1990-92	Tangerine design consultancy, London	
	1992-	leader Apple Design Team; currently Vice President of Industrial Design, Apple Computer Inc.	
AWARDS	1997	Gold and Best of Category (Consumer Products), *I. D. Magazine Annual Design Review* Award, New York; two Good Design Awards, Chicago Athenaeum	
	1998	three iF Design Awards, Hanover	
	1999	inaugural medal for design achievement, Royal Society of Arts, London; Best of Category, *I. D. Magazine Annual Design Review*, New York; D & AD Gold Award, London; *Object of the Year* Award, *The Face* magazine, London; Gold and Silver Industrial Design Excellence Awards, IDSA; three iF Design Awards, Hanover; Philadelphia Museum of Art & Collaboration COLLAB Design Excellence Award for *Designing the Future*; Winner of the inaugural World Technology Award for Design held in association with *The Economist* magazine; *Design of the Decade* Award, IDSA	
	2000	two Gold Design Excellence Awards, IDSA; D&AD Gold and Silver Product Design Awards, London; Corporate Design Achievement Award, Cooper-Hewitt National Design Museum, New York, National Design Awards; Good Design Award, Chicago Athenaeum; J. Ive awarded Honorary Doctorate, University of Northumbria, Newcastle	
	2001	nine iF Design Awards, Hanover; D & AD Gold and three Silver Product Design Awards, London; Gold Design Excellence Award, IDSA; Best of Show, *I. D. Magazine Annual Design Review*, New York	

8

6

9

7

"Identifying the opportunity and creating the 'idea' for each and every project that will actively inspire others to believe that even the improbable is possible."

Jam

Jam Design and Communication Ltd., 4th Floor, 35-39, Old Street, London EC1V 9HX, England
T +44 20 7253 8998 F +44 20 7253 9966 all@jamdesign.co.uk www.jamdesign.co.uk

»Die Gelegenheit erkennen und für jedes neue Projekt ›die Idee‹ finden, die anderen den Glauben vermittelt, dass selbst das Unwahrscheinliche möglich ist.«

« Pour chaque nouveau projet, identifier ses possibilités et créer " l'idée " qui convaincra les autres que même l'improbable est possible. »

1. **Ringos** napkin ring/Serviettenring/ronds de serviette
de table designed in collaboration with Zotefoams Plc
(produced by Jam), 1997
2. ↓ **Panel** light/Lampe/luminaire designed in collaboration
with Zotefoams Plc (limited edition by Inflate), 2000

« En design, il faut sans cesse poser des questions et chercher de nouvelles perspectives. Le design prendra de plus en plus d'importance sur le plan social et économique en continuant à créer des plates-formes pour de nouvelles expériences. Il explorera de nouvelles manières de communiquer, d'intégrer et finalement d'apprécier ce qui nous entoure. Il fournira de nouvelles valeurs de responsabilité, de viabilité et d'engagement dans une société régie par le pouvoir économique. Il stimulera également la conception d'idées et de produits nouveaux, permettant l'émergence de nouvelles activités ou l'élimination de celles devenues obsolètes.

Nous traversons actuellement une passionnante période de changement culturel qui appelle une nouvelle manière de penser – à mesure que le rythme et le style de vie se modifieront, on pensera et on communiquera de façons différentes. C'est ce qui nous excite et c'est là que nous intervenons. Nous voulons inaugurer une nouvelle attitude entre nos commanditaires et leur marché cible. En se concentrant sur le design et des projets conceptuels visant à construire et communiquer des marques, nos commanditaires profitent des effets internes et externes de ces projets, qui catalysent l'innovation, le changement et de meilleures opportunités. » JAM

3. ← **Flatscreen** coffee tables using screen for Sony's widescreen Wega television/Couchtische unter Verwendung des Bildschirms für den Wega-Breitwandfernseher von Sony/tables basses utilisant les écrans du poste de télévision grand écran Wega de Sony (limited edition, produced by Jam), 1999
4. **Moving Image** stool/Hocker/tabouret (produced by Jam), 1995

"In effect, design is about asking questions and finding new opportunities. Design will gain in social and economic significance as it continues to create platforms for new experiences. It will explore different ways to communicate, integrate and ultimately relate to what surrounds us. It will bring new values of responsibility, sustainability and commitment to a society driven by economics. Design will also stimulate the conception of new products or ideas, enabling new activities to emerge or eliminating unwanted ones.

We feel people are now in an exciting period of cultural change that requires a new way of thinking – as the pace and style of life changes, people will think and communicate in new ways. This is what excites us and it is where we fit in. We want to pioneer a new attitude between our clients and their market audience. By focusing on the use of design and conceptual projects to build and communicate brands, our clients benefit from the internal and external effects of these projects, which act as a catalyst to innovation, change and increased opportunity." JAM

»Im Grunde geht es beim Design darum, Fragen zu stellen und neue Möglichkeiten zu entdecken. Design wird an sozialer und ökonomischer Bedeutung gewinnen, indem es weiterhin Plattformen für neue Erfahrungen schafft. Es wird unterschiedliche Arten erforschen, wie wir kommunizieren, anderes integrieren und uns schließlich auf das beziehen können, was uns umgibt. Design wird neue Werte der Verantwortlichkeit, Nachhaltigkeit und Verbindlichkeit in eine von der Wirtschaft gelenkte Gesellschaft einbringen. Außerdem wird es die Konzeption neuer Produkte oder Ideen stimulieren, neue Aktivitäten ermöglichen oder unerwünschte aussondern.

Wir haben das Gefühl, dass sich die Menschen gegenwärtig in einer aufregenden Periode kultureller Veränderung befinden, die neue Denkweisen erfordert. Während sich Tempo und Stil des Alltagslebens verändern, werden die Leute auch auf neue Arten denken und kommunizieren. Das ist der Punkt, den wir spannend finden, und wo wir ansetzen. Wir wollen den Weg bahnen für eine neue Haltung im Verhältnis zwischen unseren Klienten und deren Zielgruppen. Indem wir uns auf den Einsatz von Design und konzeptionellen Projekten konzentrieren, um neue Marken aufzubauen und bekannt zu machen, profitieren unsere Auftraggeber von den internen und externen Auswirkungen dieser Projekte, die als Katalysatoren für Innovation, Veränderung und erweiterte Möglichkeiten fungieren.« JAM

5.-6. **2020 Vision** showing Corus Concept car/Ansicht des Automodells Corus/vue de la voiture conceptuelle Corus for Corus, 2000 in cooperation with Softroom

		JAM		CLIENTS
FOUNDED	1995	in London by Jamie Anley (b. 1972) and Astrid Zala (b. 1968) (with Mathieu Paillard who left Jam in 1998)		Audi Breitling
STUDIED		JAMIE ANLEY		Corian
	1995	graduated from Bartlett School of Architecture, London		Corus
		ASTRID ZALA		Evian
	1991	graduated from Goldsmith's College, London, also studied Fine Art at Wimbledon School of Art, London		Guinness Philips Lighting
EXHIBITIONS	1996	Recycling, Crafts Council		Sony UK
	1997	"Private Views", Architecture Foundation		Whirlpool Europe
	1999	Saturn Launch, Same, Brick Lane		Zotefoams
		Flat Screen Coffee Table Launch, Haus, Mortimer St.		

7

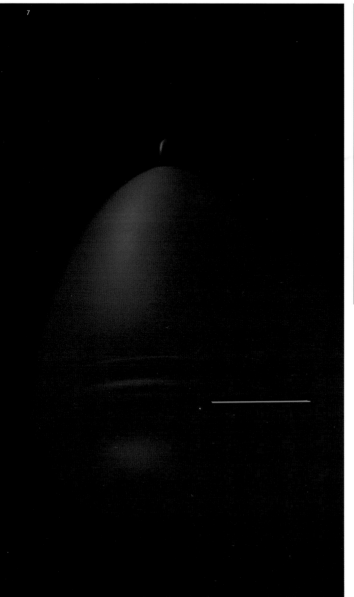

8

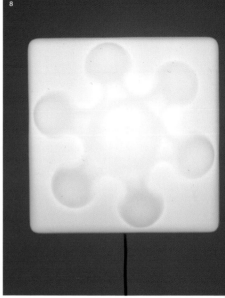

9

7. **Saturn** light/Lampe/luminaire designed in collaboration with Zotefoams, 1999

8. **Panel** light/Lampe/luminaire designed in collaboration with Zotefoams (produced by Jam), 2000 – original concept for the series/Originalentwurf für die Serie/concept original de la série: Andrea Grey

9. **Ladder** chair and stool/Stuhl und Hocker/chaise et tabouret in collaboration with SGB Youngman (produced by Jam), 1996

10. **Foam Dome**/Schaumkuppel/dôme en mousse designed in collaboration with Zotefoams (produced by Jam), 1998

11. **Three-door** concept washing machine/dreitürige Modellwaschmaschine/concept machine à laver trois portes for Whirlpool, 1999

12. **Concept kitchen**/Modellküche/concept de cuisine for Whirlpool and Corian (shown at 100 % Design exhibition), 1999 in cooperation with Softroom and Linbeck Rausch

"Objects designed by trial and error have more soul."

Hella Jongerius

Hella Jongerius, JongeriusLab, Schietbaanlaan 75b, 3021 LE Rotterdam, The Netherlands
T +31 104 770 253 F +31 104 778 300 jongeriuslab@planet.nl

»Objekte, die durch praktisches Herum-
probieren entstanden sind, haben mehr
Seele.«

« Les objets conçus sur le tas ont plus
d'âme. »

1. **Wash-basin**/Waschbecken/lavabo for JongeriusLab, 1997

»Meine schlichten und bodenständigen Entwürfe verfügen über eine Art ›schmutzigen Realismus‹. Sie sind eine Verherrlichung der Unvollkommenheiten des industriellen Produkts. Seelenlose Massenartikel befinden sich nicht länger im Einklang mit einer Ära, die von Veränderung, Tempo und Mühelosigkeit der Fabrikation beherrscht wird. Das Konzept des ›Industriellen‹ erlebt zur Zeit eine Umwandlung.

Indem ich meine Arbeit von einer konzeptionellen Perspektive aus angehe, bin ich mehr an den sozialen und menschlichen Implikationen von Design interessiert als an der äußeren Form oder an den Objekten selbst. Meiner Ansicht nach kommuniziert ein Designprodukt mit seinem Umfeld und erfüllt seinen Besitzer mit einer Identität. Aus diesem Grund suche ich nach dem Charakter, der im Inneren verborgen liegt. Damit sind meine Entwürfe in erster Linie ein Mittel, um mit dem zukünftigen Besitzer in einen Dialog zu treten. Die persönliche Note – oder auch: die Seele – verleiht Industrieprodukten eine Aura, die sie wie individuelle Einzelstücke wirken lässt. Ebenso wie in der avantgardistischen Designermode die Materialprüfung entscheidend für die Endgestaltung ist, so bestimmen die in meinen Designs verwendeten Werkstoffe häufig schon in einem frühen Stadium Form und Funktion des Endprodukts. Die Designer von heute sollten als hyper-moderne Alchemisten traditionelle Techniken nutzen und ausnutzen, um neue und bessere Lösungen zu kreieren.« HELLA JONGERIUS

"My plain and down-to-earth designs have a 'dirty realism'; they are a celebration of the imperfections of the industrial product. Soulless, mass-produced objects are no longer in tune with an era that is dominated by change, speed and ease of manufacture. The concept of 'what is industrial' is undergoing transformation.

By approaching my work from a conceptual perspective, I am interested in the social and human implications of designs rather than in their form or in the objects themselves. From my point of view, a product communicates with its environment and imbues its owner with an identity. Because of this, I search for the character that lurks within so that my designs are first and foremost a means of creating a dialogue with the future user. The personal touch – the soul – will bestow on industrial designs a sense of being individual one-offs. Just as material research is crucial to final creations in avant-garde fashion, so the materials used in my designs often determine the final product's form and function at an early stage. As hyper-modern alchemists, today's designers should use and abuse traditional techniques so as to create new and better solutions." HELLA JONGERIUS

« Mes créations simples et terre à terre sont " vulgairement réalistes ". Elles célèbrent les imperfections du produit industriel. Les objets sans âme, produits en masse, ne sont plus en harmonie avec une époque dominée par le changement, la vitesse et la fabrication facile. Le concept de " ce qui est industriel " est en mutation.

En abordant mon travail dans une perspective conceptuelle, je m'intéresse aux implications sociales et humaines des produits plutôt qu'à leurs formes ou aux objets eux-mêmes. De mon point de vue, un produit communique avec son environnement et imprègne son propriétaire d'une identité. Pour cela, je cherche à insuffler une personnalité dans mes créations pour qu'elles soient avant tout un moyen d'instaurer un dialogue avec leurs futurs utilisateurs. La note personnelle – l'âme – conférera aux designs industriels la qualité d'un exemplaire unique.

Toute comme la recherche de matières est vitale aux créations de la mode d'avant-garde, les matériaux utilisés dans mes designs déterminent souvent très tôt la forme et la fonction du produit final. Tels des alchimistes ultramodernes, les designers devraient user et abuser des techniques traditionnelles afin de créer des solutions nouvelles et meilleures. » HELLA JONGERIUS

2. **Kasese Foam chair**/Stuhl/chaise produced by JongeriusLab for Cappellini, 1999
3. **Kasese Foam chair** (folded)/Stuhl (zusammengeklappt)/chaise (pliée) produced by JongeriusLab for Cappellini, 1999
4. **Felt stool**/Hocker/tabouret for Cappellini, 2000
5. **Soft Urn vases**/Vasen for JongeriusLab, 1999

HELLA JONGERIUS		CLIENTS
BORN	1963	de Meern, the Netherlands	Arabia
STUDIED	1988-93	Academy for Industrial Design, Eindhoven	Cappellini
PRACTICE	1997	workshops at Staatliche Akademie für Bildende Künste, Karlsruhe	Donna Karan
	1998	summer workshop Domus Academy, Milan	Droog Design
	1998-99	taught design at the Design Academy, Eindhoven	Iittala
	2000	director of *Het Atelier*, Design Academy, Eindhoven	Maharam NY
AWARDS	1997	Incentive Award Industrial Design, Amsterdam Foundation of Art	Rosenthal
	1999	World Technology Award for Design, World Technology Network, London	
EXHIBITIONS	1994	Droog Design exhibition, Milan	
	1995	*Mutant Materials in Contemporary Design*, Museum of Modern Art, New York	
	1996	*Self Manufacturing Designers*, Stedelijk Museum, Amsterdam; *Thresholds in Contemporary Design from the Netherlands*, Museum of Contemporary Art, New York	
	1997	*5 Years Droog Design*, Central Museum, Utrecht, Droog Design, Milan	
	1998	*Do Normal*, San Francisco Museum of Modern Art, Droog Design Milan; *Inevitable Ornament*, Milan	
	1999	Droog Design, Oranienbaum, Milan	
	2000	*Pseudofamily*, Het Princessehof, Leeuwarden, ICA, Philadelphia; *Design World 2000*, Museum of Art and Design, Helsinki	
	2001	*Workspheres*, Museum of Modern Art, New York	

3

4

5

"Design must balance ethics and aesthetics for the good of society."

Kazuo Kawasaki

Kazuo Kawasaki, c/o Ouzak Design Formation, International Design Center Nagoya,
7F Design Lab Studio 1, 3-18-1 Sakae Naka-ku, Nagoya Aichi-ken, 460-0008 Japan
T +81 52 249 2466 F +81 52 249 2467 info@ouzak.co.jp www.ouzak.co.jp

»Design muss Ethik und Ästhetik zum
Nutzen der Gesellschaft ausbalancieren.«

« Le design doit équilibrer l'éthique et
l'esthétique pour le bien de la société. »

1. **Flex Scan L675** display/Bildschirm/écran for Eizo Nanao
Corporation, 2001
2. ↓ **Anti-Tension Frame** glasses/Brillengestelle/lunettes
for Masunaga Optical Mfg. Co., 2000

»Rolle und sozialer Einfluss von Design haben sich durch die Entwicklung der Informationsgesellschaft in einem solchen Maße gewandelt, dass wir nun die Ziele, Anwendungsgebiete und Techniken des Designs neu bewerten müssen. Erstens: Was die Techniken betrifft, so können wir Computer als ein Hilfsmittel für Design nutzen. Es sollte aber nicht unser Ziel sein, nur mittels Computer zu gestalten. In diesem Zusammenhang sind 3D-CAD/CAM und *Rapid Prototyping* die effektivsten Werkzeuge, die uns derzeit zur Verfügung stehen. Zweitens: Die zahlreichen Anwendungsbereiche für Design, von der Grafik über die Produktgestaltung bis zur Architektur und sogar dem Kunsthandwerk, welche die Gestalter in der Vergangenheit mit einem jeweils eigenen Ausdrucksmittel versorgten, werden sich unvermeidlicherweise stärker vermischen. Und zuletzt: Die Ziele von Design sollten nicht nur außerhalb des menschlichen Körpers realisiert werden, sondern auch innerhalb des Körpers – und das heißt hier, nicht nur auf die Entwicklung künstlicher Herzen und anderer menschlicher Organe beschränkt. Das alles bedeutet, dass Design die Rolle einer Vermittlungsinstanz einnehmen wird, durch die unsere idealistischen Vorstellungen von einem längeren und besseren Leben konkretisiert werden. Schließlich ist das Design eine Widerspiegelung der gesellschaftlichen Einstellungen und Standpunkte.« KATSUO KAWASAKI

"The role and social impact of design have been transformed to such an extent with the emergence of the information society that we must now reassess the objectives, areas and techniques of design. First, concerning techniques, we can use the computer as an implement of design, but it should not be our aim to design using a computer. In this regard 3D-CAD/CAM and Rapid Prototyping are the most effective tools currently available to us. Second, the many areas of design, from graphics to product to architecture and even crafts, which have historically provided designers with a means of expression, will inevitably become more closely integrated. Lastly, the objectives of design should not only be realized on the outside or around the human body but inside the living body – and here, not only in the development of artificial hearts and other internal organs. What all this means is that design will provide the agency through which our idealistic notions of a prolonged and better life will be brought to fruition – design, after all, is a reflection of the attitudes of society." KAZUO KAWASAKI

« Le rôle et l'impact social du design ont été tellement transformés par l'émergence de la société de l'information que nous devons désormais réévaluer ses objectifs, ses domaines et ses techniques. Tout d'abord, pour ce qui est des techniques, nous pouvons utiliser l'ordinateur comme un instrument de design à condition que la création sur ordinateur ne devienne pas un objectif. A cet égard, le 3D-CAD/CAM et le Prototypage Rapide sont les outils les plus efficaces dont nous disposons actuellement. Ensuite, les nombreux domaines du design qui ont depuis toujours permis aux créateurs de s'exprimer – des graphiques aux produits en passant pas l'architecture et même l'artisanat – deviendront inévitablement plus étroitement intégrés. Enfin, les objectifs du design ne devraient pas être réalisés en dehors ni autour du corps humain mais à l'intérieur, et pas uniquement à travers le développement de cœurs artificiels ou d'autres organes internes. Tout ceci signifie que le design sera l'instance au travers de laquelle nos notions idéalistes d'une vie meilleure et plus longue se concrétiseront. Après tout, le design est le reflet des attitudes de la société. » KATSUO KAWASAKI

3. Scissors/Schere/ciseaux for TAKEFU Knife Village Association, 2000
4. **Flex Scan 80A** bedside television/Bett-Fernseher/télévision de chevet for Eizo Nanao Corporation, 1999
5. **Two-Dimensional** barcode reader/Strichcode-Lesegerät/lecteur de codes-barres for Nippon Chemi-Con Corporation, 1999

KAZUO KAWASAKI

BORN	1949	Fukui, Japan
STUDIED	1992	graduated (Industrial Design), Kanazawa College of Art
	1999	M. D., Nagoya City University; Ph. D. (Medical Science), Nagoya City University
PRACTICE	1977-79	Creative Director, Product Design Department, Toshiba
	1979-80	freelance consultant designer
	1995	founded Ouzak Design Formation, Nagoya
	1996-2000	professor of School of Design & Architecture, Nagoya City University
	2000-	professor of Graduate School of Design & Architecture, Nagoya City University
AWARDS	1991	Mainichi Design Award, Japan
	1992	Special Award for excellence, ICSID (International Council of Societies of Industrial Design Group)
	1994	Kunii Kitaro Industrial Crafts Award, Japan
EXHIBITIONS	1993	BIO 13 Biennial of Industrial Design, exhibition, Ljubliana
	1994	*Japanese Design* exhibition, Philadelphia Museum of Art
	1995	*Mutant Materials in Contemporary Design*, Museum of Modern Art, New York
	1998	*Japan 2000*, Chicago Museum of Art

CLIENTS

AISIN AW Co.
Denso Corporation
Eizo Nanao Corporation
Fujitsu
Japan Industrial Design
KYODEN Corporation
Kyoto Prefecture
Masunaga Optical Mfg. Co.
Nippon ChemiCon Corp.
NTT DoCoMo
Promotion Organization
Sabae city
TAKATA LEMNOS
TAKEFU Knife Village
Association

"Inquisitive and practical, combining traditional techniques with technology and a unique aesthetic."

Tom Kirk

Tom Kirk, 13c, Camberwell Church Street, London SE5 8TR, England
T/F +44 20 7780 9288 tomkirk@excite.co.uk

»Wissbegierig und praktisch, eine Kombination traditioneller Techniken mit neuer Technologie und einer unverwechselbaren Ästhetik.«

« Recherché et pratique, associant des techniques traditionnelles à la technologie et à une esthétique qui lui soit propre. »

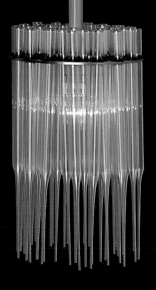

1. **GS Series** lamp/Lampe/lustre (self-production), 2000
2. ↓ **Spike No. 2** wall light/Wandleuchte/appliques
(self-production), 2000

»In dem Maße, in dem der industrielle Sektor durch die fortschreitende Computerisierung immer vielseitiger wird, verringert sich die Zahl der in Produkten verwendeten Komponenten. In Kombination mit der Einführung neu entwickelter Materialien bedeutet diese spannende Technologisierung, dass wir mit einer zunehmenden Zahl an miniaturisierten Apparaten und Objekten leben. In Zukunft werden wir zunehmend vertrauter mit alternativen Lebensräumen, wie es sie früher nur auf der Filmleinwand zu sehen gab. In Bezug auf Inneneinrichtung und Architektur bedeutet diese Entwicklung, dass wir ein vermindertes Bedürfnis nach unordentlich vollgestopften Räumen haben werden. Wir werden mehr und mehr von multifunktionalen Objekten umgeben sein, und Design wird bei der Herstellung von Alltagsprodukten eine weit größere Rolle spielen als bisher.« TOM KIRK

"As computerization continues to add versatility to industry, we are seeing a continual shrinkage in the scale of components used in products. Combined with the introduction of newly developed materials, this technology is exciting to work with and means that we are living with an increasing number of miniaturised gadgets and objects. We will be living nearer to the alternative environments that have previously been limited to celluloid. Within interiors and architecture, this will reduce our everyday need for clumsy and cluttered living spaces. We will be surrounded more and more by multifunctional objects, and design will have a far greater scope within the everyday products around us." TOM KIRK

« A mesure que l'informatisation continue de rendre l'industrie de plus en plus polyvalente, la taille des composants utilisés dans les produits se réduit. Associée à l'introduction de nouvelles matières, cette technologie excitante signifie que nous vivons avec un nombre croissant d'objets et de gadgets miniaturisés. Nous habiterons dans des environnements alternatifs comme en n'en voyait jusque-là qu'au cinéma. Dans les intérieurs et en architecture, nos espaces de vie seront mieux adaptés et moins encombrés. Nous serons de plus en plus entourés d'objets aux fonctions multiples et le design jouera un rôle beaucoup plus important dans les produits quotidiens autour de nous. » TOM KIRK

3. **CS2** table lamp/Tischlampe/lampe (self-production), 2000
4. **Turf** table light/Lampe/luminaire (self-production), 2000
5. **CS3** table lamp/Tischlampe/lampe (self-production), 2000

		TOM KIRK	CLIENTS
BORN	1972	Manchester, England	Annexe Bar and Restaurant, London (installation)
STUDIED	1990-91	Foundation Studies, Middlesex University	Boss Models
	1991-94	BA (Hons) Silversmithing and Metalwork, Camberwell College of Arts, London	The End Bar, London (installation)
PRACTICE	1991-94	exhibition construction for Crafts Council, London	Jerusalem Bar, London (installation)
	1994-95	lighting department Heal's, London	Nambe
	1995-97	sales consultant, London Lighting Company, London	Ozer Restaurant, London (installation)
AWARDS	1992	Johnson and Matthey silver bursary	Smirnoff Vodka
	1994	sponsored by Goldsmith's Hall	St. Lukes Communications
	1997	Setting-up grant awarded by Crafts Council, London	also self-production
	1998	Crafts Council and 100 % Design exhibition bursary, London	
	1999	winner *Ergonom* product development Award	
EXHIBITIONS	1994	*New Designers*, Business Design Centre, London	
	1997	*Trans-Forms*, Cable Street Gallery, London; *One Year On*, Business Design Centre, London	
	1998	*New British Design*, London; *Interior*, British Embassy, Paris	
	1999	*Create Britain*, Taiwan; *Design Resolutions*, Royal Festival Hall, London	
	2000	*Creative Britain*, Stilwerk, Berlin; *New British Design*, Paris; *Decorative Arts 2000*, Sotheby's, London; *British Design*, Arango, Florida	

"The fundamental purpose of design is to either answer or formulate essential questions."

Harri Koskinen

Harri Koskinen, c/o Hackman Designor Oy Ab, Iittala Glass, 14 500 Iittala, Finland
T +358 204 39 6318 F +358 204 39 6303 harri.koskinen@designor.com

»Der grundlegende Zweck von Design ist, essentielle Fragen entweder zu beantworten oder zu formulieren.«

« L'objectif fondamental du design est de formuler des questions essentielles ou d'y répondre. »

1. **Tools** outdoor cooking utensils/Grill-Utensilien/ ustensiles de cuisine pour l'extérieur for Hackman, 2000
2. ↓ **Block** lamp/Lampe/lampe for Design House Stockholm, 1998

« J'écris sur le futur du design, mon futur et celui de nous tous. A l'heure actuelle, je conçois des produits de consommation qui me sont commandés par des sociétés qui les fabriquent. Ces produits sont destinés à être utilisés quotidiennement dans un avenir proche. Lorsqu'elles me passent une commande, les entreprises m'expliquent une situation qu'elles veulent voir se réaliser au plus tôt : ce dont le consommateur a besoin et ce dont on a décidé qu'il aurait besoin. Les problèmes sont très réalistes, impliquant des améliorations aux produits déjà disponibles ainsi que de nouvelles perspectives. Ce qui m'intéresse dans mon travail ce sont mes intuitions, les moments où je trouve une solution qui débouchera sur des produits plus fonctionnels et plus faciles à fabriquer. A l'avenir, nous occuperons l'instant présent plus que nous le faisons actuellement. Nos victoires personnelles nous donneront davantage de raisons de nous battre. Nous développons une nouvelle conscience en la cherchant. Satisfaire nos besoins de base reste encore notre activité principale. De l'autre côté de l'océan, il y a peut-être encore des terres arables à cultiver.
Le design joue un rôle dans tout ceci, mais, d'un autre côté, il en est également très éloigné. A l'avenir, nous réfléchirons davantage à l'avenir. » HARRI KOSKINEN

3. ← **Genelec** loudspeaker (prototype)/Lautsprecher (Prototyp)/haut-parleur (prototype) for Genelec, 2000
4. **Fatty-Containers** storage system/Aufbewahrungssystem/système de rangement for Schmidinger-Modul, 1998-99

"I'm writing about the future of design, my future and the future of us all. At present, I'm working as a designer of consumer goods under commission from companies that produce them. The designs I create are meant for everyday use in the near future. When commissioning work from me, companies outline a situation envisioned for the near future: what the consumer needs and is allowed to need. The problems are very realistic, involving improvements to the products that are available now as well as new perspectives. My interest in my work lies in insights, in the moments when I figure out a solution that leads to products that are more functional and easier to manufacture.
In the future, we'll occupy the *now* more than we do at present. The things we win for ourselves will give us more to fight for. We evolve a new consciousness by searching for it. The fulfilling of basic needs remains the most important activity. Over the ocean, there might still be arable fields to farm.
Design plays a part in all of this – but, on the other hand, it is also very far removed from it. In the future, we'll give more thought to the future." HARRI KOSKINEN

»Ich schreibe über die Zukunft von Design, meine Zukunft und die Zukunft von uns allen. Gegenwärtig arbeite ich als Designer von Konsumartikeln im Auftrag der Hersteller. Die Designs, die ich entwerfe, sind für den alltäglichen Gebrauch in der nächsten Zukunft bestimmt. Wenn Firmen mich mit einer Arbeit beauftragen, skizzieren sie für mich eine Situation, die sie für die nächste Zukunft anvisieren: was der Konsument braucht, und was er brauchen darf. Die Problemstellungen sind sehr realistisch und beinhalten Verbesserungen für bereits erhältliche Produkte sowie neue Perspektiven. Was mich in meiner Arbeit interessiert, sind Einsichten und Erkenntnisse. Damit meine ich jene Momente, in denen mir eine Lösung einfällt, die zu Produkten führt, die zweckmäßiger und leichter zu handhaben sind.
In Zukunft werden wir das *Jetzt* mehr ausfüllen, als wir es gegenwärtig tun. Die Dinge, die wir für uns selbst gewinnen, werden uns mehr bieten, wofür wir kämpfen können. Wir entwickeln ein neues Bewusstsein, indem wir danach suchen. Dabei bleibt die Erfüllung elementarer Bedürfnisse die wichtigste Aktivität. Jenseits des Ozeans mag es noch urbares Ackerland zu bebauen geben.
Design spielt bei all dem eine Rolle. Auf der anderen Seite ist es aber auch sehr weit davon entfernt. In Zukunft werden wir mehr Gedanken auf die Zukunft verwenden.« HARRI KOSKINEN

5

6

7

5. **Air** food container/Vorratsdose/récipient for Arabia, 2001
6. **Slow** lamp/Lampe/lampe (one-off), 2000
7. **Shelf** system (prototype)/Regalsystem (Prototyp)/ étagères (prototype), 2000
8. **Atlas** candleholder & vase/Kerzenhalter & Vase/ bougeoir & vase for Iittala, 1996
9. **Alue** bowls/Schalen/bols for **Pro Arte Collection**, Iittala, 2000

| | | HARRI KOSKINEN | | CLIENTS |

		HARRI KOSKINEN	
BORN	1970	Karstula, Finland	
STUDIED	1993	BA, Lahti Design Insitute	
	1994	MA studies Product and Strategic Design, University of Industrial Arts and Design, Helsinki	
PRACTICE	1996	Designor Oy (Nuutajärvi Glass), Finland	
	1998-	Hackman Designor Oy (Iittala Glass), Finland	
AWARDS	1997 & 98	grant University of Art and Design, Helsinki	
	1999	grant Häme Region, Finland; grant Finnish Cultural Foundation	
	2000	winner Absolut Helsinki Prize, Helsinki Awards	
EXHIBITIONS	1997	*PTTY 90 Years*, Museum of Fine Arts, Pori, Finland	
	1998	*International Design Forum*, Singapore; *Empty Spaces*, Alvar Aalto Museum, Jyväskylä; *Talente '99*, Munich	
	1999	*Artificial Nature*, Milan; *New Scandinavia*, Museum für Angewandte Kunst, Cologne; *Finnish Modern Design*, Göteborg, Hamburg; *Empty Spaces*, Munich	
	2000	*Design World 2000*, Museum of Art and Design, Helsinki; *Privacy*, solo exhibition, Miyake Design Studio Gallery, Tokyo	

CLIENTS

Arabia
Design House Stockholm
Genelec
Hackman
Iittala
Issey Miyake
Källemo
Nuutajärvi Glass
Schmidinger-Modul

10

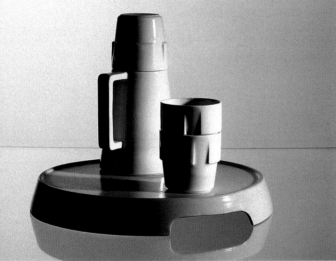

10. **Kämppä** installation/Installation at Iittala glassworks, 1999-2000
11. **Klubi** glassware/Glasware/verres for Iittala, 1996-98
12. **Ceramic** thermos set (prototype)/Thermoskanne und Tassen (Prototyp)/service Thermos (prototype), 1998-2000
13. **Relations** storm candleholder/Windlichter/photophores for Iittala, 1999
14. **Sofa bed** (prototype)/Bettcouch (Prototyp)/canapé-lit (prototype), 2000

"Design makes rubbish superfluous."

Isabelle Leijn

Isabelle Leijn, Vrolikstraat 355-c, 1092 TB Amsterdam, The Netherlands
T/F +31 20 675 1654 isabelle-leijn@planet.nl www.leijn.com

»Design macht Müll überflüssig.«

« Le design rend la camelote superflue. »

1. **Sunny Side Up** relax carpet/Liegeteppich/
tapis de détente (self-production), 2000
2. ↓ **Bollamp** lights/Lampen/luminaires (self-production),
2000

»Eine Gesellschaft ist wie eine Geleemasse. Teile davon bewegen sich, und die Masse folgt. Andere Teile wieder werden absorbiert. Die Masse bewegt und verändert sich fortwährend. Ideen und Werte verändern sich auf politischer, ökonomischer und sozialer Ebene. Neue Erfindungen verlangen neue Bräuche. Neue Bräuche verlangen neue äußere Umstände und nehmen alte Bräuche mit sich, die der Veränderung bedürfen. All dies erfordert Formgebung, und mit diesem Bedürfnis sind viele Designer beschäftigt. Sie entwerfen schöne und hässliche Objekte, entweder in futuristischem oder altmodischem Stil, aus umweltfreundlichen oder umweltschädlichen Materialien hergestellt. Was gekauft wird, wird produziert! Auf diese Weise diktiert die Masse den Weg, den die Gesellschaft einschlägt. Nicht die Designer, sondern die Leute bestimmen, was ›hip‹ ist und was nicht. *Wer kann die Massen formen?*« ISABELLE LEIJN

"Society is like a moving jelly mass. Parts of it grow and the mass follows. Other parts get drawn in again. The mass moves, it is ever-changing. On political, economical and social levels, ideas and values change. New inventions demand new customs. New customs demand new surroundings, taking with them old customs for want of change. All this needs shape, a need that many designers busy themselves with. They design beautiful and ugly objects in a style that is either futuristic or old-fashioned, made from environmentally correct or polluting material. What will be bought shall be produced! Thus the mass dictates the road society takes. Not the designer but the people decide what's hot and what's not. *Who can shape the masses?*" ISABELLE LEIJN

« La société est comme une masse gélatineuse en mouvement. Des parties se développent et la masse suit. D'autres parties sont réabsorbées dans la masse. La masse bouge, se transformant sans cesse. Sur les plans politiques, économiques et sociaux, les idées et les valeurs changent. Les nouvelles inventions exigent de nouvelles habitudes. Les nouvelles habitudes exigent de nouveaux environnements, entraînant avec elles les vieilles habitudes qui ont besoin d'évoluer. Tout ceci nécessite une mise en forme, qui occupe de nombreux designers. Ils conçoivent des objets qui sont beaux ou laids, dans un style qui est soit futuriste soit désuet, fabriqués avec des matériaux qui respectent l'environnement ou qui le polluent. Ce qui sera acheté sera produit! Ainsi la masse dicte-t-elle la voie que la société doit prendre. Ce n'est pas le designer mais le peuple qui décide de ce qui est dans le coup ou pas. *Qui peut modeler les masses ?* » ISABELLE LEIJN

3. **Chair 00**/Stuhl/chaise (self-production), 2000
4. **Cocoon** sofa/Sofa/canapé (self-production), 1999
5. **Statement 2** shelving system/Regalsystem/
bibliothèque (self-production), 1995
6. **Bed 01**/Bett/lit (self-production), 1999

ISABELLE LEIJN		CLIENTS
BORN	1964 Nijmegen, the Netherlands	Artifort
STUDIED	1982-85 Art Academy, Arnhem	Creafort
PRACTICE	1994 began career as an industrial and furniture designer	Harvink
EXHIBITIONS	1995 solo exhibition, Metri, Amsterdam	MBH
	1996 Interieur Biennial, Kortrijk	also self-production
	1997 Gallery Kis, Amsterdam	
	1998 Meubelbeurs RAI, Amsterdam	
	1999 Perles & Fracas, Brussels	
	2000 *Places and Spaces*, London; Salone del Mobile, Gallery Pit, Milan	
	2001 *Baby*, Amsterdam; Salone del Mobile, SaloneSatelitte, Milan	

"There's something I hate in the world of design: the excess of protagonism, which can make designed objects so difficult to live with."

Piero Lissoni

Piero Lissoni, Lissoni Associati srl, Via Goito 9, 20 121 Milan, Italy
T +39 026 571 942 F +39 026 571 918 lissoni@mclink.it

»Was ich an der Welt des Designs hasse, ist die Profilierungssucht, die es so schwierig machen kann, mit Design- objekten zu leben.«

« Ce que je déteste dans le monde du design : le manque d'humilité, qui rend parfois si difficile de vivre avec certains des objets conçus. »

1. **Metro2** sofa/Sofa/canapé for Living Divani, 2000
2. ↓ **Frog** chair/Stuhl/chaise for Living Divani, 2000

»Ich glaube, das Design der Zukunft wird dank technischer Fortschritte hauptsächlich durch eine bessere Qualität in der industriellen Massenfertigung gekennzeichnet sein, was zu einem Rückgang des Handwerks auf Kosten ungewöhnlicher, individueller Objekte führen wird. Designer werden stärker in die Verbesserung und Entwicklung von Materialien einbezogen, und sie werden über neuartige, kreative Produktionsmittel verfügen (z. B. Elektronik und Biotechnik). Was Möbel und die Ausstattung von Innenräumen betrifft, so werden die ›Schlüsselworte‹ lauten: Eklektizismus, Schlichtheit, Erinnerungskraft, Innovation, ethnisch, unsichtbar und elektronisch. Die Käufer werden bewusster den wirklichen Wert der Dinge erkennen und jeden Aspekt eines Objekts bedenken, statt nur dessen Marke oder den jeweils aktuellen Trend. Die Leute werden Produkte kaufen, weil sie ihnen gefallen und weil sie zufriedenstellend funktionieren. Ich glaube nicht, dass unser Übergang in das neue Jahrtausend ›die eine große Veränderung‹ mit sich bringen wird: Es wird keine plötzlichen Umwandlungen geben, sondern einen evolutionären Prozess, eine allmähliche Entwicklung, die – auf lange Sicht – einen Unterschied machen wird. Ich kann nur phantasieren, wie es sein wird ...« PIERO LISSONI

"I think that design in the future will be mainly characterized by better quality in industrial mass production thanks to technological advances, leading to a decline in craftwork at the cost of special, individual pieces. Designers will become involved in the improvement and development of materials and will have new creative means at their disposal (eg. electronics and biotechnology). As far as furniture and the use of internal spaces go, the 'keywords' will be eclecticism, simplicity, memory, innovation, ethnic, invisible and electronics. Buyers will be more conscious of where real value lies and will consider every aspect of an object rather than just its brand or the current trend. Products will be chosen because people like them and are satisfied by their function. I do not think that our passage into the new millennium will create 'the big change': there will be no sudden transformation, but a process of evolution, a gradual development that in the long term will make a difference. I can only imagine how it will be ..." PIERO LISSONI

« A mon avis, le design sera surtout marqué par une meilleure qualité de la production industrielle de masse grâce aux progrès technologiques, entraînant une déclin de l'artisanat au détriment des pièces uniques, spéciales. Les designers s'impliqueront dans l'amélioration et le développement des matériaux et disposeront de nouveaux moyens créatifs (comme l'électronique et la biotechnologie). Pour ce qui est du mobilier et de l'aménagement des intérieurs, les mots clefs seront " éclectisme ", " simplicité ", " mémoire ", " innovation ", " ethnique ", " invisible " et " électronique ". Les acheteurs seront davantage conscients des vraies valeurs et prendront en compte chaque aspect d'un objet plutôt que sa marque ou la tendance du moment. Ils choisiront les produits parce qu'ils leur plaisent et parce qu'ils seront satisfaits de leur fonction. Je doute que notre passage au prochain millénaire crée " le grand chambardement " : il n'y aura pas de transformations soudaines mais une évolution, un développement progressif qui, à long terme, fera la différence. Je ne peux qu'imaginer comment ce sera ... » PIERO LISSONI

3. **Spin** chair/Stuhl/chaise for Porro, 2000
4. **HT** shelving & cabinet system/Regal- & Schranksystem/meuble bibliothèque for Porro, 1999
5. **Pavillon** table/Tisch for Porro, 1993
6. **Basics** bed/Bett/lit for Porro, 1998
7. **Modern** shelving & cabinet system/Regal- & Schranksystem/meuble bibliothèque for Porro, 1995

		PIERO LISSONI	CLIENTS

		PIERO LISSONI		CLIENTS
BORN	1956	Seregno, Italy		Allegri
STUDIED	1985	Architectural degree, Politecnico di Milano		Artemide
PRACTICE	1986	founded Studio Lissoni with Nicoletta Canesi		Benetton
	1995	appointed art director for Cappellini		Boffi
AWARDS	1991	Compasso d'Oro selection, Milan		Cappellini
	1999	third prize TKTS Time Square competition, New York		Cassina
EXHIBITIONS	1997	*30 Years of Italian Design*, Palazzo della Triennale di Milano, Milan		Iren Uffici
	2000	*Design 4:3 – Fünfzig Jahre italienisches und deutsches Design*, Kunst- und Ausstellungshalle der Bundesrepublik Deutschland, Bonn		Kartell
				Living Divani
				Matteograssi
				Nemo
				Porro
				Wella

"It's only the future if it can't be made."

Ross Lovegrove

Ross Lovegrove, Studio X, 21, Powis Mews, London W11 1JN, England
T +44 20 7229 7104 F +44 20 7229 7032 studiox@compuserve.com

»Zukunft ist alles das, was noch nicht gemacht wurde.«

« Ce n'est l'avenir que si c'est irréalisable. »

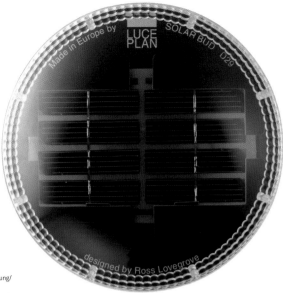

1. **Solar Bud** outdoor light/Außenbeleuchtung/
luminaire for Luceplan, 1998
2. ↓ **Bioform** wooden sculpture/Holzskulptur/
sculpture en bois (studio project), 2000

« En ce début de nouveau millénaire, nous entrons dans une ère unique de réévaluation de nous-mêmes et de notre habitat. Nous avons atteint un niveau de confiance en nos capacités créatives qui alimente un degré sans précédent de recherche dans tous les domaines, du génie génétique aux ressources énergétiques, de la médecine aux profondeurs abstraites de notre univers organique. Le processus qui nous permet de découvrir de nouvelles possibilités est rapidement accéléré par la technologie informatique, une technologie dont nous avons toujours su qu'elle ouvrirait nos esprits. De fait, c'est ce concept d'inexorabilité qui m'intrigue, surtout quand il est appliqué au monde que nous voyons et touchons ... notre monde physique. A mesure que les frontières deviennent floues, ce monde deviendra de plus en plus étrange et imprévisible – une perspective fabuleuse pour ceux d'entre nous qui croient que l'étrangeté est une conséquence de la pensée innovatrice. L'ironie de tout ceci est que, au bout du compte, la créativité engendrée par une telle liberté ramènera l'homme à la nature, à sa composition organique, à ses objectifs et à ses formes qui ne seront plus limitées par l'imagination de l'homme. Le design organique découle de la pensée organique. Il émeut les gens de l'intérieur vers l'extérieur, stimulant de profondes résonances primordiales qui transcendent les tendances superficielles. Jusqu'ici, nous ne faisions que deviner, mais la beauté extraordinaire et impérissable des œuvres d'art organiques produites par des artistes tels que Henry Moore ou Frei Otto suggère que l'association d'intuition brute et d'un degré de logique cellulaire, fractale, influencera inévitablement la forme et la matérialité du monde fabriqué par l'homme, des automobiles à l'architecture. » ROSS LOVEGROVE

"As we begin a new millennium we are entering a unique era of re-evaluation of ourselves and our habitat. We have reached a level of confidence in our creative abilities that is fuelling an unprecedented level of inquiry in all fields, from genetic engineering to fuel cells and medicine to the abstract depths of our organic universe.
The process by which we are discovering new possibilities is being rapidly accelerated by computing technology – a technology that we always knew would open our minds. Indeed, it is this concept of inevitability that intrigues me especially when applied to the world we see and touch ... our physical world. As boundaries blur, this world will become stranger and less predictable – a fabulous prospect for those of us who believe that strangeness is a consequence of innovative thinking. The irony of all this is that ultimately, creativity generated by such soup-like freedom will lead mankind full circle back to nature, its organic composition, its purpose and with it forms that will no longer be limited by man's imagination.
Organic design comes from organic thinking. It moves people from the inside out, stimulating deep primordial resonances that transcend superficial trends. So far we have only been guessing, but the extraordinary and enduring beauty of the organic works of art produced by the likes of Henry Moore and Frei Otto tends to suggest that the combination of raw intuition combined with a degree of cellular, fractal logic will inevitably begin to greatly influence the form and physicality of our man-made world from cars to architecture."
ROSS LOVEGROVE

»Zu Beginn des neuen Jahrtausends treten wir in ein einzigartiges Zeitalter der Neubewertung unserer selbst und unserer Lebensräume ein. Wir haben ein solches Vertrauen in unsere kreativen Fähigkeiten erreicht, das in einem noch nie da gewesenen Maß die Forschung in allen Bereichen anspornt, von der Gentechnik über Brennstoffelemente und Medizin bis zu den dunklen Tiefen unseres organischen Universums. Dieser Prozess, der uns neue Möglichkeiten eröffnet, wird durch die Computertechnologie stark beschleunigt – eine Technologie, von der wir immer wussten, dass sie unseren Horizont erweitern würde. Tatsächlich ist es das Konzept des Unvermeidlichen, das mich fasziniert, besonders in seiner Anwendung auf die Welt, die wir sehen und berühren – also unsere sinnlich wahrnehmbare Welt. In dem Maß, in dem sich die Grenzen verwischen, wird diese Welt fremder und weniger berechenbar, was phantastische Aussichten für jene von uns bietet, die Fremdheit für eine Folge innovativen Denkens halten. Es ist die Ironie dieser Situation, dass eine von solch unbegrenzter Freiheit hervorgebrachte Kreativität die Menschheit letzten Endes im Zirkelschluss zurück zu einer Natur führen wird, deren organische Struktur, Zweck und damit Formen nicht länger von der menschlichen Vorstellungskraft begrenzt sein werden. Organisches Design kommt von organischem Denken. Es berührt die Menschen in ihrem Innersten und stimuliert tiefverwurzelte, archaische Reaktionen, die über oberflächliche Trends hinausgehen. Das alles sind nur Vermutungen. Aber die außerordentliche und bleibende Schönheit der organischen Kunstwerke, die von Künstlern wie Henry Moore und Frei Otto geschaffen wurden, legt nahe, dass die Verbindung von unverfälschter Intuition und einem gewissen Grad an zellularer, fraktionierter Logik zwangsläufig die Form und physische Beschaffenheit unserer durch Menschenhand geschaffenen Welt stark beeinflussen wird – und zwar vom Autodesign bis hin zur Architektur.« ROSS LOVEGROVE

5

5. **Air One** polystyrene seating/Sitz aus Polystyren/
siège de polystyrène for Edra, 2000
6. **Aircraft seat**/Flugzeugsitz/siège d'avion for Japan
Airlines, 1997-2000
7. **Air One** polystyrene seating (detail)/Sitz aus Polystyren
(Detail)/siège de polystyrène (détail) for Edra, 2000

6

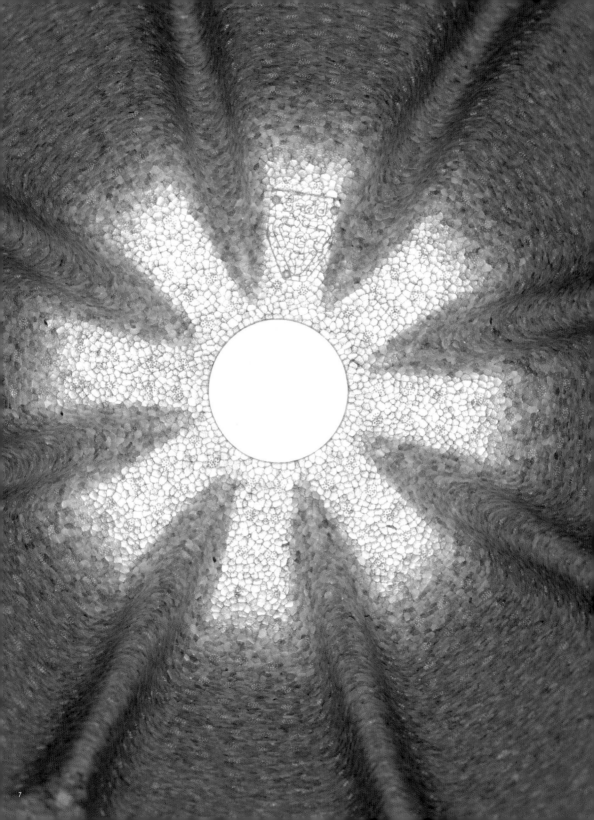

ROSS LOVEGROVE		CLIENTS
BORN	1958 Cardiff, Wales	Apple Computer
STUDIED	1980 BA (Hons) Industrial Design, Manchester Polytechnic	Bernhardt
	1983 MA Industrial Design, Royal College of Art, London	Biomega
PRACTICE	1983-84 worked at Frogdesign, Altensteig	Cappellini
	1984-87 worked as an in-house designer for Knoll International, Paris	Ceccotti
	1986-90 established a design partnership in London	Connolly Leather
	1990 established own design office, Studio X, London	Driade
AWARDS	1998 George Nelson Award, USA; iF Design Award, Hanover	Edra
	1999 Medaille de la Ville de Paris	Fratelli Guzzini
	2000 *I. D. Magazine Annual Design Review* Award, New York	Frighetto
	2001 nominated Designer of the Year by the magazine *Architektur & Wohnen*, Hamburg	Hackman
EXHIBITIONS	1996 *Ross Lovegrove Objects*, Stockholm	Hansgrohe
	1997 *Ross Lovegrove – Design*, Danish Museum of Decorative Art, Copenhagen; *Organic Dreams*, IDÉE, Tokyo	Herman Miller
	1999 *Sensual Organic Design*, Yamagiwa Corporation, Tokyo	Japan Airlines
		Junghans
		Kartell
		Knoll International
		Loom
		Luceplan
		Matoso
		Moroso
		Motorola
		Olympus Cameras
		Tag Heuer
		Toyo Architects
		Zanotta

9

8. **Agaricon** table lamp/Tischlampe/
lampe de table for Luceplan, 2001
9. **Water bottle**/Wasserflasche/
bouteille d'eau for Ty Nant, 2001

"Our goal is to solve business problems by connecting brand, technology and people in innovative and compelling ways."

Lunar Design

Lunar Design, 537, Hamilton Avenue, Palo Alto, California 94 301, USA
T + 650 326 7788 F +650 326 2420 info@lunar.com www.lunar.com

»Unser Ziel ist es, Probleme im Unternehmensbereich zu lösen, indem wir Marke, Technologie und Menschen auf innovative und unwiderstehliche Weise in Verbindung bringen.«

« Notre objectif est de résoudre des problèmes commerciaux en reliant les marques, la technologie et les consommateurs par des moyens innovateurs et irrésistibles. »

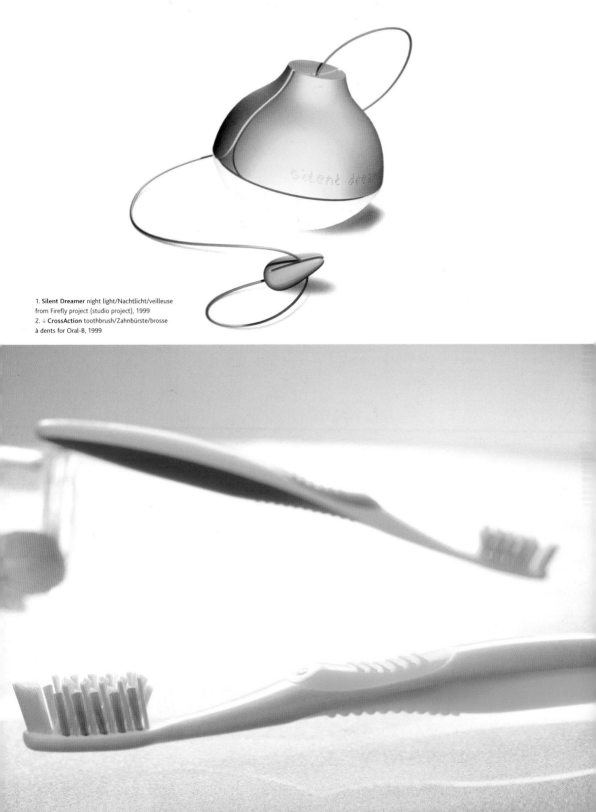

1. **Silent Dreamer** night light/Nachtlicht/veilleuse
from Firefly project (studio project), 1999
2. ↓ **CrossAction** toothbrush/Zahnbürste/brosse
à dents for Oral-B, 1999

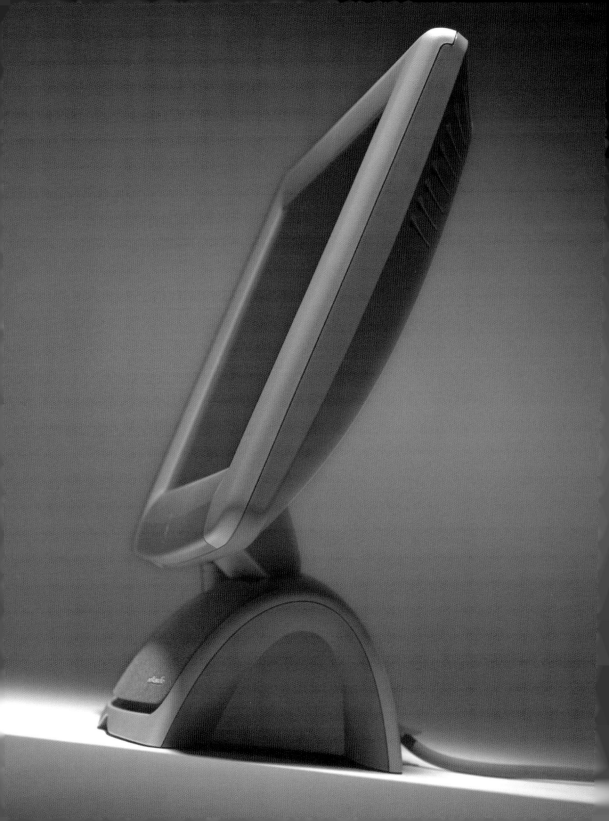

« En quelques années, l'Internet a révolutionné la manière de faire des affaires. Il a déjà déclenché la transition de la " production de masse" au "sur mesure de masse". Quiconque ayant une idée de produit peut le vendre directement sur le Net. Les entrepreneurs n'ont plus besoin d'attendre qu'un détaillant présente leurs produits. Les consommateurs ne sont plus limités à la marchandise en stock dans les magasins. Pour les designers, le "sur mesure de masse" représente un sérieux défi : celui de développer des produits souples et des systèmes modulaires qui offrent des choix censés aux consommateurs. A mesure que la technologie devient de plus en plus transparente et compacte, les produits servent des objectifs toujours plus complets. La taille et l'aspect des articles de demain refléteront de plus en plus leur capacité à rendre un service, à informer sur les avantages de telle ou telle marque, à traduire les préférences des consommateurs. De fait, pour se différentier, les marques s'attacheront surtout à relier les gens à la technologie de façons simples et attrayantes. Les designers d'aujourd'hui sont investis d'une lourde responsabilité : ils doivent créer des produits qui communiquent les promesses d'une marque, qui puissent être fabriqués de manière efficace à un haut niveau de qualité, et qui " parlent " de manière convaincante à ceux qui les achèteront et les utiliseront. Les produits du futur devront également respecter davantage l'environnement. C'est d'autant plus important que des marchés de consommateurs émergent dans les pays en voie de développement, ce qui ne manquera pas d'étirer encore les ressources naturelles. »
LUNAR DESIGN

3. « HP Pavilion FX70 flat panel display/Flachbildschirm/écran plat for Hewlett Packard, 1999
4. Sprout night light/Nachtlicht/veilleuse from Firefly project (studio project), 1999

"In just a few years, the Internet has revolutionized the way the world does business. It has already triggered the move from 'mass production' to 'mass customization'. In fact, almost anyone with a product idea can sell goods directly over the Web. Entrepreneurs don't have to wait for a retailer to carry their products. And consumers are no longer limited to merchandise that stores have in stock. For product designers, mass customization presents a compelling challenge: to develop flexible products and modular systems that give consumers meaningful choices.
Just as technology is becoming increasingly transparent and compact, the purpose of products is becoming increasingly comprehensive. The size and appearance of tomorrow's products will, more and more, reflect their ability to deliver a service, to inform consumers of their brand's benefit proposition, and to reflect customers' preferences. Indeed, connecting people to technology in easy and engaging ways will become the primary way to differentiate a brand.
Designers today carry a great responsibility. They must create products that communicate a brand promise, that are efficient to manufacture at high quality levels, and that resonate strongly with the people who will buy and use them. Anything less thoughtful won't attract the emerging generation of discerning consumers. Future products will soon have to be more ecologically friendly, too. This need is particularly important as consumer markets emerge in developing countries, further straining natural resources." LUNAR DESIGN

»Innerhalb weniger Jahre hat das Internet die Form des globalen Wirtschaftens revolutioniert. Bereits jetzt hat es den Aufbruch von der ›Massen-Produktion‹ zur ›Massen-Kundenauftragsfertigung‹ in Gang gesetzt. Fast jeder, der eine Produktidee hat, kann seine Waren direkt über das ›World Wide Web‹ verkaufen. Unternehmer brauchen nicht mehr darauf zu warten, dass ein Einzelhändler ihre Produkte ins Sortiment nimmt. Und die Verbraucher sind nicht länger auf Waren beschränkt, die in den Geschäften vorrätig sind. Für Produktdesigner stellt die Anpassung an den speziellen Kundenbedarf die faszinierende Herausforderung dar, flexible Produkte und modulare Systeme zu entwickeln, die den Konsumenten sinnvolle Wahlmöglichkeiten bieten.
In gleichem Maß, wie Technologien zunehmend transparent und kompakt werden, wird der Zweck von Produkten umfassender. Größe und Aussehen der Produkte von morgen werden immer stärker deren Fähigkeit widerspiegeln, die Dienstleistung zu bieten, über den Nutzwert einer Marke zu informieren und sich den Vorlieben der Konsumenten anzupassen. Tatsächlich wird die Frage, inwieweit es gelingt, Menschen auf einfache und attraktive Weise mit Technologie in Verbindung zu bringen, zu einem der wichtigsten Profilierungsmerkmale für eine Marke.
Die Designer tragen heutzutage eine große Verantwortung. Die von ihnen entworfenen Produkte müssen die Verheißungen einer Marke übermitteln, effizient und auf hohem Qualitätsniveau herzustellen sein und eine starke, ansprechende Wirkung auf die Menschen ausüben, die sie kaufen und benutzen. Produkte, die weniger durchdacht sind, können die aufkommende Generation urteilsfähiger Konsumenten nicht für sich gewinnen. Darüber hinaus müssen zukünftige Produkte auch umweltfreundlicher sein. Diese Notwendigkeit ist besonders wichtig im Hinblick darauf, dass in den Entwicklungsländern neue Märkte entstehen, wodurch die natürlichen Ressourcen noch weiter belastet werden.«
LUNAR DESIGN

		LUNAR DESIGN	CLIENTS
FOUNDED	1985	co-founded by Jeff Smith (b. 1953 Springfield, IL) and Gerard Furbershaw (b. 1952 New York, NY)	Apple Computer
STUDIED		JEFF SMITH	Acuson
		BA Industrial Design, University of Illinois	Cisco Systems
		GERARD FURBERSHAW	Electrolux
		BA Architecture, University of Southern California and BA Industrial Design,	Glad Products
		San Hosé University	Hewlett-Packard
AWARDS	1995	D&AD Award, London; Good Design Award, Chicago Athenaeum;	Microsoft Corporation
		Grand Prize, Absolut Design Competition	Motorola
	1996	Appliance Manufacturer Excellence in Design Best Overall And Winner; People's Choice	Oral-B
		Award, Society of Plastics Engineers; SMAU Cadd Industrial Design Award;	Palm, Inc.
		iF Design Award, Hanover	Philips
	1997	two Silver Industrial Design Excellence Awards, IDSA; three Good Design Awards, Chicago	SGI
		Athenaeum; SMAU Cadd Industrial Design Award	Sony
	1998	two Design Distinction Awards, *I. D. Magazine Annual Design Review*, New York;	
		Silver Industrial Design Excellence Award, IDSA; two Good Design Awards, Chicago	
		Athenaeum	
	1999	three Gold Medical Design Excellence Awards; Gold and Silver Industrial Design Excellence	
		Awards, IDSA; five Good Design Awards, Chicago Athenaeum; two Silver *Design of the Decade*	
		awards, IDSA	
	2000	Good Design Award, Chicago Athenaeum; Silver Industrial Design Excellence Award, IDSA;	
		four iF Design Awards, Hanover	
EXHIBITIONS	1996	*The Dumb Box – Designing the Desktop CPU*, San Francisco Museum of Modern Art	
	1997	Showplace for Excellence in Industrial Design, Georgia Institute of Technology, Atlanta	
	2000	*Design Matters*, Museum of Contemporary Art, Miami; *National Design Triennial –*	
		Design Culture Now, Cooper-Hewitt National Design Museum, New York	
	2001	*Global Tools*, Künstlerhaus, Vienna	

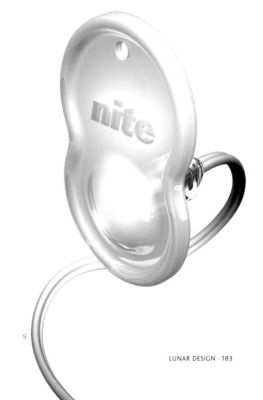

5. **Glimo** night light/Nachtlicht/veilleuse from Firefly project (studio project), 1999
6. **HMD-A200, FD Trinitron** monitor/Monitor/écran d'ordinateur for Sony, 1999
7. **Daisy Glow** night light/Nachtlicht/veilleuse from Firefly project (studio project), 1999
8. **Travel Tote**/Reise-Organizer/guide personnel de voyage from *Service-as-Product* range (studio project), 1998
9. **PoP** night light/Nachtlicht/veilleuse from Firefly project (studio project), 1999

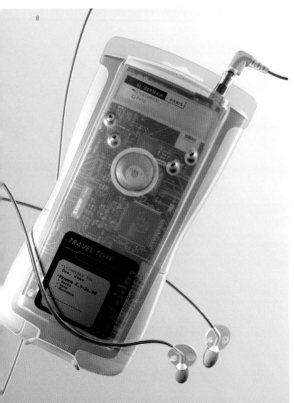

"Exploring the properties of materials in order to create forms which have organic and sculptural qualities that are enhancing and enhanced by light."

Sharon Marston

Sharon Marston, Studio 38, 21, Clerkenwell Green, London EC1R 0DP, England
T/F +44 20 7490 7495 enquiries@sharonmarston.com www.sharonmarston.com

»Die Eigenschaften von Materialien erforschen, um organische und skulpturale Formen zu gestalten, die durch Licht intensiviert werden.«

« Explorer les propriétés des matériaux afin de créer des formes ayant des qualités organiques et spirituelles qui rehaussent et sont rehaussées par la lumière. »

1. **Cocoon** table lamp/Tischlampe/lampe de table
(self-production), 1999
2. ↓ **SQ Pleat** pendant lamp (detail)/Hängelampe (Detail)/
lustre (détail) (self-production), 1999

»Designer lassen sich in zwei Kategorien einordnen: Die einen arbeiten auf einer logischen Ebene, die anderen auf einer emotionalen. Ich selbst würde mich zur zweiten Kategorie zählen. Zentraler Aspekt meiner Entwürfe ist ein Gefühl, das sich auf eine zunehmend konfus und unsicher werdende Zukunft bezieht. Das ist eine sehr spannende Position für Designer, da die gegenwärtigen technischen Fortschritte viele neue Räume schaffen, in denen sich Design entwickeln kann.

Als Konsumenten bewegen wir uns heute auf eine Welt zu, die das Grundkonzept von Design im Sinne von ›Weniger ist Mehr‹ in Frage stellt. Damit sind wir mit einer Welt voller Wahlmöglichkeiten konfrontiert. Diese Vermehrung resultiert teilweise aus den Fortschritten im Bereich der Fertigungstechniken und aus dem massiven medialen Bombardement durch multinationale Konzerne.

Ich halte das für eine positive Entwicklung, weil auf diese Weise eine reiche Auswahl an verschiedenen Farben, Materialien, Größen, Funktionen und Preise geboten wird. Und da wir menschliche Wesen sind, betrachten wir uns als Individuen und wollen unsere unterschiedlichen Geschmäcker und Vorlieben geltend machen. Die Auswahl der Objekte, mit denen wir uns umgeben, definiert und prägt unsere Identität, indem wir uns unterscheiden. Die Designer der Zukunft müssen sich dieser Aspekte bewusst sein, wenn sie neue Produkte entwickeln. Dabei müssen sie gleichermaßen auf unsere körperlichen wie auf unsere emotionalen Bedürfnisse eingehen.« SHARON MARSTON

"Designers can be said to fall into two categories: those who design on a logical level and those who design on an emotional level. I would put myself in the latter of these two categories. I create designs that are built around emotion for a future that is becoming increasingly confused and uncertain. This is a very exciting position to be in as current advances in technology are creating many new spaces in which design can develop.

As consumers, we are now moving forward into a world that challenges the fundamental concept of design based on the idea of 'Less is More'. Now we are faced with a world of choices. This proliferation is partly the result of advances in manufacturing processes and the massive media bombardment by multinational companies.

I believe that this is a positive step, for people are now offered the options of different colours, materials, sizes, functions and price variations. As humans, we consider ourselves individuals and like to assert our different tastes. Our decisions on the objects we surround ourselves with define who we are and provide us with identity through difference. Designers in the future will have to be aware of these issues when developing new products. They must design not only for our physical needs but for our emotional needs as well." SHARON MARSTON

« On distingue deux catégories de designers : ceux qui créent sur un plan logique, et ceux qui créent sur un plan émotionnel. Je me place dans la seconde. Je crée des lampes construites autour de l'émotion pour un avenir de plus en plus confus et incertain. C'est une situation passionnante car les progrès technologiques actuels nous offrent de nombreux nouveaux espaces dans lesquels le design peut se développer.

En tant que consommateurs, nous nous dirigeons vers un monde qui remet en question le concept fondamental du design, à savoir "moins il y en a, mieux c'est". Nous sommes confrontés à un monde de choix. Cette prolifération résulte en partie des progrès des procédés de fabrication et du bombardement médiatique des multinationales.

C'est une étape positive, car on peut désormais opter entre différents prix, couleurs, matières, tailles et fonctions. En tant qu'êtres humains, nous nous considérons comme des individus et aimons affirmer nos goûts personnels. Nos décisions sur les objets qui nous entourent définissent qui nous sommes et nous offrent une identité par le biais de la différence. Les créateurs du futur devront en tenir compte en développant de nouveaux produits. Ils devront répondre à nos besoins physiques mais également à nos besoins émotionnels. » SHARON MARSTON

3. **SQ Pleat** pendant lamp/Hängelampe/lustre (self-production), 1999
4. **Aqua** floor lamp/Stehlampe/lampadaire (self-production), 1998
5. **Cocoon** floor lamp/Stehlampe/lampadaire (self-production), 1998
6. **Spiral Pleat** table lamp/Tischlampe/lampe de table (self-production), 1998

SHARON MARSTON

BORN	1970	Hereford, England
STUDIED	1986-88	Btec Diploma Art & Design, Herefordshire College of Art & Design
	1988-92	BA (Hons) Jewellery Design, Middlesex University
PRACTICE	1997-	independent designer/maker
EXHIBITIONS	1997	*Design Resolutions*, Royal Festival Hall, London
	1998	*UK 98 British Festival*, Tokyo; *British and Hungarian Jewellery Design*, Vienna; 100 % Design, London
	1999	*Sotheby's Decorative Arts*, London
	2000	*British Design Excellence*, Manila; International Contemporary Furniture Fair, New York

CLIENTS

Harvey Nichols
Jaeger
The Metropolitan Hotel
also self-production

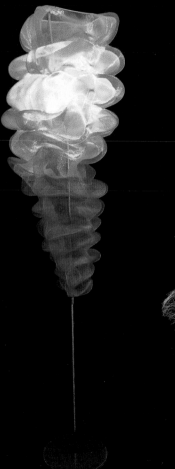

4

5

6

"My favourite design is in my mind,
not yet born."

 Ingo Maurer

Ingo Maurer, Ingo Maurer GmbH, Kaiserstrasse 47, 80 801 Munich, Germany
T +49 89 381 6060 F +49 89 381 60620 postmaster@ingo-maurer.com www.ingo-maurer.com

*»Mein Lieblingsdesign existiert in mei-
nem Kopf, es ist noch nicht geboren.«*

« Mon design préféré est dans ma tête,
pas encore né. »

»Kunst ist das, was eine Person in einem Objekt sieht. Kunst kann ein Nagel oder ein Stück Natur sein, je nach persönlicher Empfindung. Ich kann keine Grenze zwischen Kunst und Design erkennen. Und ich habe auch keine Philosophie. Ich versuche, meiner Intuition, meinem Instinkt, meinen zwanzig Verpflichtungen zu folgen. Wobei das Wichtigste natürlich die Qualität ist. In Zukunft wird die größte Herausforderung für Designer darin liegen, verantwortlich gegenüber den Menschen und der Umwelt zu handeln und mit Sinn und Verstand zu entwerfen.« INGO MAURER

"Art is what a person sees in an object. Art could be a nail or a piece of nature, depending on one's perception. I cannot see any borderline between art and design. I do not have a philosophy. I try to follow my intuition, my instinct, my twenty responsibilities, and, of course, most important is quality. The main challenge for a designer in the future will be to act responsibly towards human beings and the environment and to design with sense." INGO MAURER

« L'art est ce que la personne voit dans un objet. Il peut s'agir d'un clou ou d'un fragment de la nature, selon la perception de chacun. Je ne vois aucune frontière entre l'art et le design. Je n'ai pas de philosophie. J'essaie de suivre mon intuition, mon instinct, mes vingt responsabilités. Bien sûr, ce qui compte avant tout, c'est la qualité. A l'avenir, le plus grand défi du designer sera d'agir de manière responsable envers les êtres humains et l'environnement et de créer en se servant de sa raison. » INGO MAURER

1. page/Seite 189 **XXL Dome** pendant lamps in Westfriedhof subway station, Munich/Hängelampen in der Münchner U-Bahn-Station Westfriedhof/ plafonniers de la station de métro Westfriedhof, Munich (self-production), 1999
2. **Bob** table light/Tischlampe/lampe (self-production), 2000
3. **Paragaudi** lamp/Lampe/luminaire (self-production), 1997

	INGO MAURER	CLIENTS
BORN	1932 Reichenau island, Lake Constance	self-production
STUDIED	Typography courses in Germany and Switzerland	
	1954-58 Graphics Diploma, Munich	
PRACTICE	1960-63 freelance designer in New York and San Francisco	
	1966 founded "Design M" in Munich	
AWARDS	1986 created *Chevalier des arts et des lettres* by the French Ministry of Culture	
	1998 nominated Designer of the Year by the magazine *Architektur & Wohnen*, Hamburg	
	1999 prize for design, City of Munich	
	2000 prize for design, City of Barcelona; Lucky Strike Designer Award, Raymond Loewy Foundation, Switzerland	
EXHIBITIONS	1985 installation for *Lumières – Je pense à vous*, Centre Georges Pompidou, Paris	
	1986 *Ingo Maurer Lumière aha Soho*, Institut Français d'Architecture, Paris; light show for *Design à la Villa Medici*, Rome	
	1988 installation for *Design heute. Maßstäbe – Formgebung zwischen Industrie und Kunst-Stück*, Deutsches Architekturmuseum, Frankfurt/Main	
	1989 *Ingo Maurer – Lumière Hasard Réflexion*, Fondation Cartier, Paris	
	1991 *Münchener Räume*, Stadtmuseum, Munich	
	1993 *Licht licht*, Stedelijk Museum, Amsterdam	
	1998 *Projects 66* (with Fernando and Humberto Campana), Museum of Modern Art, New York	
	1999 installation for Issey Miyake, La Villette	

3

"The attempt to achieve simple things meets what you might call a 'biological' need for simplicity. Since we are complicated beings, let us at least be surrounded by simple objects."

Alberto Meda

Alberto Meda, Via Savona 97, 20 144 Milan, Italy
T +39 02 422 90157 F +39 02 477 16169 a.meda@planet.it

»Das Bemühen um Einfachheit in der Gestaltung von Objekten entspricht einer Art ›biologischem‹ Bedürfnis: Da wir komplizierte Wesen sind, sollten wir uns zumindest mit einfachen Dingen umgeben.«

« La tentative d'accomplir des choses simples répond à ce qu'on pourrait appeler un besoin " biologique " de simplicité. Puisque nous sommes des êtres complexes, entourons-nous au moins d'objets simples. »

1. **Floating Frame** chair/Stuhl/chaise for Alias, 2000
2. ↓ **Fortebracco** task lamp/Arbeitslampe/lampe
d'architecte for Luceplan (designed with Paolo Rizzatto),
1998

"The design process is not linear, it is rather a complex activity similar to a game's strategy, but strangely it is a game where the rules are continuously changing and that is what makes it so fascinating and mysterious.

The designer collects his ideas from various sources within his own world of reference where he looks for creative suggestions. I am personally interested in the world of technology, because it seems to me to be the contemporary expression of the imaginative capability of man, of his ingenuity fed by scientific knowledge. Technology widens the scope of knowledge, but it is necessary to understand that technological development must no longer proceed without justification, without consideration of its repercussions. Self-directed technology can be very dangerous. Technology must be tamed in order to realize things that have the simplest possible relation with man – we must reject technologically driven industrial goods that have no regard for human needs and no communicative rationality. Technology is not an end in itself, but a means of producing simple things capable of enhancing expressively the space around them. Paradoxically, the more complex technology becomes, the better it can generate objects with a simple, unitary, 'almost organic' image.

Design should be seen as a strategy that fishes in the realms of techno- ↓

« Le design n'est pas un processus linéaire, c'est une activité assez complexe qui ressemble à un jeu stratégique mais où, bizarrement, les règles changeraient constamment. C'est ce qui le rend si fascinant et mystérieux. Le designer puise ses idées dans différentes sources au sein de son propre monde de références où il cherche des suggestions créatives. Personnellement, je m'intéresse à la technologie, parce qu'elle me paraît être l'expression actuelle de la capacité imaginative de l'homme, de son ingéniosité nourrie de connaissance scientifique. La technologie élargit le champ de la connaissance, mais son développement ne doit pas avancer sans justification, sans prendre en considération ses répercussions. La technologie pour la technologie peut être très dangereuse. La technologie doit être apprivoisée afin de réaliser des objets qui aient avec l'homme la relation la plus simple possible. Nous devons rejeter les produits industriels qui ne prennent pas en compte les besoins humains, qui n'ont aucune rationalité communicative. La technologie n'est pas une fin en soi mais un moyen de produire des objets capables d'améliorer de manière expressive l'espace autour d'eux. Paradoxalement, plus la technologie devient complexe, plus elle est en mesure de générer des objets à l'image simple, unitaire, " quasi organique". Le design devrait être considéré comme une stratégie s'inspirant du domaine de l'imaginaire technologique. Son but n'est pas d'invoquer une image mettant en avant la pensée scientifique et technique, et donc la technologie en soi, mais d'utiliser cette dernière comme un moyen esthétique et figuratif ↓

3. ← Meda conference chair/Konferenzstuhl/fauteuil de conférence for Vitra, 1996
4. Meda chair (work drawings)/Stuhl (Entwurfsskizzen)/chaise (dessins) for Vitra, 1997

»Der Designprozess verläuft nicht linear, sondern stellt eine komplexe Aktivität dar, die einer Spielstrategie ähnelt. Komischerweise ist es ein Spiel, dessen Regeln sich ständig ändern. Aber genau das ist es, was es so faszinierend und geheimnisvoll macht. Designer beziehen ihre Ideen aus verschiedenen Quellen innerhalb ihres eigenen Bezugssystems, wo sie nach kreativen Anregungen suchen. Mein persönliches Bezugssystem ist die Welt der Technik, weil mir die Technik der zeitgemäße Ausdruck des Vorstellungsvermögens des Menschen, seiner von wissenschaftlicher Erkenntnis gespeisten Erfindungsgabe zu sein scheint. Die Technik erweitert das Spektrum unseres Wissens. Wir müssen jedoch einsehen, dass die technische Entwicklung nicht länger ohne Rechtfertigung und ohne Rücksicht auf ihre Auswirkungen fortschreiten darf. Eine Technologie, deren Zweck nur in sich selber liegt, kann sehr gefährlich werden. Die Technik muss gezähmt werden, damit man Objekte realisieren kann, die eine einfache Beziehung zum Menschen ermöglichen. Abzulehnen sind rein technisch orientierte Industrieerzeugnisse, die keine Rücksicht auf menschliche Bedürfnisse nehmen und keiner kommunikativen Logik folgen. Technologie ist kein Selbstzweck, sondern ein Mittel zur Herstellung einfacher Dinge, die auf ausdrucksvolle Weise ihre Umwelt bereichern können. Je komplexer die Technik wird, desto besser ist sie paradoxerweise geeignet, Objekte mit einer einfachen, einheitlichen und beinahe ›organischen‹ Erscheinungsform zu erzeugen. Man sollte Design als eine Strategie betrachten, mit der man sich Anregungen aus dem ↓

BORN	1945	Lenno Tremezzina, Como, Italy
STUDIED	1969	MA Mechanical Engineering, Politecnico di Milano
PRACTICE	1973-79	technical manager, Kartell
	1979	established own design office
	1983-87	lecturer, industrial technology Domus Academy, Milan
	1995-	lecturer Politecnico di Milano
AWARDS	1989	Compasso d'Oro, Milan
	1992	Design Plus Award, Frankfurt/Main
	1994	Compasso d'Oro, Milan; European Design Prize, Frankfurt/Main
	1995	iF Design Award, Hanover
	1996	iF Design Award Hanover
	1997	Best of Category, *I. D. Magazine Annual Design Review*, New York
	1999	Designer of the Year, Salon du Meuble, Paris
EXHIBITIONS	1990	*Creativitalia* and solo exhibition, Design Gallery, Tokyo
	1992	*Il Giardino delle Cose*, Triennale, Milan; *Mestieri d'Autore*, Siena
	1993	*Design, Miroir du Siècle*, Paris
	1995	*Mutant Materials in Contemporary Design*, Museum of Modern Art, New York
	1996	*Meda-Rizzatto*, Amsterdam; *Lighting Affinities*, Milan
	1999	Salon du Meuble, Paris

CLIENTS

Alfa Romeo
Alessi
Alias
Ansaldo
Carlo Erba
Cinelli
Colombo Design
Fontana Arte
Gaggia
Ideal Standard
Italtel Telematica
Kartell
Luceplan
Legrand
Mandarina Duck
Mondedison
Omron Japan
Philips
Vitra

5

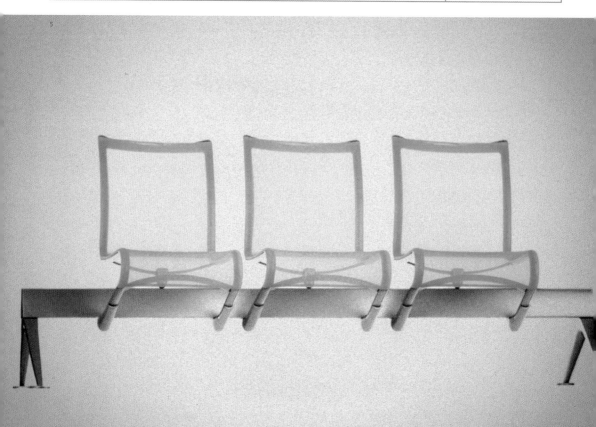

d'interpréter et d'explorer les performances possibles. Je ressens le besoin de produire des objets ayant une qualité culturelle reconnaissable, qui aient un " sens " en plus d'une " forme ". En d'autres termes, le design devrait servir à fabriquer des produits résolvant des problèmes irrésolus. » ALBERTO MEDA

5. **Floating Frame** bench seating system/Sitzbanksystem/système de banquette for Alias, 2000
6. **Partner** shelving system/Regalsystem/système d'étagères for Kartell (designed with Paolo Rizzato), 1999 (exploded to show components/explodiert, um die einzelnen Komponenten sichtbar zu machen/décomposé pour montrer les différents composants)
7. **Words of Light** table lamp/Tischlampe/lampe de table for Luceplan (designed with Paolo Rizzato), 2000

logical fantasy. Its purpose is not to conjure up an image that emphasizes scientific and technical thinking, and therefore technology for its own sake, but to use technology as a means of aesthetic-figurative interpretation and exploration of possible performances. I feel the necessity to produce things with a recognizable cultural quality – things that make 'sense', in addition to 'shape'. In other words, design should be approached with a view to making products capable of solving unsolved problems."
ALBERTO MEDA

Reich der technischen Phantasie holt. Es geht nicht darum, ein Image zu erzeugen, das wissenschaftliches und technisches Denken ins Zentrum stellt – und damit die Technologie zum Selbstzweck macht. Design sollte vielmehr bewirken, Technik als Instrument einer ästhetisch-figurativen Interpretation und Erforschung möglicher Funktionen einzusetzen. Ich halte es für notwendig, Dinge mit einer erkennbaren kulturellen Qualität herzustellen – Dinge, die einen ›Sinn‹ haben, und nicht nur eine ›Form‹. Mit anderen Worten: Man sollte an die Gestaltung von Design mit dem Ziel herangehen, Produkte anzufertigen, die ungelöste Probleme lösen können.« ALBERTO MEDA

"Keep a thing for seven years and you'll find a use for it." (IRISH PROVERB)

Jasper Morrison

Jasper Morrison, Office for Design

»Behalte einen Gegenstand sieben Jahre lang, und du wirst eine Verwendung dafür finden.« (IRISCHES SPRICHWORT)

« Conservez un objet pendant sept ans et vous finirez par lui trouver une utilité. » (PROVERBE IRLANDAIS)

1. **Glo-ball** pendant lamp/Hängelampe/plafonnier
for Flos, 1998
2. ↓ **Three** sofa/Sofa/canapé for Cappellini, 1992

Il y a plusieurs avenirs possibles pour le de-sign, mais imaginons d'abord le meilleur. Le design (le vrai) sature progressivement tous les domaines de l'industrie, apportant une qualité esthétique et matérielle exception-nelle aux produits, qui peuvent être commer-cialisés à des prix abordables, enrichissant notre quotidien au-delà de toute espérance. A présent, un avenir moins désirable: les gens du marketing s'emparent de l'industrie et le saturent avec leur idée du design (pas le vrai), inondant le monde d'articles inutiles dont personne ne sait quoi faire, à part les offrir à d'autres. Comme d'habitude, le futur réside quelque part entre ces deux extrêmes. » JASPER MORRISON

3. ← **Air-Chair**/Stuhl/chaise for Magis, 1999
4. **Tin Family** kitchen containers/Behälter für die Küche/
récipients de cuisine for Alessi, 1998

"There are many possible futures of design, but let's imagine an ideal one first. Design (the real thing) gradually saturates all areas of industry bringing exceptional aesthetic and material quality to products, which can be marketed at affordable levels, enriching our daily lives beyond imagination. And now a less desirable future: marketing people take over industry and saturate it with their idea of design (not the real one), flooding the world with useless articles that nobody needs, which can only be bought as gifts for others. As usual, the future lies somewhere between these extremes." JASPER MORRISON

»Es gibt viele Zukunftsmöglichkeiten für das Design, aber lassen Sie mich zunächst eine Idealversion beschreiben: Design (das wahre) durchdringt allmählich alle Industrie-bereiche und verleiht den Produkten eine außergewöhnliche ästhetische und materielle Qualität. Diese Produkte werden dann zu ver-nünftigen Preisen vermarktet und bereichern unser Alltagsleben mehr als man es sich heute vorstellen kann. Und jetzt ein weniger wün-schenswertes Zukunftsszenario: Marketing-Manager übernehmen die Herrschaft über die Industrie und durchdringen sie mit ihrer Vor-stellung von Design (nicht das wahre). Sie überschwemmen die Welt mit nutzlosen Wa-ren, mit denen niemand etwas anzufangen weiß, außer, sie zu verschenken. Wie immer liegt die Zukunft irgendwo zwischen diesen beiden Extremen.« JASPER MORRISON

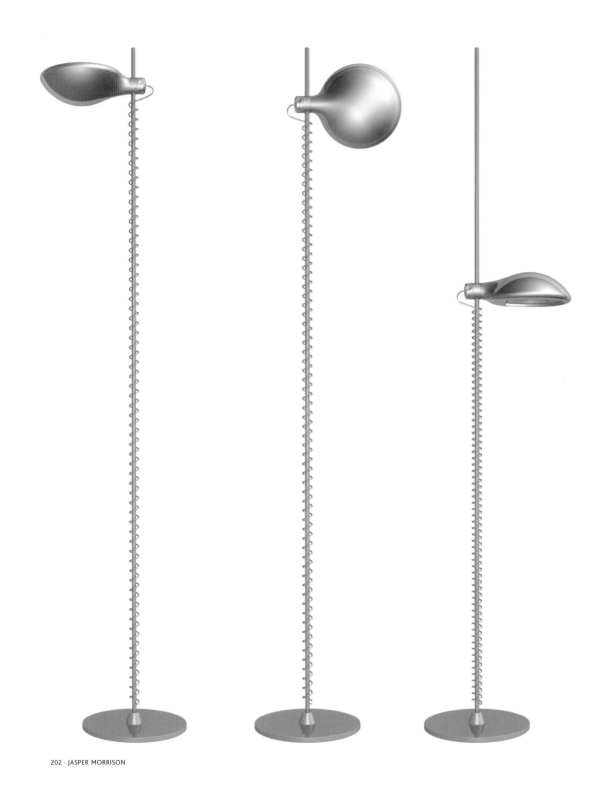

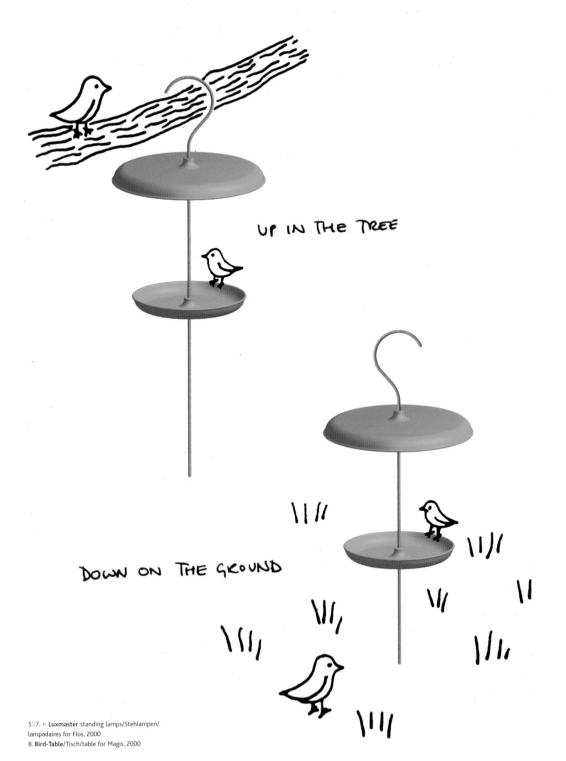

UP IN THE TREE

DOWN ON THE GROUND

5.-7. ← **Luxmaster** standing lamps/Stehlampen/
lampadaires for Flos, 2000
8. **Bird-Table**/Tisch/table for Magis, 2000

9

9. **Lima** folding outdoor chair/Klappstuhl für draußen/
chaise de jardin pliable for Cappellini, 1996
10. **Hi Pad** chairs/Stühle/chaises for Cappellini, 1999
11. **Low Pad** lounge chair/Klubsessel/trausat for Cappellini,
1999
12. **Plan** drawers/Schubladen/tiroirs for Cappellini, 1999

"Think Right – *Penser Juste*"

Pascal Mourgue

Pascal Mourgue – Patrice Hardy, 2, Rue Marcelin Berthelot, 93 100 Montreuil-Sous-Bois, France
T +33 1 48 51 59 38 F +33 1 48 51 59 51 mourgue.hardy@wanadoo.fr

»Richtig denken«

« Penser juste »

1. **Le Paresseux** armchair/Sessel/fauteuil for Cinna-Ligne
Roset, 1999
2. ↓ **Smala** sofa/Sofa/canapé for Cinna-Ligne Roset, 2000

»Ein gutes Designprodukt ist immer mit einer konzeptionellen Innovation verknüpft. Dabei reicht es nicht, nur auf die Form abzuzielen. Alle guten Produkte, d.h. alle Produkte, die kommerziell erfolgreich sind, sind auf die eine oder andere Weise innovativ. Es ist ziemlich einfach, einer Idee Form zu verleihen. Auf der anderen Seite ist es jedoch sehr schwierig, ohne gedankliche Auseinandersetzung eine Form zu gestalten. Meine Arbeit als Designer besteht darin, Ideen zu formulieren, die auf Innovation beruhen.« PASCAL MOURGUE

"A good product is always linked to a conceptual innovation. Researching only through form is not enough. All good products, meaning those that are commercially successful, have a subtle touch of innovation. It is quite easy to get an idea into shape. On the other hand, with no thoughts it is very difficult to create a form. As a designer, my work lies in formulating ideas based on innovation."
PASCAL MOURGUE

« Un bon produit est toujours lié à une innovation conceptuelle. La recherche uniquement formelle n'est pas suffisante. Tous les bons produits en termes commerciaux ont ce subtil dosage d'innovation. Il est très facile de donner forme à une idée. D'un autre côté, sans pensée, il est très difficile de créer une forme. En tant que designer, mon travail consiste à formuler des idées basées sur l'innovation. »
PASCAL MOURGUE

3. **10 Line** chair/Stuhl/chaise for Artelano, 1997
4. **Dune** chair/Stuhl/chaise for Fermob, 1995
5. **Smala** table/Tisch for Cinna-Ligne Roset, 2000
6. **Câlin** armchair/Sessel/fauteuil for Cinna-Ligne Roset, 1994

PASCAL MOURGUE		CLIENTS
BORN	1943 Neuilly, France	Artelano
STUDIED	1962 graduated in Sculpture, Ecole Boulle, Paris	Baccarat
	1964 graduated in Interior Design, ENSAD (Ecole Nationale Supérieure des Arts Décoratifs)	Cartier
PRACTICE	1969 designer for Mobel Italia	Cassina
	1970s furniture designer for Prisunic	Cinna-Ligne Roset
	1973 co-founded design office with Patrice Hardy	Fermob
AWARDS	1984 & 92 Designer of the Year, Salon du Meuble, Paris	Knoll International
	1985 First Prize, Fondation Cartier Competition, Paris	Marcadet-Mobilier
	1988 First Prize, La Critique du Meuble Contemporain	Scarabat
	1996 First Prize – Industrial Design, French Ministry of Culture, Paris	Toulemonde-Bochart
	1998 *Prix du Nombre d'Or du Mobilier Contemporain*, Salon du Meuble, Paris	Vinco
EXHIBITIONS	1985 *Vivre en Couleurs*, Fondation Cartier, Paris	
	1988 *Avant-Première*, Victoria & Albert Museum, London	
	1989 *De Main de Maître*, Seibu-Yuraku-Cho, Tokyo	
	1990 *Mondo Materialis*, Pacific Design Center, Los Angeles	
	1994 *Pascal Mourgue – Designer and Sculptor*, Choisy-le-Roi, France	
	1997 *Made in France*, Centre Georges Pompidou, Paris; *Les Feux de la Rampe – Hommage à Pascal Mourgue*, Galeries Lafayette Haussmann, Paris	
	1999 *Masques Intimes*, Ligne Roset showroom, Moscow	
	2001 *Regards Intimes*, V. I. A. Gallery, Paris	

"I approach design in a fairly subliminal way, which is lucky because I don't have time to think about it too much ..."

Marc Newson

Marc Newson, Marc Newson Ltd., 1, Heddon Street, London W1R 7LE, England
T +44 20 7287 9388 F +44 20 7287 9347 pod@marc-newson.com www.marc-newson.com

»Mein Zugang zu Design ist ein ziemlich unbewusster. Glücklicherweise, denn ich habe keine Zeit, besonders viel darüber nachzudenken ...«

« J'aborde le design d'une manière assez subliminale, ce qui est aussi bien parce que je n'ai pas le temps de trop y penser ... »

1. **Sygma** clothes hook/Kleiderhaken/patère for Alessi,
1997-99
2. ↓ **W. & L.T.** retail shelving system/Regalsystem
für Geschäfte/présentoir de boutique for Walter Van
Beirendonck, 1996-97

"Without doubt, design will play a more important role in our lives in the future whether we like it or not. Certainly, it will play a much bigger role in large companies. In a sense, it's as if design is being re-born as we speak, strangely coinciding with the new millennium. As well, I suppose the word 'design' will become increasingly familiar to most people. My hope is that it will not simply become a commercial catch-phrase, but come to define something that implies quality and improvement." MARC NEWSON

« Il ne fait aucun doute que le design jouera un rôle plus important dans notre vie à l'avenir, que ça nous plaise ou non. Il jouera certainement un rôle plus important dans les grandes entreprises. Dans un sens, c'est comme s'il renaissait en ce moment même, coïncidant étrangement avec le nouveau millénaire. De même, je suppose que le terme "design" deviendra de plus en plus familier pour tout le monde. J'espère seulement qu'il ne sera pas uniquement une accroche commerciale mais qu'il sera synonyme de qualité et d'amélioration. » MARC NEWSON

3. ‹ **W. & L. T.** retail shelving system/Regalsystem für Geschäfte/présentoir de boutique for Walter Van Beirendonck, 1996-97
4. **Megapode** watch/Armbanduhr/montre for Ikepod, 1998
5. **Stavros** bottle opener/Flaschenöffner/ouvre-bouteilles for Alessi, 1997-99
6. **Titan** soap dish/Seifenschale/porte-savon for Alessi, 1997-99
7. **Hi, Med, Low** drinking glasses/Trinkgläser/verres for Iittala, 1998

»Zweifellos wird Design in Zukunft eine wichtigere Rolle in unserem Leben spielen, ob uns das gefällt oder nicht. Und ganz sicher wird es eine wesentlich größere Bedeutung für große Unternehmen haben. In gewissem Sinne scheint es, als werde Design gerade jetzt neu geboren, was eigenartigerweise mit dem Beginn des neuen Jahrtausends zusammenfällt. Außerdem nehme ich an, dass der Begriff ›Design‹ den meisten Menschen immer vertrauter wird. Ich hoffe nur, dass es sich dabei nicht einfach zu einem kommerziellen Schlagwort entwickelt, sondern dass es etwas definieren wird, das Qualität und Verbesserung beinhaltet.« MARC NEWSON

8. & 10. **Interior** for Syn recording studio in Tokyo/
Inneneinrichtung für das Syn-Aufnahmestudio in Tokio/
décoration intérieure de studio d'enregistrement Syn à
Tokyo, 1996
9. **Interior** for Andoni shop/Inneneinrichtung für den
Andoni-Laden/intérieur de boutique Andoni, 1988
11. **Orgone** plastic chair/Plastikstuhl/chaise en plastique
for Pod, 1998
12. **Bath Plug**/Badewannenstöpsel/bouchon de baignoire
for Alessi, 1997
13. **David Gill** chair/Stuhl/chaise for B&B Italia, 1998

11

12

13

14.-19. **021C** concept vehicle for Ford (exterior and interiors)/Konzept-Fahrzeug für Ford (Innen- und Außenansichten)/concept de véhicule pour Ford (intérieur et extérieur), 2000

18

19

MARC NEWSON			CLIENTS
BORN	1963	Sydney, Australia	Alessi
STUDIED	1984	BA jewellery and sculpture, Sydney College of Arts	Biomega
PRACTICE	1987-91	lived and worked in Tokyo	Cappellini
	1991	established design studio in Paris	Flos
	1997	established Marc Newson Ltd. in London	Ford
AWARDS	1984	Australian Crafts Council Award	IDÉE
	1989	George Nelson Award, USA	Iittala
	1990	First Prize Salon du Meuble Creator of the Year Award	Ikepod Watch Company
	1999	Sydney Design Convention Award	Magis
	2001	shortlisted for Perrier-Jouët Selfridges Design Award, London	Moroso
EXHIBITIONS	1990	*Fresh Produce by Marc Newson*, Gold and IDÉE, Tokyo	
	1991 & 92	solo exhibitions, Carla Sozzani, Milan	
	1995	*Marc Newson & Bucky*, Fondation Cartier, Paris	
	1997	*Marc Newson*, Villa de Noailles, France	
	1998	solo exhibition, Museum Boijmans Van Beuningen, Rotterdam	
	1999	*Marc Newson*, McLellan Gallery, Glasgow; *Jasper Morrison, Marc Newson, Michael Young*, Reykjavik Art Museum	

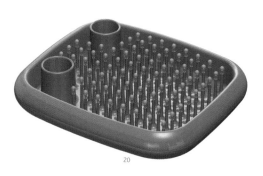

20

21

22 23

20. **Dish Doctor** drainer/Abtropfgestell/égouttoir for Magis, 1997
21. Gemini salt grinder and pepper mill/Salz- und Pfeffermühle/salière et poivrière for Alessi, 1999
22.-23. **Falcon 900B** long-range executive jet (interior)/ Langstreckenflieger (Innenausstattung)/jet privé long-courrier (intérieur), 1998-99
24.-25. **MN01** bicycle/Fahrrad/bicyclette for Biomega, 1998-99
26. **Rock** doorstop/Türstopper/butoirs de porte for Magis, 1997
27. **IO** table/Tisch for B&B Italia, 1998

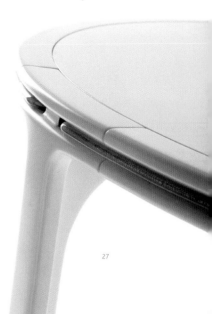

"Reality is what we make it."

Stephen Peart

Stephen Peart, Vent Design, Unit 15, 1436, White Oaks Road, Campbell, California, 95 008 USA
T +408 559 4015 F +408 559 4036 vent1design@earthlink.net

»Realität ist das, was wir dazu machen.«

« La réalité est ce qu'on en fait. »

1. **Computercap**/Computerhelm/casque ordinateur
for Virtual Vision, 1996
2. ↓ **Animal** wetsuit/Tauchanzug/combinaison de plongée
for O'Neill, 1990

»Wir befinden uns mitten in einer ökonomischen und spirituellen Revolution, wobei Design heute mehr auf Entdeckungen und Visionen basiert als auf den Kosten von Waren. Wir konstruieren Dinge, weil wir es können und nicht, weil wir sie brauchen. Dinge sollten als Werkzeug, Gebäude, Möbel, Produkte oder Medien angesehen werden – und wir sollten nicht zum Werkzeug für die Existenz von Dingen werden. Die Leute halten Design für cool, und das ist es auch. Aber im Gestalten von Design liegt auch eine Verantwortung. Indem wir etwas herstellen, billigen wir persönlich dessen Existenz und beeinflussen das Schicksal zahlreicher Ressourcen. Wenn wir Dinge konstruieren, sollten wir die verwendeten Werkstoffe und deren Nebenwirkungen in Betracht ziehen. Die meisten der heute hergestellten Chemikalien kommen ungeprüft auf den Markt. Nehmen Sie zum Beispiel die von Mobiltelefonen ausgehende Elektronenemission: Sie mag nicht tödlich für Sie sein, aber sie könnte Ihr Leben sehr beeinträchtigen. Das Entsorgen all dieser Dinge auf Mülldeponien ist vielleicht unser geringstes Problem. Das heißt nicht, dass wir eine Revolution anzetteln sollten statt als Designer zu arbeiten. Aber wir sollten uns darüber im Klaren sein, welche Konsequenzen die von uns gestalteten Produkte haben. Wir müssen unsere natürlichen Spielräume schützen. Sie sind zu kostbar, um sie zu verlieren.«
STEPHEN PEART

"We are in the midst of an economic and spiritual revolution with design now being based more on discovery and vision than on the cost of goods. We build things because we can, not because we need to. Things should be tools, buildings, furniture, products or media – we should not become tools for the existence of things.
People think of design as cool and it is, but there is responsibility in design. By creating something, you are personally approving its existence and directing the fate of many resources.
When we build things we should consider their side effects and the substances used. Most chemicals made today are untested. Take, for example, the electronic hardware emissions produced by cell phones: They may not kill you but they could make you very unhappy. Throwing things into landfill sites may be the least of our worries. This doesn't mean that we should start a revolution and stop designing, but we must be aware of the consequences of the products we create. We need to protect our physical playground, it's too much fun to lose." STEPHEN PEART

« Nous sommes au beau milieu d'une révolution économique et spirituelle où le design est désormais basé davantage sur la découverte et la vision que sur le coût des produits. Nous construisons des choses parce que nous le pouvons, pas parce que nous en avons besoin. Les choses devraient être des outils, des bâtiments, des meubles, des produits ou des médias. Nous ne devons pas devenir les outils des choses. Les gens pensent que le design, c'est cool, et ils ont raison, mais il implique également une responsabilité. En créant quelque chose, on approuve son existence et on influe sur le sort de nombreuses ressources. Quand on construit quelque chose, on devrait tenir compte de ses effets secondaires et des composants utilisés. La plupart des substances chimiques fabriquées aujourd'hui ne sont pas testées. Prenez par exemple les émissions des matériaux électroniques utilisés dans les téléphones cellulaires : elles ne vous tueront peut-être pas mais elles peuvent sérieusement vous gâcher la vie. On ne se soucie guère des dépotoirs dans lesquels on déverse tous ces déchets. Ça ne veut pas dire qu'il faut faire la révolution et bannir le design, mais qu'on doit être conscient des conséquences des produits qu'on crée. Nous devons protéger notre terrain de jeux, il est trop beau pour qu'on le perde. » STEPHEN PEART

3. **Shoe of the Future** concept project/Projekt für Schuhe/projet de chaussure for Reebok, 1996
4. **EMMA** floor system/Bodensystem/système de fixation de carrelage for Herman Miller (concept project, designed with Ross Lovegrove), 1995-1999
5. **Enterprise** ear-mounted telephone headset/am Ohr befestigter Telefonhörer/oreillettes pour téléphone for Plantronics, 1993
6. **Persona** Internet answering machine/Internet-Anrufbeantworter/répondeur Internet for Sun Microsystems, 1998

STEPHEN PEART

BORN	1958	Durham, England
STUDIED	1975-79	BA (Hons) Industrial Design, Sheffield City Polytechnic
	1979-82	MA Industrial Design, Royal College of Art, London
PRACTICE	1982-87	Design Director Frogdesign, Altensteig and California
	1987	founded Vent Design, Campbell, California
AWARDS	1985	Best of Category, *I. D. Magazine Annual Design Review* Award, New York
	1986	Gold Industrial Design Excellence Award, IDSA
	1991	Gold Industrial Design Excellence Award, IDSA
	1993	iF Design Award, Hanover; Special Award for Design Innovation in the Field of Computer and Communication Technology, Roter Punkt Award, Design Zentrum Nordrhein-Westfalen, Essen; Silver Industrial Design Excellence Award, IDSA
	1994	American Society of Interior Designers (ASID) Interior Design Product Award; Roter Punkt Award, Design Zentrum Nordrhein-Westfalen, Essen; *I. D. Magazine Annual Design Review* Design Distinction Award and Best of Category, New York
	1995	shortlisted for BBC Design Awards
	1996	Good Design Award, Chicago Athenaeum; Best of Category, *I. D. Magazine Annual Design Review* Award, New York
	1997	Industrial Design Excellence Award, IDSA
EXHIBITIONS	1995	*Mutant Materials in Contemporary Design*, Museum of Art, New York; *National Design Triennial – Design Culture Now*, Cooper-Hewitt National Design Museum, New York

CLIENTS

Apple Computer
GE Plastics
Herman Miller
Jetstream
Knoll Group
Nike
O'Neill
Plantronics
Sun Microsystems
Virtual Vision
Visioneer

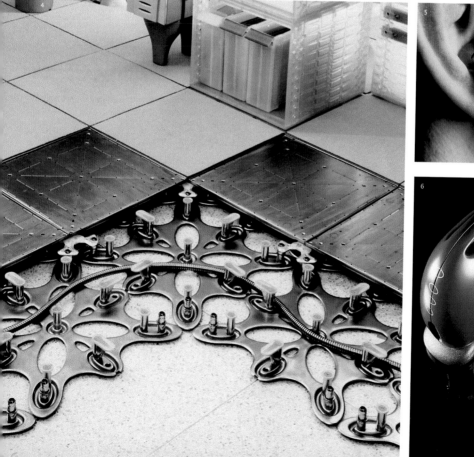

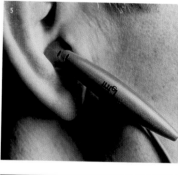

"The best is yet to come."

Jorge Pensi

Jorge Pensi, Jorge Pensi Diseño, Pza. Berenguer 1, 08 002 Barcelona, Spain
T +34 93 310 3279 F: +34 93 315 1370 pensi@idgrup.ibernet.com

»Das Beste kommt erst noch.«

« Le meilleur est encore à venir. »

1. **Peppermint** armchair/Sessel/fauteuil for Kron, 2000
2. ↓ **Chocolate** sofa/Sofa/canapé for Perobell, 1999

« Un designer aborde un objet un peu comme un auteur, tissant une histoire visuelle et conceptuelle à partir d'une image originale qu'il a dans la tête. La principale différence est que le designer travaille généralement avec un commanditaire qui spécifie le thème et le cadre dans lequel le processus créatif doit se dérouler. Le client est la pierre d'achoppement du processus créatif, celui qui fera " croire " au designer à son inspiration avant même que n'apparaissent les premières images mentales (qui aient un sens). Dans certains projets, l'image est créée d'avance, alors que dans d'autres, il ne s'agit que d'un concept brut et flou qui doit être étayé par plusieurs modèles tridimensionnels et des prototypes. En ce sens, le design ressemble à l'architecture et repose sur l'expérimentation.

Le designer vit entre deux mondes, le subjectif et l'objectif. Le premier se base sur des symboles, l'originalité et la nature relativement immuable et intrinsèque des objets. Il est lié à la magie de la créativité, à l'influence de l'histoire et de la mémoire, aux grands maîtres et visionnaires du design. Le second est le monde réel, qui dépend des marchés, des investissements, des coûts, des calendriers des fabricants et de la production. Le premier monde représente le désir et l'autre, la réalité. Plus nos désirs se rapprochent de la réalité, plus le design sera bon. La capacité d'un objet à susciter des émotions vient d'un processus de développement, où les désirs ne peuvent être trahis par la réalité et où le lien entre les deux mondes reste intact. » JORGE PENSI

3. ← **Duna** chair/Stuhl/fauteuil for Cassina, 1998
4. **Splash** armchair/Stuhl/fauteuil for Amat, 1999

"A designer approaches an object in a similar way to an author – visually and conceptually weaving a story from an original mind's eye image. The most important difference, however, is that the designer usually works with a client, who specifies the theme and framework in which the creative process must take place. The client is the first input of the creative process, the person responsible for making the designer 'believe' in the inspiration before the first mental images (that make any sense) appear. In some projects the image is created in advance, while in others it is merely a rough, fuzzy concept that needs to be verified by several three-dimensional models and prototypes. In this sense, design is similar to architecture in that it relies on a process of trial and error.

The designer lives between two worlds – the subjective and the objective. The first world is based on symbols, originality and the relatively immutable and intrinsic nature of objects. It is connected to the magic of creativity, the influence of history and memory, and the great masters and visionaries of the design field. The second world is the real world, which is related to markets, investments, costs, the manufacturer and the production schedule. One world represents desire and the other, reality. The closer our desires are to reality, the better the design will be. The ability of an object to stir emotions comes from a process of development, where desires cannot be betrayed by reality and where the connection between the two worlds remains intact." JORGE PENSI

»Ein Designer geht in seiner Arbeit an einem Objekt ähnlich vor wie ein Schriftsteller – indem er aus einem ursprünglich geistigen Bild visuell und konzeptionell eine Geschichte entwickelt. Der wichtigste Unterschied ist jedoch, dass Designer in der Regel mit Auftraggebern zusammenarbeiten, die das Thema und den Rahmen vorgeben, in dem der kreative Prozess stattzufinden hat. Der Auftraggeber gibt den ersten Impuls für den kreativen Prozess und ist verantwortlich dafür, dass der Designer an die Inspiration ›glaubt‹, noch bevor die ersten (einigermaßen sinnvollen) mentalen Bilder auftauchen. Bei einigen Projekten entsteht das Bild vorher, während es bei anderen lediglich ein grobes, vages Konzept gibt, das durch mehrere dreidimensionale Modelle und Prototypen verifiziert werden muss. In diesem Sinne lässt sich Design auch mit Architektur vergleichen, da es ebenso wie diese auf einem Prozess des Experimentierens beruht. Designer leben im Wechsel zwischen zwei Welten – der subjektiven und der objektiven. Die erste Welt basiert auf Symbolen, Originalität und der relativ unveränderlichen und spezifischen Natur von Objekten. Sie steht in Verbindung mit der Magie der Kreativität, dem Einfluss von Geschichte und Erinnerung sowie mit den großen Meistern und Visionären des Designs. Die zweite Welt ist die reale Welt, die mit Handelsmärkten, Investitionen, Kosten, dem Hersteller und dem Produktionsplan verbunden ist. Die eine Welt repräsentiert das Begehren und die andere die Realität. Je näher unsere Begierden der Realität sind, desto besser wird das Design sein. Die Fähigkeit eines Objekts, Emotionen zu wecken, ist auf einen Entwicklungsprozess zurückzuführen, in dem die Begierden nicht von der Realität verraten werden können und die Verbindung zwischen beiden Welten intakt bleibt.« JORGE PENSI

JORGE PENSI		CLIENTS
BORN	1949 Buenos Aires, Argentina	Akaba
STUDIED	1965-73 architecture, Facultad de Arquitectura, UBA, Buenos Aires	Amat
PRACTICE	1975 emigrated to Spain and adopted Spanish nationality	Andreu World
	1977-84 collaborated with Alberto Liévore as part of Group Berenguer in Barcelona	B.Lux
	1985 established own design practice in Barcelona	Cassina
AWARDS	1988 Award Selection from SIDI	Ciatti
	1987 & 95 Silver Delta Award, Assoziazione del Diesegno Industriale	Disform
	1990 *Design-Auswahl 90* Award, Design Center Stuttgart	Driade
	1997 *National Design Prize*, Spanish Ministry of Industry and BCD (Barcelona Design Centre), Golden Delta Award, Assoziazione del Diesegno Industriale	Inno Interior
		Knoll International
EXHIBITIONS	1984 *SIDI (Salón Internacionale de Diseño para el Habitát) ON Diseño*	Kron
	1988-94 *Design in Catalonia*, touring exhibition, Milan, Tokyo, Singapore and USA	Kusch+Co
		Perobell
		Punt Mobles
		Santa & Cole
		SIDI
		Thonet

5. **Gimlet** stools/Hocker/tabouret for Mobles 114, 1998
6. **Techne** office seating system/Büromöbel/sièges de bureau for Kitto, 2000
7. **Nite** table & pendant lamp/Tisch- & Hängelampe/lampe suspendue for B. Lux, 1998
8. **Hega** table & sideboard/Anrichte & Tisch/table & console for Azcue, 2000
9. **Goya** wall-bookcase/Wand-Buchregal/bibliothèque for Casprini, 1998

"A good designer has to be part artist, part engineer, psychologist, sociologist, planner, marketing man and communicator: part everything, and part nothing!"

Roberto Pezzetta

Roberto Pezzetta, c/o Electrolux Zanussi S. P. A.,
Uffici di Corso Lino Zanussi 30, 33 080 Porcia (Pordenone), Italy
T +39 0434 39 6215 F: +39 0434 39 6045 roberto.pezzetta@notes.electrolux.it www.zanussi.com

»Ein guter Designer muss ein bisschen Künstler, ein bisschen Ingenieur, Psychologe, Soziologe, Planer, Marketing-Experte und Vermittler sein: ein bisschen alles … und ein bisschen nichts!«

« Un bon designer doit être un peu artiste, ingénieur, sociologue, planificateur, expert en marketing et en communication : un peu tout … et n'importe quoi ! »

1. **ZHC95ALU** extractor fan/Abzugshaube/hotte de cuisine
from **Aluminium Range** for Zanussi, 2000
2. ↓ **Softech** built-in electric oven/elektrischer Einbauherd/
four électrique encastrable for Zanussi, 1996

»Ein Kollege sagte einmal zu mir, Design repräsentiere eine elitäre Wahl. Das ist wahr. Und es trifft ebenfalls zu, dass jeder Berufsstand von einer Ideologie getragen wird, die man nicht ignorieren kann. Es ist keine leichte Aufgabe, Konflikte zu klären und Ideologien auf ein neues, gemeinsames Ziel auszurichten. Ein charakteristisches und inhärentes Merkmal des ›Handwerks‹ von Designern ist deren Bewusstsein, sich nicht im Besitz einer absoluten Wahrheit zu befinden. Gerade die Tatsache, dass dieser Beruf von anderen Berufen häufig nicht zu unterscheiden ist oder mit ihnen in Deckung gebracht werden kann, bedeutet, dass Designer – mehr als andere Leute – eine Neigung zu Zweifel und Relativismus haben, was sie beständig über die Grenzen ihrer eigenen Wahrheiten hinaus forschen lässt.

Hier ein Rat, zuallererst an mich selbst und dann an alle gerichtet, die es interessiert: Man muss in dynamischen Begriffen denken; man darf es sich nicht zu leicht machen, indem man immer nur festen Regeln und bewährten Lösungen folgt, sondern man muss aus der Perspektive kontinuierlichen Forschens und Experimentierens handeln, den Mut zu unerwarteten Vorschlägen haben und – zusätzlich zum Bleistift – diese essentielle Eigenschaft der Designer gebrauchen: die Neugierde.« ROBERTO PEZZETTA

"A colleague once told me that design represents an aristocratic choice. This is true, and it is also true that every profession is sustained by an ideology that you cannot ignore. Settling conflicts and reorienting ideologies towards a common goal are not easy tasks to accomplish. A peculiar and inherent characteristic of the designer's 'craft' is the awareness of not being in possession of absolute truth. The very fact that this profession is often indistinguishable from and superimposable on others means that, more than other people, the designer is predisposed to doubt and relativism, and is capable of continuously searching beyond his own truths.

A piece of advice directed first and foremost to myself and then to anyone who is willing to listen: think in dynamic terms, do not take the easy way out by following the rules and approved solutions, act in the perspective of continuous research, find the courage to make unexpected proposals, and, in addition to your pencil, use that quintessential quality of designers – curiosity."
ROBERTO PEZZETTA

« Un collègue m'a dit une fois que le design représentait un choix aristocratique. C'est vrai, comme il est également vrai que chaque profession est soutenue par une idéologie qu'on ne peut ignorer. Régler des conflits et réorienter les idéologies vers un objectif commun ne sont pas des tâches faciles. Une des caractéristiques singulières et inhérentes à "l'art" du designer est la conscience de ne pas être le détenteur d'une vérité absolue. Le seul fait que la profession elle-même soit souvent indissociable et superposée à d'autres signifie que les designers sont particulièrement prédisposés au doute et au relativisme, et qu'ils sont capables de chercher continuellement au-delà de leurs propres vérités.

Un petit conseil, tout d'abord à moi-même puis à tous ceux que cela intéresse : il faut penser en termes dynamiques, ne pas chercher une porte de sortie facile en suivant les règles et les solutions établies, agir dans la perspective de recherches continues, trouver le courage de faire des propositions inattendues et, outre son crayon, utiliser cette qualité fondamentale des designers : la curiosité. »
ROBERTO PEZZETTA

3. **Oz** refrigerator/Kühlschrank/réfrigérateur for Zanussi, 1994-98
4. **Ambience 9** electric oven/Elektroherd/four électrique from **Aluminium Range** for Zanussi, 2000
5. **ZD699ALU** dishwasher (detail)/Spülmaschine (Detail)/lave-vaisselle (détail) from **Aluminium Range** for Zanussi, 2000

ROBERTO PEZZETTA			CLIENTS
BORN	1946	Treviso, Italy	Nordica
STUDIED		self-taught	Zanussi/Electrolux
PRACTICE	1967-69	worked in R&D for Zoppas	Zoppas
	1969-74	product designer for Zoppas	
	1974-77	product designer for Zanussi	
	1977-78	product designer for Nordica	
	1978-82	product designer for Zanussi	
	1982-	head of industrial design, Zanussi Electrodomestici Industrial Design Center	
	1993-	Director of Design, Electrolux European Design Management Team	
AWARDS	1981	Compasso d'Oro, Milan	
	1987, 89 & 91	Compasso d'Oro selection, Milan	
	1987, 91 & 99	*Goed Industrieel Ontwerp* Award, Netherlands	
	1988	Gold Medal, BIO 12 Biennial of Industrial Design, Ljubliana	
	1990	Sami du Design Award, Salon des Arts Ménagers, Paris	
	1997	Design Prestige Award, Brno	
	1997	conferred *Master of Labour* by the President of the Italian Republic	
	1998	Premio De Diseño award, Cuba; Honour Selection for Compasso d'Oro, Milan	
	1999 & 2000	Good Design Award, Chicago Athenaeum	
EXHIBITIONS	1990	*Civiltà delle Macchine*, Turin	
	1992	*Organic Design*, Design Museum, London	
	1997	Expo L'ocio, Madrid	
	1998	Biennale Internationale du Design de Saint-Etienne	
	1999	*Roberto Pezzetta*, Forum for Form, Stockholm; *The Shape of Colour Red*, Glasgow; *Design in the Digital Age*, Victoria & Albert Museum, London	
	2000	*Les Bons Génies de la Vie Domestique*, Centre Georges Pompidou, Paris	

4

5

"Design must offer people an alternative way of living – it must answer the aspirations of people in terms of well-being and happiness."

Christophe Pillet

Christophe Pillet, 81 Rue Saint-Maur, 75011 Paris, France
T +33 1 48 06 78 31 F +33 1 48 06 78 32 cpillet@club-internet.fr

»Design muss den Menschen eine alternative Lebensform anbieten. Es muss den Sehnsüchten der Menschen im Hinblick auf Wohlbehagen und Glück entsprechen.«

« Le design doit offrir aux gens une autre manière de vivre. Il doit répondre à leurs aspirations de bien-être et de bonheur. »

1. **Sunset Lounge** armchair/Sessel/fauteuil for Cappellini, 1998
2. ↓ **Ultra Living** sofa/Sofa/canapé for E&Y, 1998

« Si, par le passé, le design s'est concentré principalement sur des solutions à des problèmes spécifiques de fonction, d'ergonomie et d'esthétique, à l'avenir, il tendra de plus en plus à se libérer de ces préoccupations pour se consacrer avant tout à l'invention d'environnements pour des particuliers. S'émancipant des systèmes qui l'ont généré, il travaillera à une échelle plus globale sur des modes de vie alternatifs et innovateurs, sur des scénarios imaginaires motivés par le désir d'un meilleur style de vie. » CHRISTOPHE PILLET

3. ← Saucepan/Kochtopf/faitout for the **Pots and Pans** microwave experimental project for Whirlpool, 2000
4. Remote control/Fernbedienung/télécommande for the **Pots and Pans** microwave experimental project for Whirlpool, 2000
5. Pasta cooker/Nudelkocher/cuit-pâtes for the **Pots and Pans** microwave experimental project for Whirlpool, 2000
6. Kettle/Kessel/bouilloire for the **Pots and Pans** microwave experimental project for Whirlpool, 2000

"If in the past design has concentrated mainly on producing solutions for specific problems of function, ergonomics, economy and aesthetics, it will tend in the future to liberate itself more and more from these specific concerns in order to become a discipline primarily devoted to the invention of environments for individuals. Freeing itself from the systems that generated it, design will work on a more global scale on alternative and innovative lifestyles, on scenarios imagined that are driven by the desire for a better way of living."
CHRISTOPHE PILLET

»War das Design in der Vergangenheit hauptsächlich darauf konzentriert, Lösungen für bestimmte Probleme im Hinblick auf Funktion, Ergonomie, Ökonomie und Ästhetik anzubieten, so wird es sich in Zukunft mehr und mehr von diesen spezifischen Anliegen befreien und zu einer Disziplin werden, die sich in erster Linie dem Erfinden von individuellen Umwelten widmet. Indem es sich von den Systemen verselbstständigt, die es hervorgebracht haben, wird Design auf einer globaleren Ebene an alternativen und innovativen Lebensformen arbeiten, an imaginativen Szenarios, die von dem Wunsch nach einer besseren Lebensform motiviert werden.« CHRISTOPHE PILLET

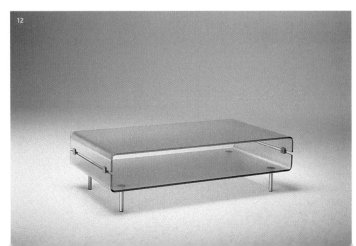

7. **Air Can** lamp/Lampe/lampe for AV Mazzega, 1999
8. **Nath's Sofa**/canapé for Domeau & Perès, 1998
9. **Marie Claire** 2000 virtual project/virtuelles Projekt/ projet virtuel for the magazine *Marie Claire*, 2000
10. **Video Lounge** chaise longue/Liege for Domeau & Perès, 1998
11. **C&C** table on castors/Tisch auf Rollen/table à roulettes for Fiam, 2000
12. **C&C** table/Tisch for Fiam, 2000

"Design is the whole experience
of living."

Karim Rashid

Karim Rashid, 357, W. 17th Street, New York, NY 10011, USA
T +1 212 929 8657 F +1 212 929 0247 office@karimrashid.com www.karimrashid.com

*»Design ist das ganze Erlebnis des
Daseins.«*

« Le design est l'expérience de la vie. »

1. **Pendant** lamp/Hängelampe/lustre from
Soft Collection for George Kovacs Lighting, 1999
2. ↓ **Omni** reconfigurable seating object/variables Sitz-
objekt/banquette modulable for Galerkin Furniture, 1999

« Les produits doivent être en rapport avec nos émotions et enrichir l'imagination et l'expérience populaire. La diversité, la variété, la multiplicité et le changement font partie d'un ensemble de concepts. Le design industriel est un acte créatif, politique et physique. C'est un procédé interactif qui dépasse la forme physique elle-même. Son résultat se manifeste par des lignes esthétiques, son contenu s'inspirant de toutes les possibilités de notre monde moderne.
Les nouveaux objets qui façonnent nos vies sont des hybrides transconceptuels, multi-culturels. Ils peuvent exister n'importe où dans différents contextes, naturels et synthétiques, inspirés par les télécommunications, l'information, le ludique et le comportement. Notre culture de l'objet capte l'énergie et le phénomène de cette nouvelle ère numérique universelle. Ce qui m'intéresse le plus en design, c'est l'apparition de nouveaux procédés industriels, de nouveaux matériaux, de nouveaux marchés planétaires. Ils nous permettent d'espérer remodeler nos vies. Les nouvelles cultures exigent de nouvelles formes, de nouvelles matières et de nouveaux styles. Je définis mon travail en termes de minimalisme sensuel ou de " sensualisme ", où les objets communiquent, attirent et inspirent tout en restant relativement dépouillés. Ils parlent simplement et directement, sans superflu. Mon travail est un mariage de géométrie pure et organique.
Pour ce qui est des arguments controversés d'excès, de durabilité et de séduction du marché, j'estime que chaque nouvel objet devrait en remplacer trois. *La qualité des produits détermine le marché.* Les objets ne devraient pas être des obstacles mais des capteurs d'expérience. J'essaie d'en développer qui luttent contre le stress, qui apportent de la joie et simplifient nos tâches tout en augmentant notre degré d'implication et ↓

"Products must deal with our emotional ground and increase the popular imagination and experience. Diversity, variance, multiplicity and change are part of every whole construct. Industrial design is a creative act, a political act, a physical act and a socially interactive process that is greater than the physical form itself – its result is manifested in aesthetic forms, the content inspired by all the possibilities of our contemporary conditions.
I believe that the new objects that shape our lives are trans-conceptual, multi-cultural hybrids, objects that can exist anywhere in different contexts, that are natural and synthetic, that are inspired through telecommunications, information, entertainment and behaviour. Our object culture can capture the energy and phenomena of this contemporary universal culture of the digital age. The birth of new industrial processes, new materials, global markets are my great interests in design that all lend hope to reshaping our lives. I feel that new culture demands new forms, material and style. I define my work as sensual minimalism, or 'sensualism', where objects communicate, engage and inspire yet remain fairly minimal. They can speak simply and directly, without superfluousness. My work is a marriage of organic and pure geometry.
In the controversial arguments about excess, sustainability and market seduction, I believe that every new object should replace three. *Better products edit the marketplace.* I believe objects should not be obstacles in life but raptures of experience. I try to develop objects as de-stressers – objects that bring enjoyment and simplify tasks while increasing ↓

»Designprodukte müssen sich mit unserer emotionalen Grundhaltung befassen, sowie Vorstellungskraft und Erfahrungsschatz der Allgemeinheit bereichern. Mannigfaltigkeit, Verschiedenheit, Vielfalt und Veränderung sind Bestandteile jeder Gesamtkonzeption. Die Gestaltung von Industriedesign ist ein kreativer, politischer, physischer Akt und ein sozial interaktiver Prozess, der über die sinnlich wahrnehmbare Form hinausgeht. Das Resultat manifestiert sich in ästhetischen Gestaltungsformen, während der Inhalt durch all die Möglichkeiten unserer modernen Lebenswelt inspiriert wird.
Neue Objekte, die unser Leben formen, sind konzeptübergreifende und multikulturelle Mischformen. Sie können überall und in verschiedenartigen Zusammenhängen existieren. Sie sind natürlich und synthetisch und werden durch Telekommunikation, Information, Unterhaltung und Verhaltensweisen angeregt. Unsere Kultur des Objekts fängt die Energie und Phänomene dieses neuen und universellen digitalen Zeitalters ein. Ich interessiere mich besonders für das Aufkommen neuer Produktionsmethoden, neuer Materialien und globaler Märkte – Aspekte, die alle zur Hoffnung auf eine Umgestaltung unserer Lebenswelten berechtigen. Meiner Ansicht nach erfordert eine neue Kultur die Entwicklung neuer Formen, Werkstoffe und Stile. Ich definiere meine Arbeit als sinnlichen Minimalismus oder ›Sensualismus‹, wobei die Objekte kommunizieren, berühren und inspirieren und doch ziemlich minimalistisch bleiben. Ihre Sprache ist einfach und direkt, ohne Überflüssiges. Ich sehe meine Arbeit als eine Verschmelzung des Organischen mit dem rein Geometrischen.
In der Kontroverse über die Themen Überfluss, Nachhaltigkeit und die Verlockungen des Marktes, vertrete ich den Standpunkt, dass jedes neue Objekt drei andere ersetzen sollte. *Bessere Produkte ordnen und korrigieren den Markt.* Ich finde, Designprodukte sollten keine Hindernisse für das Alltagsleben darstellen, sondern mit Begeisterung wahrgenommen und erlebt werden. Ich versuche, Objekte zu entwickeln, die ›ent-spannend‹ wirken. Sie sollen Freude bereiten und Tätigkeiten vereinfachen, während sie gleichzeitig unser Engagement und unser ästhetisches Niveau erhöhen. Unser Alltag wird bereichert durch das Erlebnis, dass Schönheit, Komfort, Luxus, Funk- ↓

3. ← OH stacking chair/Stapelstuhl/chaise encastrable for Umbra, 1999
4. **Softscape** conceptual environment for future living/ Entwurf für zukünftige Lebensraumgestaltung/environnement conceptuel pour la vie de demain, 1998

5

6

7

d'appréciation de la beauté. Lorsque nous vivons dans une alliance parfaite de beauté, de confort, de luxe, de performance et d'utilité, nos vies s'en trouvent enrichies. La beauté est une relation profonde entre l'intérieur et l'extérieur, une osmose d'esthétiques. Elle n'est pas une question de goût mais une appréciation acquise, un processus empirique. Cette profondeur sous-jacente signifie que le contenu joue un rôle primordial dans la beauté des choses. Les peintures, les objets d'art, l'architecture, l'espace, tous expriment leur esthétique au travers de leur contenu. Le visuel et le concept ne font qu'un. Tout ce qui est beau a un contenu. » KARIM RASHID

5. **Blobject** chairs/Stühle/chaises (limited edition of 10), 1999
6. **Syntax** chairs/Stühle/chaises from **Decola Vita Furniture Collection** for Idée, 1998
7. **Sofa Two**/Sofa/canapé for Galerkin Furniture, 1999

our level of engagement and of beauty. Our lives are elevated when we experience beauty, comfort, luxury, performance and utility acting seamlessly together. Beauty is a deeper, inseparable relationship between the inner and the outer, an osmosis of aesthetics. Beauty is not a question of taste, or personal likes and dislikes but a learned appreciation, an experiential process. This underlying depth of beauty means that content plays a primary role in the beauty of things. Paintings, objects, art, architecture, space, all manifest their aesthetics through their content. The visual effect and the concept are one. Something beautiful has content." KARIM RASHID

tionalität und Zweckmäßigkeit nahtlos ineinander greifen. Schönheit ist eine tiefere, unauflösbare Verbindung zwischen dem Inneren und dem Äußeren, eine Osmose der Ästhetik. Schönheit ist keine Frage des Geschmacks oder der persönlichen Vorlieben und Abneigungen, sondern ein erlerntes Verständnis, ein Erfahrungsprozess. Diese tiefere Dimension von Schönheit bedeutet, dass bei der Schönheit von Dingen der Inhalt eine entscheidende Rolle spielt. Gemälde, Objekte, Kunst, Architektur, Räume – in all diesen Dingen manifestiert sich ihre Ästhetik durch ihren Inhalt. Optische Wirkung und Konzept sind eins. Alles, was schön ist, besitzt Inhalt.« KARIM RASHID

KARIM RASHID

BORN	1960	Cairo, Egypt (Canadian national)
STUDIED	1978-82	BA Industrial Design (Distinction), Carleton University, Ottawa
	1983	post-graduate design studies, Massa Lubrense, Italy sponsored by ADI/ISIA, Rome
PRACTICE	1981-82	Mitel Corporation, Kanata, Canada
	1984	Rodolfo Bonetto Industrial Design Studio, Milan
	1984-91	senior designer/partner, KAN Industrial Designers, Toronto
	1985-91	senior designer/co-founder, Babel Inc. and North Studio, Toronto
	1992-	principal designer, Karim Rashid Inc., New York
	1993-95	Visiting Associate Professor, Industrial Design, Pratt Institute, New York
	1993-	Associate Professor, Industrial Design, The University of the Arts, Philadelphia
AWARDS	1993	Best of Year in Product Design, *I. D. Magazine Annual Design Review* Award, New York
	1995-2000	11 Good Design Awards, Chicago Athenaeum
	1999	Design Journal Gold Award; two Good Design Awards, Chicago Athenaeum; George Nelson Award, USA; DaimlerChrysler Design Award
	2001	Designer of the Year, Interior Design Show, Toronto; Gold IDEA Award, IDSA; 3 *I. D. Magazine Annual Design Review* Distinctive Awards, New York
EXHIBITIONS	1998	*Decola Vita* solo show, IDÉE Gallery, Tokyo
	1999	*Collab Award* exhibition, Philadelphia Museum of Art
	2000	*National Design Triennial – Design Culture Now*, Cooper-Hewitt National Design Museum, New York
	2001	*Pleasurscape*, Rice University Gallery, Houston; *Workspheres*, Museum of Modern Art, New York; *010101*, San Francisco Museum of Art

CLIENTS

Black & Decker
Canada Post Corporation
Citibank
ClassiCon
Estée Lauder
Fasem
Fujitsu
Giorgio Armani
Guzzini
IDÉE
Issey Miyake
Sony
Swid Powell
Tommy Hilfiger
Zanotta
Zeritalia

8

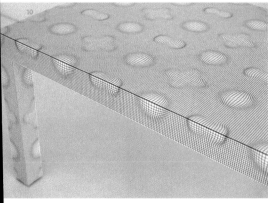

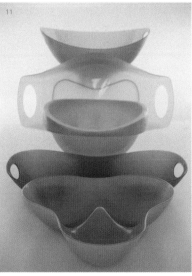

8. **Ribbon** future desktop landscape/Arbeitsplatz
der Zukunft/bureau du futur for Totem, 1999
9. **Sofa One**/Sofa/canapé for Galerkin Furniture, 1999
10. **Morphscape** table/Tisch (one-off), 2000
11. **Sumo** bowl/Schale/bol, **Jambo** tray/Tablett/plateau,
Rimbowl and **Tribowl** bowls/Schalen/bols for Umbra, 1999
12. **Garbo** and **Garbino** wastepaper baskets/Papierkörbe/
corbeilles à papier for Umbra, 1996

"Exact/precise/intensive observation
and planning are the preconditions
for designing objects that have
visible souls."

Prospero Rasulo

Prospero Rasulo, Via Sebenico 13, 20 124 Milan, Italy
T +39 02 668 8840 F +39 02 668 8842 prrasulo@tin.it

*»Intensive Beobachtung und Planung
sind die Vorbedingungen für das Gestalten von Objekten, die eine sichtbare
Seele haben.«*

« L'observation et une planification
exactes/précises/intensives sont les
conditions préalables à la conception
d'objets pourvus d'une âme visible. »

1. **Alma** chair/Stuhl/chaise for BRF, 2000
2. ↓ **Skinny** table/Tisch/table basse for Zanotta, 1999

»Mein künstlerischer Hintergrund kennzeich-
net und beeinflusst die Art, wie ich Dinge
wahrnehme und verstehe. Indem wir die materiellen Güter, die uns umgeben, mit Auf-
merksamkeit und Neugier betrachten, können
wir den für unsere Inspiration notwendigen
Wunsch in uns entdecken, Objekte mit Herz
und Gefühl zu entwerfen. Ein bestimmtes
Material, ein Zeichen oder eine Farbe kann
als Katalysator für die emotionale Beziehung
zwischen Objekten und Menschen fungieren.
Für mich muss jedes Produkt eine autonome
Ausdruckskraft haben. Zusammen mit seiner
klaren Funktionalität wird das Produkt damit
zu einem dauerhaften Objekt, denn es wird
auch mit der Zeit verblüffend präsent bleiben.
Beim Design kommt es in erster Linie auf das
Spiel der Anziehung an.« PROSPERO RASULO

"My artistic background character-
izes and influences the way I
observe and comprehend things.
By looking with attention and
curiosity at the material goods that
surround us, we are able to find the
necessary desire that inspires us
to create objects with heart and
emotion. A certain material, sign
or colour can act as a catalyst for
an emotional relationship between
objects and people. I believe that
every product should have an au-
tonomous expressive energy. With
this, together with an obvious use-
fulness, the product will become a
durable object because over time
it will continue to offer the surprise
of its presence. Design is ultimately
about the game of attraction."
PROSPERO RASULO

« Ma formation artistique caractérise et influence la façon dont j'observe et je com-
prends les choses. C'est dans l'examen atten-
tif et curieux des biens matériels qui nous entourent que nous puisons le désir nécessaire
qui nous inspire la création d'objets avec cœur
et émotion. Une certaine matière, une couleur
ou un signe servent parfois de catalyseur à
une relation émotionnelle entre les objets et
les hommes. Pour moi, chaque produit devrait
avoir une énergie expressive autonome. Ceci,
associé naturellement à son utilité, en fait
un objet durable parce que, avec le temps, il
continue d'offrir la surprise de sa présence. Le
design est avant tout un jeu de séduction. »
PROSPERO RASULO

3. **Alma** chairs/Stühle/chaises for BRF., 2000
4. **Bone** table/Tisch for BRF, 2000
5. **Qua** lamp/Lampe/applique for Foscarini, 1998

PROSPERO RASULO

BORN 1953 Stigliano, Matera, Italy
STUDIED 1973 graduated (art & design), Accademia di Belle Arti di Brera, Milan
PRACTICE 1980-82 designed for Studio Alchimia and collaborated with Alessandro Mendini researching "redesign" and the "banal object"
 1982 began working as an industrial designer
 1987 founded Oxido Gallery, Milan
EXHIBITIONS
 1986-88 *Sexy Design*, Milan & Parma; *L'Immagine Imprudente*, Milan, Reggio Emilia and Mantova; *Abitare con Arte*, Verona, Paris
 1994 *Piatto Fax*, Milan; *Trash Furniture*, Milan
 1998 *Eco Mimetico*, Milan

CLIENTS

Antonio Lupi
Arcade
Arflex
BRF
Fiam Italia
Foscarini
L'Oca Nera
Mandelli
Poltronova
Rosenthal
Zanotta

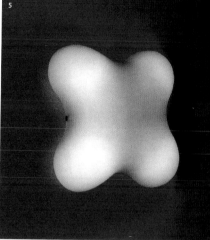

"Low-tech choices for a digital era."

Timo Salli

Timo Salli, Muotoilutoimisto Salli Ltd., Meritullinkatu 11, 00 170 Helsinki, Finland
T +358 9 681 37700 F +358 9 278 2277 salli@timosalli.com

»Low-tech-Alternativen für ein digitales Zeitalter.«

« Des choix non technologiques pour une ère numérique. »

1. **Jack in the Box** television set/Fernseher/meuble de
télévision (self-production), 1997
2. ↓ **Zik Zak** collapsible chair/Klappstuhl/chaise pliante
(one-off for Snowcrash exhibition), 1997

"I question how we look at things and whether this behaviour can be a motive to make functional objects. Could a fireplace replace a television? When stared at, both have a deeper purpose – they erase your memory until it is downloaded. Connecting the function of a mirror with that of a lamp is a way of producing a double meaning for one object. When the light is turned off it can be used as a mirror to reflect daylight, while during the evening it can be used both as a light-source and as a mirror, to see with and to be seen. Our homes are saturated with objects that we no longer notice. By reinterpreting the relics in the home, I aim for a more direct and meaningful contact between people and furniture." TIMO SALLI

« Je m'interroge sur la manière dont nous regardons les choses et me demande si ce comportement justifie la création d'objets fonctionnels. Une cheminée peut elle remplacer une télévision ? Lorsqu'on les fixe du regard, toutes deux ont un but plus profond : elles effacent notre mémoire jusqu'à être téléchargées. Associer la fonction d'un miroir à celle d'une lampe est une manière de produire un double sens pour un même objet. Lorsque la lampe est éteinte, elle sert de miroir en réfléchissant la lumière du jour, tandis que le soir, elle sert à la fois de source lumineuse et de miroir, pour voir et être vu. Nos maisons sont saturées d'objets que nous ne remarquons plus. En réinterprétant les reliques du foyer, je vise un contact plus direct et profond entre les gens et les meubles. » TIMO SALLI

»Ich hinterfrage die Art, wie wir Dinge ansehen und denke darüber nach, ob dieses Verhalten ein Motiv für die Herstellung funktionaler Objekte sein kann. Könnte ein Kamin an die Stelle eines Fernsehers treten? Wenn man sie länger ansieht, haben beide Gegenstände einen tieferen Zweck: Sie löschen das eigene Gedächtnis, bis es heruntergeladen ist. Indem man die Funktion eines Spiegels mit der einer Lampe verbindet, kann man einem einzelnen Objekt eine doppelte Bedeutung verleihen. Wenn das Licht ausgeschaltet ist, kann man es als Spiegel benutzen, der das Tageslicht reflektiert, während man es am Abend sowohl als Lichtquelle wie als Spiegel verwenden kann, um damit zu sehen und gesehen zu werden. Unsere Wohnungen sind voller Objekte, die wir nicht mehr bewusst wahrnehmen. Mit meiner Neuinterpretation häuslicher Relikte bezwecke ich einen direkteren und tiefer gehenden Kontakt zwischen Mensch und Möbel.« TIMO SALLI

3. ← **Tramp** easy chair (prototype)/Sessel (Prototyp)/chauffeuse (prototype) for Cappellini, 1997
4. **Meccano** chair/Stuhl/chaise (one-off material study), 1995

TIMO SALLI		CLIENTS
BORN	1963	Helsinki, Finland
STUDIED	1992	BA Furniture Design, Lahti Design Institute
	1996	MA Craft & Design, University of Industrial Arts and Design, Helsinki
PRACTICE	1993	established own design studio
AWARDS	1993	honourable mention, IKEA mötet, Helsinki
	1997	Young Finland Prize, Helsinki
	1998	Young Design Prize, Hamburg
	1999-2001	State Grant, Helsinki
EXHIBITIONS	1997	*Young Forum*, Nagoya Design Centre; *Snowcrash*, Milan; *New Simplicity?*, Helsinki
	1998	*Finnish Design*, Design Forum, Helsinki; *Nomadhouse*, Milan; *Alvar Aalto Symposium*, Jyväskylä
	1999	*New Scandinavia*, Museum für Angewandte Kunst, Cologne; *Snowcrash*, Milan; *Biennale dei Giovani Artisti Dell Europa e Mediteraneo*, Rome; *Taivas Kattona*, Tampere; *Italy-Europa*, Verona; *Empty Spaces*, Munich
	2000	*Objects and Concepts*, Museum of Applied Arts, Helsinki; *100*, Helsinki; Designers Block, London

CLIENTS

Designium
Fat Douglas
Helsinki Cultural Capital 2000
SITRA
Sandgate
Snowcrash
Stanza
Suomen Messut
TEKES

5

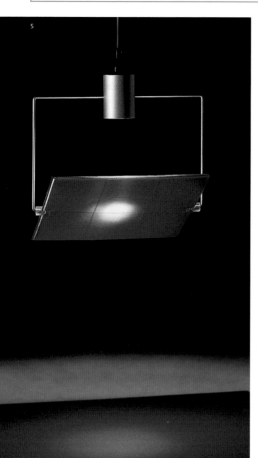

6

7

5. **ScreenLamp** light (prototype)/Leuchte (Prototyp)/
luminaire (prototype), 1998
6. **Firecase** fireplace (prototype)/Kamin (Prototyp)/
cheminée (prototype), 2000
7. **LampLamp** mirror lamp/Spiegel-Lampe/lampe miroir
(self-production), 2000
8. **Power Ranger** chair/Stuhl/chaise (one-off), 1996
9. **TimoTimo** lamp (prototype)/Lampe (Prototyp)/
lustre (prototype), 1999

8

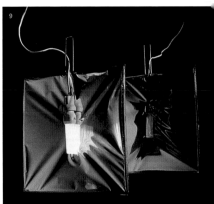

9

"... Places to live in will become temples,
and objects will be their idols."

Marta Sansoni

Marta Sansoni, Via Luigi Carlo Farini 10, 50 121 Florence, Italy
T/F +39 055 2 34 21 27 martasansoni@yahoo.it

»... Wohnstätten werden zu Tempeln,
und Objekte werden ihre Idole sein.«

«... Les lieux à vivre deviendront des
temples et les objets seront leurs
idoles. »

1. **Tralcio Muto** tray/Tablett/plateau for Alessi, 2000
2. ↓ **Folpo** hand mixer/Handmixer/fouet for Alessi, 1998

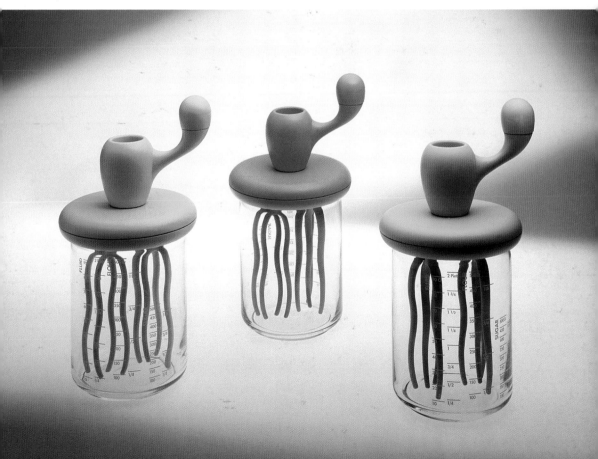

»Ich stelle mir Objekte vor, die sich, obgleich durch eine starke formale Persönlichkeit gekennzeichnet, nicht aufdrängen. Objekte, die hergestellt wurden, um aktuelle Bedürfnisse zu befriedigen, die aber über den Gebrauch hinaus auch zur Kontemplation einladen. Objekte, die sich in die häusliche Umgebung einfügen, die nicht allzu selbstverliebt, arrogant oder prätentiös sind. Objekte, die wir niemals müde werden anzusehen oder fürchten zu berühren.

Nichtsdestoweniger glaube ich, dass das Design der Zukunft nicht auf die konventionelle Kombination aus Ästhetik, Funktion, Produktion und Kommerzialisierung angewiesen sein wird. Stattdessen sollte es Objekte realisieren, die neben den genannten Merkmalen mit wirklich therapeutischen Eigenschaften ausgestattet sind: der Fähigkeit zu trösten, zu beschützen und ein Gefühl von Wohlbefinden und Friedfertigkeit zu erzeugen. Folglich möchte ich gerne Objekte entwerfen, die nicht nur zweckmäßig sind, sondern die sich auch zum Spielen und zum Liebkosen eignen. Dinge, die man umarmen, die man auf einen Altar stellen kann, in einen von der Außenwelt abgeschirmten, kostbaren und stillen häuslichen Schrein, den allerletzten Ort individueller Freiheit.

Ich liebe Objekte, die provokative Emotionen und Empfindungen hervorrufen. In zunehmendem Maße müssen die emotionalen Bedürfnisse ebenso befriedigt werden wie die praktischen. In diesem Kontext kann die ästhetische Planung einen wesentlichen Beitrag für den Schutz der menschlichen spirituellen Integrität leisten. Vielleicht kann ich an den Bedingungen für Wohlbefinden, Glück und emotionale Stabilität mitarbeiten, indem ich eine spirituelle Konzeption von Orten entwerfe, in denen man leben und von Objekten, mit denen man leben kann.« MARTA SANSONI

"I imagine objects that, although characterized by a strong formal personality, are not intrusive; objects made to meet contemporary needs, that invite use beyond contemplation; objects that can fit in with the domestic environment; objects that are not too self-celebrating, arrogant or pretentious; objects that we are never tired of seeing or afraid of touching.

Nevertheless, I believe that future design will not have to rely on the conventional combination of aesthetics, function, production and commercialization, but rather should realize objects that, together with these characteristics, are provided with real therapeutic qualities: the capacity for reassuring, protecting and generating a feeling of well-being and peacefulness ...

Thus, I would like to design objects that are suitable not only for use but also for playing with, to be caressed; things to be embraced, things to be put on an altar in a secluded, precious and quiet domestic shrine, the very last place of individual freedom.

I love objects that are capable of evoking emotions and feelings that are provocative. Increasingly, emotional needs have to be satisfied as much as the practical ones; in this context, aesthetic research can play a crucial role in protecting human spiritual integrity. Perhaps the only thing that remains for me to do is to help create those conditions that are essential to well-being, happiness and emotional stability, through a projection toward a spiritual conceptualization of places to live in and of objects to live with." MARTA SANSONI

« J'imagine des objets qui, bien que caractérisés par une forte personnalité formelle, ne sont pas envahissants ; des objets conçus pour satisfaire des besoins contemporains ; qui nous invitent au-delà de la contemplation ; qui s'intègrent dans l'environnement domestique ; que nous ne nous lassons jamais de voir et n'avons pas peur de toucher.

Néanmoins, je pense que le design du futur ne dépendra plus du mélange conventionnel d'esthétique, de fonction, de production et de commercialisation, mais qu'il réalisera des objets qui, aux côtés de toutes ces caractéristiques, seront dotés de véritables vertus thérapeutiques : la capacité à rassurer, à protéger et à générer un sentiment de bien-être et de paix ... J'aimerais donc créer des objets qui soient non seulement utiles, mais également ludiques, que l'on aime caresser, des choses à étreindre, à placer sur un autel dans une châsse domestique isolée, précieuse et tranquille, le dernier retranchement de la liberté individuelle.

J'aime les objets capables d'évoquer des émotions et des sentiments provocants. Nos besoins émotionnels doivent de plus en plus être pris en compte au même titre que nos besoins pratiques. Dans ce contexte, la recherche esthétique peut jouer un rôle crucial pour protéger l'intégrité spirituelle de l'homme. La seule chose qui me reste peut-être à faire est d'aider à créer ces conditions essentielles au bien-être, au bonheur et à la stabilité émotionnelle, au travers d'une projection vers une conceptualisation spirituelle des lieux à vivre et des objets avec lesquels vivre. » MARTA SANSONI

3. **Evoluzioni** two-sectioned silver candelabrum/zweiteiliger Kandelaber/chandelier en argent en deux parties for Pampaloni, 1998
4. **Evasioni** silver vase/Silbervase/vase en argent for Pampaloni, 1998
5. **Evoluzioni** silver salt and pepper cruet/silberner Salz- und Pfefferstreuer/salière et poivrière en argent for Pampaloni, 1998
6. **Mother and Son** ceramic centrepiece/Keramik-Tafelaufsatz/centre de table en céramique for Flavia, 1998

MARTA SANSONI

BORN	1963	Florence, Italy
STUDIED	1990	graduated in Architecture, University of Florence
PRACTICE	1990-98	assistant to Professor Remo Buti, Architecture Faculty, University of Florence
EXHIBITIONS	1990	*Memory Containers-Alessi*, Crusinallo
	1991	*Square with a Monument at the Keihanna Interaction Plaza* design competition, Kansai Science City, Osaka; *Una Porta per Venezia* competition, Biennale di Venezia
	1994	*I Designers per la Ceramica*, Museum for Archeology and Ceramics, Florence
	1995	*Assopiastrelle*, Palazzina Ducale della Casiglia, Modena
	1996	*Evasioni* project, Pampaloni Argenterie, Florence
	1998	*Evoluzioni* project, Pampaloni Argenterie, Florence

CLIENTS

Alessi
Ceramica Bardelli
Flavia Bitossi
Gruppo Colorobbia
Pampaloni
Stayer

4

5

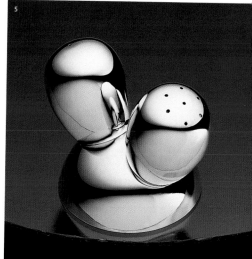

6

"An innovative approach is needed for modern textile and surface design, while new and existing methods of application and production need to be continuously explored."

Santos & Adolfsdóttir

Leo Santos-Shaw & Margrét Adolfsdóttir, 4, Middle Ground, Fovant, Salisbury, Wiltshire SP3 5LP, England
T/F +44 1722 714 669 sa-tex@dircon.co.uk

»Modernes Textil- und Oberflächen-design erfordert einen innovativen Ansatz, während bestehende Methoden der Anwendung und Fertigung konti-nuierlich erforscht werden müssen.«

« Le textile moderne et le design de surface ont besoin d'une approche innovatrice tandis que les méthodes d'application et de production exis-tantes doivent être continuellement explorées. »

1. **SA00k2** layered, dyed, printed and laser-cut polyester-
polyamide/beschichteter, gefärbter, bedruckter und mit
Laser geschnittener Schichten-Polyesteramid/polyester
polyamide multicouche teint, imprimé et découpé au
laser (self-production), 1999

2. ↓ **SA09c** dyed and laser-cut polyester-polyamide/
gefärbter und mit Laser geschnittener Schichten-Poly-
esteramid/polyester polyamide teint et découpé au laser
(self-production), 1998

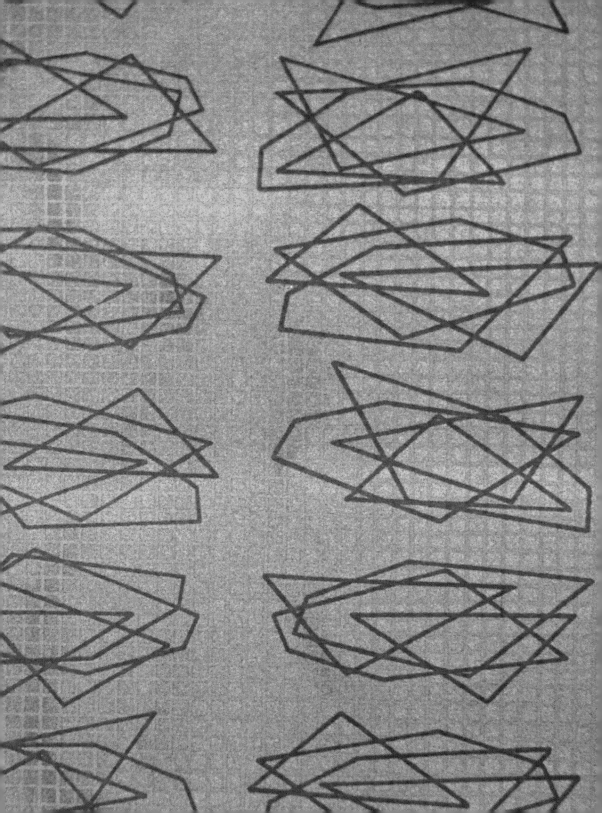

« Les développements expérimentaux et les progrès technologiques rapides de la dernière décennie ont abouti à des matières nouvelles et excitantes dans tous les domaines du design. A l'avenir, celui-ci sera toujours aussi passionnant mais chargé de considérations plus sociales, économiques, écologiques et technologiques. L'utilisation croissante et l'influence de l'informatique commencent dès les premières étapes de la création et se poursuivent tout au long de la fabrication et de la réalisation. Du fait du développement de matériaux et de techniques de plus en plus sophistiqués, les designers doivent sans cesse remettre en question leurs méthodes de travail. L'ordinateur a sans doute entraîné le changement le plus visible en introduisant un effet tridimensionnel dans les images en deux dimensions en même temps qu'une nouvelle esthétique visuelle et, naturellement, la vitesse.

Les exigences écologiques du 21ème siècle modifieront considérablement l'aspect et la fonction du design dans de nombreux domaines. Grâce à une meilleure prise de conscience des effets nocifs des matériaux utilisés dans la fabrication, les entreprises font désormais de l'environnement une de leurs préoccupations majeures, se rendant compte que les ressources mondiales seront bientôt épuisées si des mesures ne sont pas prises rapidement. Les déchets seront de plus en plus recyclés et exploités d'une manière utile. Les substances toxiques utilisées dans la fabrication de produits et de matériaux seront progressivement remplacés par des alternatives moins nocives. Travailler avec l'environnement plutôt que contre lui deviendra également un facteur extrêmement important sur le plan esthétique et "humain".

L'enseignement du design connaîtra aussi d'importants développements. Dans les ate- ↓

3. ← SA08d2 printed silk taffeta/bedruckter Seidentaft/ taffetas de soie imprimé (self-production), 1999
4. SA08f printed acetate taffeta/bedruckter Azetat-Taft/ taffetas d'acétate imprimé (self-production), 1999

"Experimental developments and rapid advances in technology over the last decade are producing new and exciting materials in all areas of design. The future of design will be as exciting as ever but with more social, economic, environmental and technological considerations. The increasing use and influence of the computer begins at the very initial stages of design, continuing through manufacturing and realization. Owing to the increasing development of sophisticated materials and techniques, designers are continuously re-examining areas of working practices. The computer has brought about probably the most visible change in design, introducing the sense of three-dimensions into two-dimensions into real three-dimensions, together with a new visual aesthetic and of course, speed.

The ecological requirements of the 21st century will greatly affect the appearance and function of design in many areas. Because of an increasing awareness of the harmful environmental effects of manufacturing materials, companies are making ecology a prime concern – being aware that the world's resources will soon be depleted if major changes are not made. Waste products will increasingly be recycled and reused positively. Toxic chemicals used in the production of products and materials are gradually being replaced by less harmful alternatives. Ecology and working with the environment rather than against it will be an extremely important factor in future design also on an aesthetic and 'human' level. ↓

»Die experimentellen Entwicklungen und raschen technologischen Fortschritte der letzten Dekade bringen in allen Bereichen des Designs neue und aufregende Materialien hervor. Das Design der Zukunft wird weiterhin spannend bleiben, allerdings werden soziale, ökonomische, ökologische und technische Überlegungen eine größere Rolle spielen. Der zunehmende Gebrauch und Einfluss des Computers beginnt bereits im Anfangsstadium jeder Gestaltung und setzt sich durch alle Phasen der Realisierung und Produktion fort. Aufgrund der Weiterentwicklung immer ausgeklügelter Materialien und Techniken müssen Designer ihre Arbeitsmethoden fortwährend überprüfen. Der Computer hat zweifellos die sichtbarste Veränderung im Design bewirkt, indem er eine reale Dreidimensionalität in die bildnerische Gestaltung einführte, zusammen mit einer neuen visuellen Ästhetik und Geschwindigkeit.

Die ökologischen Anforderungen des 21. Jahrhunderts werden Erscheinungsform und Funktion des Designs in vielen Bereichen stark beeinflussen. Dank eines gewachsenen Bewusstseins für die umweltschädlichen Auswirkungen von Industriestoffen machen Unternehmen die Ökologie zu einem Hauptanliegen, da sie sich darüber im Klaren sind, dass die natürlichen Ressourcen der Erde bald erschöpft sein werden, wenn nicht entscheidende Maßnahmen ergriffen werden. Deshalb werden Abfallstoffe immer öfter einem Recycling zugeführt und für positive Zwecke wiederverwendet. Giftige, für die Herstellung von Produkten und Werkstoffen eingesetzte Chemikalien werden allmählich durch weniger schädliche Alternativen ersetzt. Die Ökologie und das Bemühen, für die Umwelt statt gegen sie zu arbeiten, wird für das zukünftige Design zu einem äußerst wichtigen Faktor werden, und zwar auch auf ästhetischer und ›menschlicher‹ Ebene.

Ebenfalls von großer Bedeutung ist die Entwicklung der Designausbildung. Eine am Ausbildungsplatz praktizierte und auf Forschungs- und Entwicklungsanstalten ausgeweitete Teamarbeit wird den ›individuellen Schöpfer‹ eines Produkts oder Konzepts ↓

		SANTOS & ADOLFSDÓTTIR	CLIENTS
FOUNDED	1998	Fovant, England by Leo Santos-Shaw (b. 1964 London) and Margrét Adolfsdóttir (b. 1958 Reykjavik)	Barneys
STUDIED		LEO SANTOS-SHAW	Calvin Klein
	1987-88	Foundation Art & Design, Liverpool Polytechnic	C+B Scene
	1988-91	BA (Hons) Printed Textiles, Middlesex Polytechnic	Perry Ellis
		MARGRÉT ADOLFSDÓTTIR	Thierry Mugler
	1982-83	Foundation Art & Design, St Eriks Folkhogskola, Stockholm	Thomas Cook
	1984-88	HND Textiles, Icelandic College of Arts & Crafts, Reykjavik	Whistles
	1988-91	BA (Hons) Printed Textiles, Middlesex Polytechnic	
AWARDS	1995	Craft Development Award, Southern Arts, England	
	1996	Craft Development Award, Southern Arts, England	
EXHIBITIONS	1995	*Contemporary Design in Iceland*, Geysir Gallery, Reykjavik	
	1996	Applied Textile exhibition, Northern Gallery for Contemporary Art, Sunderland	
	1997	Triennale Internationale de Tournai – Nordic Textile Art, Tournai	
	1998	*Young Nordic Design*, Helsinki	
	1999	*Meister der Moderne*, Munich; *Nordic Transparency*, Stedelijk Museum, Amsterdam	
	2000	*Millennium*, Saevar Karl Gallery, Reykjavik; Experimental Textiles, Casa Pitti, Florence; *Mot-Design in Iceland*, Kjarvalstadir Art Museum, Reykjavik	

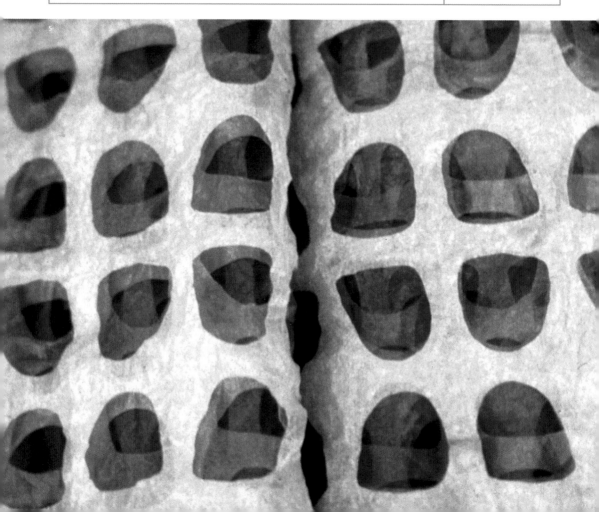

liers des écoles, y compris dans la recherche plastique, le travail d'équipe remplacera le " créateur individuel " d'un produit ou d'un concept. L'accent mis sur la formation professionnelle dans les écoles et les universités ainsi que la participation croissante de designers de tous les horizons venant donner des conférences encouragera une culture pluridisciplinaire, le travail d'équipe et la créativité dans le bureau de design. L'avenir du design est entre les mains des générations à venir. »
SANTOS & ADOLFSDÓTTIR

5. **SA092** three layer laser-cut polyester-polyamide/dreischichtiger, mit Laser geschnittener Polyesteramid/polyester polyamide trois couches, découpé au laser (self-production), 1998
6. **SA08el** printed silk taffeta/bedruckter Seidentaft/taffetas de soie imprimé (self-production), 1999
7. **SA09f** two layer dyed and laser-cut polyester-polyamide/zweischichtiger, gefärbter und mit Laser geschnittener Polyesteramid/polyester polyamide deux couches, teint et découpé au laser (self-production), 1999

The development of design education is also of great importance. Teamwork in the educational workplace, extending into design research practices will replace the 'individual creator' of a product or concept. The emphasis on vocational learning in colleges and universities and the increasing engagement of a broad range of designers from varying disciplines as visiting lecturers, will encourage a multi-disciplinary culture, teamwork and creativity in the design studio. The future of design is in future generations." SANTOS & ADOLFSDÓTTIR

ablösen. Der Schwerpunkt auf berufsbezogenes Lernen an den Schulen und Universitäten sowie das wachsende Engagement von Designern aus unterschiedlichen Disziplinen als Lehrende werden die interdisziplinäre Kultur, Teamarbeit und Kreativität in den Designstudios fördern. Die Zukunft des Designs liegt bei den kommenden Generationen.«
SANTOS & ADOLFSDÓTTIR

6

"Design objects with simplicity and personality."

Michael Sodeau

Michael Sodeau Partnership, Studio 26, 26, Rosebery Avenue, London EC1R 4SX, England
T +44 20 7833 5020 F +44 20 7833 5021 michael@msp.uk.com

»Objekte mit Einfachheit und Persönlichkeit gestalten.«

« Concevoir des objets avec simplicité
et personnalité. »

1. **Single** and **Twin** vases/Vasen for MSP, 1998
2. ↓ **RedRug/BlueRug** three-dimensional carpets/
dreidimensionale Teppiche/tapis tridimensionnels
for Christopher Farr, 2000

« Tandis que nous entrons dans le 21ᵉ siècle, ma vision du design est celle de la simplicité. Il est essentiel qu'en tant que créateur, je sois conscient des différents aspects du design liées à l'environnement, aux matériaux et à la fabrication ainsi qu'aux besoins des consommateurs du 21ᵉ siècle.

Ce dernier facteur change constamment : si les environnements domestiques et professionnels évoluent et fusionnent, il en va de même pour les objets qui sont censés y fonctionner. A mesure que le design avance dans le futur, c'est le monde tel qu'il se déroule et les moyens de vivre confortablement dans cet environnement toujours changeant qui deviennent les principales préoccupations des créateurs. Les designers de l'ère de la communication ont désormais à leur disposition des lignes ISDN qui transmettent leurs images et leurs dessins directement aux fabricants sur une simple pression d'un bouton, ainsi que des systèmes capables de faire des prototypes d'objets en quelques heures afin que designers et fabricants puissent détecter tous les problèmes avant que l'objet en question n'entre dans la chaîne de production. Tout ceci a accéléré le passage du concept au produit fini et a considérablement influencé l'offre proposée aux consommateurs. Si tous ces facteurs ont modifié le design, il est essentiel de ne pas perdre de vue le "pourquoi" de notre travail. Je m'intéresse avant tout à la relation entre l'objet et son utilisateur ; à ce qu'on attend d'un objet (en terme de fonctionnalité) et à la manière dont celui-ci doit fonctionner pour améliorer la vie quotidienne de l'utilisateur. J'aspire à donner à l'objet un certain degré de personnalité et de caractère afin de créer un lien entre lui et son utilisateur. » MICHAEL SODEAU

3. ← **Woven** floor lights/Stehlampen/lampadaires for MSP, 1998
4. **Line** stacking chairs/Stapelstühle/chaises encastrables (prototype), 1999

"My vision for design as we enter the 21st century is one of simplicity. It is essential that as a designer I am aware of the various issues that are associated with design in terms of the environment, materials and manufacturing coupled with the needs of the 21st-century consumer.

This last factor is a constantly changing one: as domestic and work environments change and merge so do the associated objects required by consumers to perform within them. As design progresses into the future, it is the world as it unfolds that is the designer's major concern, and what is required to live with comfort in this changing environment. In this, the communication-age designers now have at their disposal ISDN lines that can send drawings and images direct to the manufacturer at the touch of a button as well as rapid prototyping facilities that can prototype objects in a matter of hours so that designers and manufacturers can access any problems before the object goes into production. This has speeded up the process of design concept to manufacture and greatly impacted on what is available to the consumer.

While all these factors have had an impact on design it is essential that 'what' and 'why' we design is not lost. My interest lies in the relationship between objects and users. What is required from the object (in terms of functionality) and how the object needs to perform to enhance the user's day-to-day life. My aim is to give objects a degree of personality and character so as to create a bond between object and user." MICHAEL SODEAU

»Meine Vision vom Design im beginnenden 21. Jahrhundert ist eine der Einfachheit. Für mich als Designer ist es wesentlich, dass ich mir der verschiedenartigen Probleme bewusst bin, die mit Design verknüpft sind – Probleme im Hinblick auf Umwelt, Materialien und Fabrikation, verbunden mit den Bedürfnissen der Konsumenten des 21. Jahrhunderts. Der letztgenannte Faktor ist einer, der sich kontinuierlich verändert: Ebenso wie sich unsere Wohn- und Arbeitswelten wandeln und miteinander verschmelzen, tun dies auch die Objekte, die benötigt werden, um in der jeweiligen Umgebung zu funktionieren. In dem Maße, in dem Design in die Zukunft fortschreitet, wird die sich entfaltende Welt und die Frage, was notwendig ist, um komfortabel in ihr zu leben, zum Hauptinteresse für Designer. Hierfür stehen den Gestaltern des Kommunikationszeitalters nun ISDN-Verbindungen zur Verfügung, mit denen sie per Knopfdruck Zeichnungen und Bilder direkt an den Hersteller senden können, sowie Computerprogramme, die innerhalb weniger Stunden Prototypen von Objekten anfertigen, so dass Gestalter und Hersteller jedes eventuelle Problem abschätzen können, bevor das Objekt in Serienproduktion geht. All das hat den Gestaltungsprozess von der Konzeption bis zur Fabrikation beschleunigt und das den Konsumenten zur Verfügung stehende Warenangebot verändert. Neben dem großen Einfluss dieser Faktoren auf das Design der Vergangenheit und Gegenwart dürfen wir nicht die Frage aus den Augen verlieren, ›was‹ und ›warum‹ wir designen. Mein Interesse gilt der Beziehung zwischen Objekten und ihren Anwendern: Was wird vom Objekt verlangt (im Sinne von Funktionalität), und wie muss das Objekt funktionieren, um das Alltagsleben des Benutzers zu bereichern? Mein Ziel ist es, Objekten ein gewisses Maß an Persönlichkeit und Charakter zu verleihen, so dass eine emotionale Verbindung zwischen Objekt und Anwender entsteht.«
MICHAEL SODEAU

MICHAEL SODEAU		CLIENTS

MICHAEL SODEAU

BORN	1969	London, England
STUDIED	1994	BA (Hons) Product Design, Central St Martin's College of Art and Design, London
PRACTICE	1995	co-founded Inflate, London
	1997	co-founded Michael Sodeau Partnership, London with Lisa Giuliani
AWARDS	2000	winner Best Design Award, 100% Design, London
EXHIBITIONS	1998	*Interior*, Paris; *New British Design*, Athens; *Caned*, London; *Happening*, Tokyo; *Landed*, New York
	1999	*Premillennium Tension*, British Council, Cologne; *Being There*, Tokyo, London; *Child's Ply*, London
	2000	*Michael Sodeau*, Stockholm; *TWIST*, London; *Child's Form*, London
	2001	*Michael Sodeau*, New York

CLIENTS

Asplund
Christopher Farr
Dinny Hall
Gervasoni
Inflate
Isokon Plus
SCP
Wedgwood
also self-production

5

5. **Wing** storage unit and **Flip** tables and shelves/Schrank, Tische und Regale/buffet, tables et étagères for Isokon Plus, 1999 & 2000
6. **Wing** storage unit/Schrank/buffet for Isokon Plus, 1999
7. **Satellite** tables/Tische for MSP, 1997
8. **Tea Time** teaset/Teeservice/service à thé (prototype), 1999
9. **Walking on Water** hand-knotted rug/handgeknüpfter Teppich/tapis noué à la main for Christopher Farr, 1998
10. **Lounge chairs**/Sessel/fauteuils (prototype), 1999

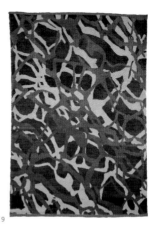

"One-byte design – to create forms that go beyond functional beauty to heart-touching designs that fascinate our instincts the minute they are held or seen."

Sony Design Center

Design Center, Sony Corporation, 6-7-35 Kitashinagawa, Shinagawa-ku, Tokyo 141-0001, Japan
www.world.sony.com

»One-Byte-Design: Die Gestaltung von Formen, die über die funktionale Schön-heit hinaus zu Herzen gehen und in dem Moment, in dem wir sie berühren oder sehen, unsere Instinkte fesseln.«

« Le design d'un octet : créer des formes qui vont au-delà de la beauté fonction-nelle, qui émeuvent, qui fascinent nos instincts dès qu'on les tient ou qu'on les voit. »

1. **Cybershot DSC-F505** digital camera/
Digitalkamera/appareil photo numérique
for Sony, 1999, design: Kaoru Sumita
2. ↓ **SDM-N50** LCD monitor/Bildschirm/écran à cristaux
liquides for Sony, 1999, design: Masakazu Kanatani

»Design lässt sich als eine Sprache definieren, die Menschen ermöglicht, mit innovativen Technologien zu kommunizieren. Als Interpreten menschlicher Bedürfnisse und Anliegen müssen Designer bejahen, dass wir – als menschliche Wesen – die Richtung kontrollieren, in die sich Technologie entwickelt, anstatt von ihr beherrscht zu werden. Darüber hinaus entspricht es unserer menschlichen Natur, dass sich mit der Zeit Vernunft und Emotionen der Umwelt entsprechend verändern. Folglich müssen wir das gegenwärtige System der Massenproduktion erneuern, das nur der Effizienz Rechnung trägt und die verschiedenen Arten von Konsumenten alle als eine einzige Gruppe betrachtet. Um Produkte und Dienstleistungen hervorzubringen, welche die individuelle Vernunft ansprechen, muss die höchste soziale Infrastruktur – die Verschmelzung von Handwerk und Massenproduktion – entworfen werden.«
MITSURU INABA, CORPORATE VICE PRESIDENT, CREATIVE (DESIGN) CENTER

"Design can be referred to as the language that enables people to communicate with innovative technologies. As interpreters of people's needs and concerns, designers must affirm that we, as human beings, control the direction that technology is headed – rather than being ruled by it. Furthermore, it is in our human nature that rationality and human emotions change over time according to environment. Thus, we need to renovate the current mass-production system that only takes into consideration efficiency and classifies the various types of consumers all in one group. To originate products and services that appeal to the rationale of individuals, the ultimate social infrastructure – the fusion of handcraft and mass-production – needs to be designed."
MITSURU INABA, CORPORATE VICE PRESIDENT, CREATIVE (DESIGN) CENTER

« Le design peut être défini comme un langage qui permet à l'homme de communiquer avec les technologies innovatrices. Interprètes des besoins et des préoccupations des gens, les designers doivent affirmer qu'en tant qu'êtres humains, nous contrôlons la direction que prend la technologie et que ce n'est pas elle qui nous gouverne. En outre, notre nature humaine fait que le rationalisme et les émotions varient avec le temps et selon l'environnement. Par conséquent, nous devons rénover l'actuel système de production de masse qui ne prend en considération que l'efficacité et qui range tous les types de consommateurs dans le même sac. Pour créer des produits et des services qui parlent à la logique des individus, il convient de concevoir l'infrastructure sociale ultime : la fusion de l'artisanat et de la production de masse. »
MITSURU INABA, CORPORATE VICE PRESIDENT, CREATIVE (DESIGN) CENTER

3. **Playstation 2** for Sony, 1999, design: Teiyu Goto
4. **VAIO LX Series** personal computer/Personalcomputer/ordinateur PC for Sony, 1999, design: Haruo Oba
5. **Handycam DCR-PC100** camcorder/Videokamera/vidéocaméra for Sony, 1999 – design: Hiroki Oka
6. **VAIO SR Series** laptop computer/Laptop/ordinateur portable for Sony, 1999, design: Shinichi Ogasawara

		SONY DESIGN CENTER	CLIENTS
FOUNDED	1961	Tokyo, Japan	Sony Corporation
SINCE	1997	Sony Corporation Design Center has been headed by Mitsuru Inaba (b. 1942 Tokyo), who graduated from Musashino Art University (1968), Rhode Island School of Design (1969). The current design team includes: Teiyu Goto (b. 1953), Kaoru Sumita (b. 1946), Shinichi Ogosawara (b. 1954), Haruo Oba (b. 1962), Masakazu Kanatani (b. 1956), Shin Miyashita (b. 1955), Takuya Niitsu (b. 1955), Hiroki Oka (b. 1956) and Junichi Nagahara (b. 1966)	
AWARDS	2000	Grand Prize, Gold Prize and four G-Mark/Good Design Awards, JIDPO, Tokyo; Packaging Design Award, Japan Packaging Competition; nine iF Design Awards, Hanover; *Design team of the Year* and ten Roter Punkt Awards, Design Zentrum Nordrhein-Westfalen, Essen; SMAU (Salone Macchine Attrezzature Ufficio) Industrial Design Award, Milan	
EXHIBITIONS	2000	*Sony Digital Dream*, Tokyo, Osaka; *Design Innovation (Roter Punkt) Design Team of the Year*, Design Zentrum Nordrhein-Westfalen, Essen	

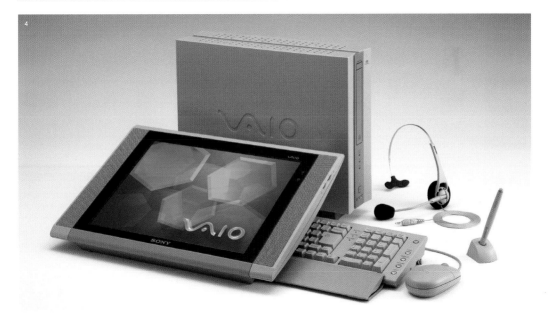

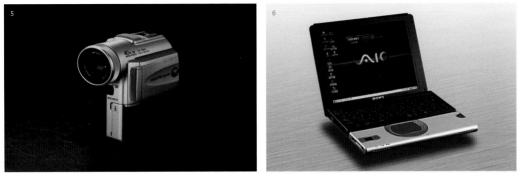

"The 21st century will be immaterial and human."

Philippe Starck

Philippe Starck, Agence Philippe Starck, 18/20, rue du Faubourg de Temple, 75011 Paris, France
T +33 1 48 07 54 54 F +33 1 48 07 54 64 starck@starcknetwork.com www.philippe-starck.com

»Das 21. Jahrhundert wird immateriell und menschlich sein.«

« Le 21ᵉ siècle sera immatériel et humain. »

1. **Low Cost Clock**/Wecker/réveil for Seven Eleven, 1998
2. ↓ **Gaoua** duffle bag on wheels/Reisetasche auf Rollen/
sac de voyage à roulettes for Samsonite, 2000

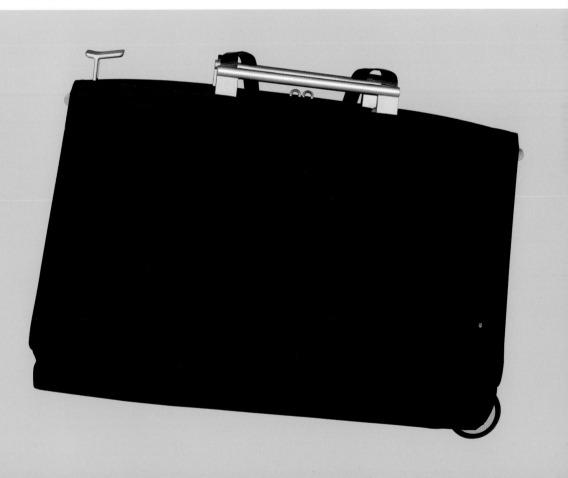

« Aujourd'hui, le problème est de ne pas produire plus afin de vendre plus. La question fondamentale est celle du droit du produit à exister. Le designer a le droit et le devoir de s'interroger sur la légitimité du produit, c'est là sa raison d'être. Selon la conclusion à laquelle il parvient, l'une des choses les plus positives qu'un designer puisse faire est de refuser de faire quoi que ce soit. Ce n'est pas toujours facile. Il devrait néanmoins refuser quand l'objet existe déjà et fonctionne parfaitement bien. Le répéter simplement serait un acte vénal, qui aurait de sérieuses conséquences, appauvrissant les richesses de la terre, limitant et ternissant l'esprit des gens ... Nous devons remplacer la beauté, qui est un concept culturel, par la bonté, un concept humaniste. L'objet doit être de bonne qualité et satisfaire un des paramètres modernes essentiels, à savoir avoir la longévité ... un bon produit est un produit qui dure. »
PHILIPPE STARCK

3. ← **StarckNaked** seamless tubular garment with integrated pantihose/nahtloses Schlauchkleid mit integrierter Strumpfhose/collants intégrés à un tube, sans coutures for Wolford, 1998
4. **Street Lamp**/Straßenlaterne/réverbère for JC Decaux, 1992

"Today, the problem is not to produce more so that you can sell more. The fundamental question is that of the product's right to exist. And it is the designer's right and duty, in the first place, to question the legitimacy of the product, and that is how he too comes to exist. Depending on what answer he comes up with, one of the most positive things a designer can do is to refuse to do anything. This isn't always easy. He should refuse, nevertheless, when the object already exists and functions perfectly well. Simply to repeat it would be a venal act, and one which has serious consequences, impoverishing the wealth of the Earth, and impoverishing and dulling the minds of people ... We have to replace beauty, which is a cultural concept, with goodness, which is a humanist concept. The object must be of good quality, it must satisfy one of the key modern parameters, which is to be long-lived ... A good product is a product which lasts." PHILIPPE STARCK

»Heutzutage besteht die Aufgabe nicht darin, mehr zu produzieren, um mehr verkaufen zu können. Die entscheidende Frage ist vielmehr die nach der Existenzberechtigung eines Produkts. Die Designer haben das Recht und die Pflicht, zunächst einmal die Legitimität eines Produkts in Frage zu stellen, woraus sich wiederum ihre eigene Daseinsberechtigung ergibt. Je nachdem, welche Antwort der Designer darauf findet, ist eines der positivsten Dinge, die er oder sie tun kann, sich zu weigern, überhaupt etwas zu tun. Das ist allerdings nicht immer leicht. Trotzdem sollte ein Designer einen Auftrag ablehnen, wenn das Objekt bereits existiert und vollkommen zufriedenstellend funktioniert. Es einfach bloß zu wiederholen, wäre ein korrupter Akt. Und zudem einer, der ernsthafte Konsequenzen hat, indem er die natürlichen Reichtümer der Erde aussaugt und die Menschen geistig verarmen lässt und verdummt ... Wir müssen das kulturelle Konzept der Schönheit durch das humanistische Konzept der Redlichkeit ersetzen. Ein Designobjekt muss von guter Qualität sein, und es muss einem der wichtigsten modernen Parameter genügen, nämlich der Langlebigkeit ... Ein gutes Produkt ist ein Produkt, das bestehen bleibt.« PHILIPPE STARCK

5. **TeddyBearBand** toy/Kuscheltier/nounours (Catalogue GOOD GOODS-La Redoute) for Moulin Roty, 1998
6. **Kayak Starck**/Kajak (Catalogue GOOD GOODS-La Redoute) for Rotomod, 1998

7. **Ero's** chair/Stuhl/chaise for Kartell, 1999

		PHILIPPE STARCK	CLIENTS
BORN	1949	Neuilly, France	3 Suisses
STUDIED		self-taught	Alain Mikli
	1968	studied briefly at Ecole Nissim de Camondo, Paris	Alessi
PRACTICE	1968	established first company to produce inflatable objects	Aprilia
	1979	founded the Starck Product company	Baleri
	1993-96	worldwide artistic director for Thomson Consumer Electronics	Cassina
AWARDS	1982	VIA *Carte blanche* Award, Paris	Driade
	1986	Delta de Plaia à Barcelona	Fiam
	1988	Grand Prix National de la Création Industrielle, France	Flos
	1995	Primero Internacional de Diseno Barcelona	Fluocaril
	1997	Harvard Excellence in Design Award, USA	Hansgrohe
	1998	received a Commandeur dans l'Ordre des Arts et des Lettres from the French government	IDÉE
	1999	nominated Designer of the Year by the magazine *Architektur & Wohnen*, Hamburg	JCDecaux
	2000	Chevalier dans l'Ordre National de la Légion d'Honneur	Kartell
EXHIBITIONS	1988	*Avant Premiere*, Victoria & Albert Museum, London	Saba
	1989	*L'Art de Vivre*, Cooper-Hewitt National Design Museum, New York	Samsonite
	1990	*Les Années VIA*, Musée des Arts Décoratifs, Paris	Seven Eleven
	1994	*Philippe Starck*, Design Museum, London	Telefunken
	1995	*Mutant Materials in Contemporary Design*, Museum of Modern Art, New York	Thomson
			Vitra
			XO

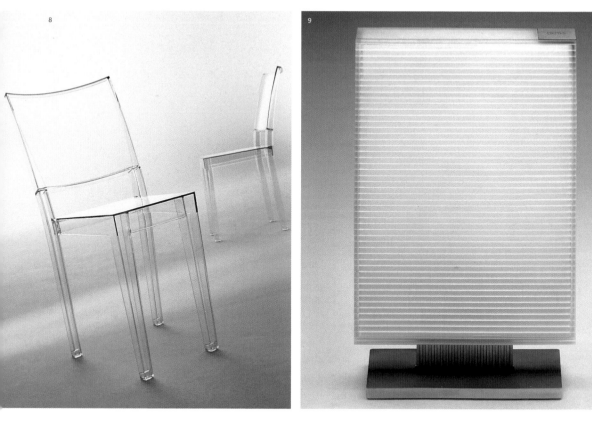

8

9

10

12

13

11

8. **La Marie** chair/Stuhl/chaise for Kartell, 1998
9. **Magic Slab** light/Leuchte/luminaire for Flos, 2000
10. **Motó 6,5** motorcycle/Motorrad/motocyclette for Aprilia, 1995
11. **Low Cost Watch**/Armbanduhr/montre for Seven Eleven, 1998
12.–13. **Starck with Virgin theme CD** (Catalogue GOOD GOODS-La Redoute) for La Redoute, 1998

"Hands and machines are equal. Each works in its own way, each has its own beauty. The designer must find the right balance of human touch and mechanical structures."

Reiko Sudo

Reiko Sudo, c/o NUNO Corporation, B1F AXIS Bldg., 5-17-1 Roppongi, Minato-ku, Tokyo 106-0032, Japan
T +81 3 3 582 7997 F +81 3 3 589 3439 nuno@nuno.com www.nuno.com

»Hand und Maschine sind gleichwertig. Beide funktionieren auf ihre eigene Weise, beide haben ihre eigene Schönheit. Der Designer muss die richtige Balance zwischen menschlicher Note und mechanischer Konstruktion finden.«

« Les mains et les machines sont égales. Toutes deux fonctionnent à leur manière, toutes deux ont leur beauté. Le designer doit trouver le juste équilibre entre le doigté humain et les structures mécaniques. »

1. **Electric Fan No. 9-354** fabric/Stoff/tissu for NUNO Corporation, 2000
2. ↓ **Cheesewheels No. 9-292** fabric/Stoff/tissu for NUNO Corporation, 1998

»Design bringt Freude und Glanz ins Alltagsleben. Mein Ziel als Textildesigner ist es, Gewebe zu gestalten, die von unserer Epoche (dem gegenwärtigen Moment) als schön angesehen werden. Wir bei Nuno glauben, dass der ›Stoff‹ – eines der ältesten der Menschheit bekannten Materialien – den Menschen der Gegenwart immer noch etwas zu sagen hat, und deshalb ist unser Ziel die Produktion ›zeitgemäßer Stoffe‹. Während wir unsere Inspiration aus der Jahrtausende alten Geschichte der Textil- und Webkultur beziehen, lassen wir gleichzeitig neuen Ideen freien Lauf und wenden die modernsten Technologien an in unserem Streben nach den aktuellsten kreativen Ausdrucksformen. In diesem Sinne sind unsere Stoffe keineswegs typisch für serienmäßig hergestellte Konsumartikel, sondern in Qualität und Originalität näher an traditionellen Webarbeiten oder Kunstwerken. Da unsere Stoffe jedoch industriell hergestellt werden – und keine handgefertigten Einzelstücke sind – können wir gleichzeitig die Produktionskosten niedrig halten. Diese Herangehensweise, mit der wir das Beste aus beiden Welten herausholen, führt zu einer Verflechtung von Schönheit und Zweckmäßigkeit in unseren modernen Stoffen, welche ihnen die Vitalität verleiht, das Leben von heute zu verschönern. Abschließend und als zukünftige Herausforderung für Textildesigner möchte ich die Frage aufwerfen: Was wäre, wenn wir holographische oder virtuelle ›meta-realistische‹ Bilder in Textilien integrieren könnten?« REIKO SUDO

"Design brings pleasure and lustre to everyday life. As a textile designer my aim is to create textiles that our times (the present moment) will regard as beautiful. At Nuno, we believe that 'fabric' – one of the oldest materials known to humankind – can still speak to people in this day and age, and so we set our sights on 'contemporary fabric-making'. While deriving inspiration from the age-old history of fabrics and weaving culture, we give free rein to new ideas and employ the latest technologies in the quest for the most up-to-date creative expressions. In this sense, the fabrics we make are not at all typical of mass-produced commercial products; rather they are closer to traditional weaving or artworks in quality and originality. Yet at the same time, since our fabrics are industrially milled – not hand-loomed one-off creations – we can keep costs down. This best-of-both-worlds approach makes for a paradoxical weave of beauty and utility that gives our contemporary fabrics the vitality to grace today's living. Finally, as a future challenge for textile designers I raise the question: what if we were able to realise holographic or virtual 'meta-realistic' imagery in textiles?" REIKO SUDO

« Le design apporte du plaisir et de l'éclat à la vie quotidienne. En tant que designer de textiles, mon objectif est de créer des tissus que notre époque (le moment présent) considérera beaux. Chez Nuno, nous pensons que le tissu – l'un des matériaux les plus anciens utilisés par l'homme – a encore des choses à dire aujourd'hui et nous aspirons à être des " tisserands contemporains ". Tout en puisant notre inspiration dans l'histoire ancestrale du tissu et de la culture du tissage, nous donnons libre cours à de nouvelles idées et utilisons les dernières technologies dans notre quête des expressions créatives les plus actuelles. En ce sens, nos tissus ne sont pas typiques de la production de masse commerciale. Par leur qualité et leur originalité, ils sont plus proches des tissages traditionnels et artistiques. Toutefois, parce qu'ils sont réalisés industriellement – et ne sont pas des créations uniques tissées à la main – nous pouvons réduire les coûts. Cette démarche, qui consiste à prendre le meilleur des deux mondes, débouche sur un tissage beau et utile qui donne à nos tissus modernes une vitalité parfaitement adaptée à la vie actuelle. Enfin, en guise de défi aux designers de textile, je soulève une question : et si nous étions capables d'intégrer des images " métaréalistes " virtuelles ou holographiques dans nos tissus ? » REIKO SUDO

3. **Kareha No. 9-304** fabric/Stoff/tissu for NUNO Corporation, 1998 – co-designed with Yoko Ando
4. **Punchcard (Mongami) No. 9-303** fabric/Stoff/tissu for NUNO Corporation, 1998 – co-designed with Zazu Hiro Veno
5. **Sakuraso No. 9-288** fabric/Stoff/tissu for NUNO Corporation, 1998 – co-design: Keiji Otani
6. **Hoshigaki No. 9-298** fabric/Stoff/tissu for NUNO Corporation, 1998 – co-designed with RyoRo Sugiura

REIKO SUDO		CLIENTS
BORN	1953	Niihari, Ibaragi, Japan	Nuno Corporation
STUDIED	1975-77	assistant to Prof. Hideho Tanaka at the Faculty of Textiles, Musashino Art University, Tokyo	
PRACTICE	1977-84	freelance textile designer working for (among others) Kanebo and Nishikawa	
	1984-89	textile designer, Nuno Corporation	
	1989-	director of Nuno Corporation; lecturer at the Faculty of Textiles, Musashino Art University	
AWARDS	1994	Roscoe Award, USA	
	2000	JID Award, Japan Interior Designer's Association	
EXHIBITIONS	1977	*Textile Exhibition*, Tokyo	
	1984	*Textiles Accessories*, Tokyo	
	1985	*Japan Creative*, Tokyo	
	1986	*Tokyo in Tokyo*, Minneapolis	
	1989	*Transfiguration*, Brussels	
	1990 & 91	*Color, Light, Surface*, Cooper-Hewitt National Design Museum, New York & Kyoto Industrial Center	
	1994	*2010 – Textiles and New Technology*, Crafts Council, London; *Japanese Design – A Survey Since 1950*, Philadelphia Museum of Art	
	1995	*Nuno – Japanese Textiles for the Body*, University of Oregon Museum of Art	
	1996	*Tokyo Creation Festival*, Tokyo; *Textile Magician*, Museum of Modern Art, Jerusalem; *Japanese Textile Design Exhibit*, Indira Ghandi National Centre for the Arts, India	
	1998	*Plastic Times – Plastic + Design*, Tel Aviv Museum of Art	
	1998-99	*Structure and Surface, Contemporary Japanese Textiles*, Museum of Modern Art, New York, The Saint Louis Art Museum of Art	
	2000	*Design World 2000*, Helsinki	

"I believe design is like poetry: absolute and precise with the minimal use of means employed to achieve the maximal result."

Ilkka Suppanen

Ilkka Suppanen, Studio Ilkka Suppanen, Punavuorenkatu 1A 7b, 00 120 Helsinki, Finland
T +358 9 622 78737 F +358 9 622 3093 info@suppanen.com www.suppanen.com

»Für mich ist Design wie Poesie: absolut und präzise mit einem minimalen Einsatz an Mitteln, um das maximale Resultat zu erzielen.«

« Pour moi, le design est comme la poésie : absolu et précis, utilisant le moins de moyens possible pour obtenir le meilleur effet. »

1. **Game-shelf**/Regal/étagère for Snowcrash, 1999
2. ↓ **Flying carpet** sofa/Sofa/canapé for Cappellini, 1998

« La situation du design aujourd'hui est la même que celle de la psychologie au 19ème siècle : une pratique avec très peu de recul et de réputation. A l'époque, la psychologie n'était même pas considérée comme une science. Elle ne l'est devenue que grâce aux travaux d'avant-garde de " M." Freud. Or, comme nous le savons, le 20e siècle tout entier a été celui de la psychologie. En tant que discipline, elle n'est devenue l'une des sciences les plus populaires et citées que grâce à la persévérance et la forte personnalité de Freud.
Comme la psychologie à ses débuts, le design est une pratique qui, contrairement à sa grande sœur l'architecture, n'est pas encore considérée comme scientifiquement importante. J'aimerais pouvoir prédire que le design connaîtra un avenir similaire à celui qu'a connu autrefois la psychologie et que lui aussi deviendra un jour une science respectée. Peutêtre faut-il pour cela qu'un pionnier de la puissance et de la portée de Freud fasse l'unanimité. » ILKKA SUPPANEN

3. ← **Airbag** chair/Sessel/siège for Snowcrash, 1997 – co-designed with Pasi Kolhonen
4. **AV Rack** cabinet/Vitrinenschrank/armoire (self-production), 1998

"I believe the situation of design today is similar to that of psychology in the 19th century — a practice with very little history or reputation. Psychology was not even regarded as a science then. It only became such as a result of the pioneering work of 'Mr' Freud. And as we know, the whole of the 20th century was the century of psychology. As a discipline, it became one of the most popular and quoted sciences only because of the perseverance and strong personality of Freud.
Like psychology in its early days, design is a practice that is not yet seen as scientifically important. It is quite unlike its 'big brother', architecture. I wish I could predict that design will have a future similar to that which psychology once had and that it too will become a respected science. Perhaps this will only happen if something like the strength and vision of Freud is widely embraced." ILKKA SUPPANEN

»Ich glaube, das heutige Design befindet sich in einer ähnlichen Situation wie die Psychologie im 19. Jahrhundert – es ist eine Disziplin mit wenig Geschichte oder Ansehen. Damals wurde die Psychologie noch nicht einmal als Wissenschaft betrachtet. Das wurde sie erst dank der Pionierarbeit des ›Herrn Freud‹. Und wie wir wissen, war das gesamte 20. Jahrhundert das Jahrhundert der Psychologie. Die Psychologie wurde nur aufgrund der Beharrlichkeit und starken Persönlichkeit von Freud zu einer der populärsten und einflussreichsten Wissenschaftslehren.
Ebenso wie die Psychologie in ihren Anfangstagen ist Design eine Disziplin, die bislang nicht als wissenschaftlich relevant angesehen wird. Im Gegensatz zu seiner ›großen Schwester‹, der Architektur. Ich wünschte, ich könnte dem Design eine ähnliche Zukunft prophezeien, wie sie die Psychologie einst hatte, und dass es ebenfalls zu einer allgemein geachteten Wissenschaft werden wird. Vielleicht wird das nur eintreten, wenn so etwas wie die Stärke und Vision eines Freud allgemein Anerkennung erfährt.« ILKKA SUPPANEN

ILKKA SUPPANEN		CLIENTS
BORN	1968 Kotka, Finland	Artek
STUDIED	1988 Faculty of Architecture, Helsinki University of Technology	Cappellini
	1989 University of Art and Design, Helsinki	Castelli-Haworth
	1992 Gerrit Rietveld Academy, Amsterdam	Kinnasand
PRACTICE	1995 founded Studio Ilkka Suppanen	Luhta
	1995-2000 taught design at the University of Art and Design, Helsinki	Nokia Multimedia Terminals
	1996 co-founded the Snowcrash design co-operative	Proventus Design
	1998-99 research project in collaboration with Nokia Multimedia Terminals	Snowcrash
	2000- creative director of Snowcrash	Saab
AWARDS	1995 First Prize *Habitare* competition, Finland; winning entry, international *Textile for New Building* competition, Frankfurt/Main	also self-production
	1998 nominated for Dedalus Prize, Bra, Italy; Young Designer of the Year, Germany	
	2001 Young Designer of the Year, Finland	
EXHIBITIONS	1992 the Fifth International Exhibition of Architecture, Venice	
	1997 *Snowcrash*, Galleria Facsimile, Milan	
	1998 *Modern Finnish Design*, Bart Center, New York	
	1999 *New Scandinavian Design*, Stedelijk Museum, Amsterdam	
	2001 *Work Spheres*, Museum of Modern Art, New York	

5

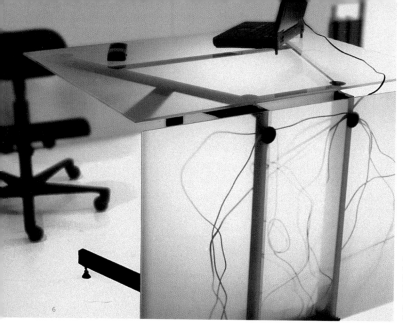

6

5. **Promotiva** office/Büro/bureau, Helsinki, 1997
6. **Luminet** office system/Büromöbel/système de bureau
for Luminet, 1996
7. Detail of **Airbag** chair/Sessel/siège for Snowcrash,
1997 – co-designed with Pasi Kolhonen
8. **Roll-light** floor lamp/Stehlampe/lampadaire for
Snowcrash, 1997

7

8

"The best products come from design thinking that is interwoven with your long-term business strategy."

Tangerine

Tangerine Product Direction and Design, 8, Baden Place, Crosby Row, London SE1 1YW, England
T +44 20 7357 0966 F +33 20 7357 0784 martin@tangerine.net www.tangerine.net

»Die besten Produkte entstehen aus einem gestalterischen Denken, das mit einer langfristigen Unternehmens-strategie verflochten ist.«

« Les meilleurs produits sont issus d'une pensée de design conjuguée à une stratégie commerciale à long terme. »

1. **Jasperware** experimental design/experimentelles Design/design expérimentel for Waterford Wedgwood, 1997

2. ↓ **Club World seat-bed**/Stuhl & Bett/fauteuil & lit for British Airways, 2000

"Really positive things are happening at the start of the 21st century in the areas of brand and multi-media design. Companies have begun to recognise that their brands are of tremendous value, expressing far more than just the identity of a company; in many cases even typifying the attitude and behaviour of the company. The surge of growth in the multi-media sector will connect customers to companies in rich and varied ways, enabling more diverse and extended forms of dialogue to take place.

The hope I have for the future (and we have encountered many examples of it recently) is that companies will wake up to the fact that the customer cannot be fooled for too long. The best products do not come from planning based on the benchmarking of competitors, or from widgets spun out of R&D departments. The best products come from observing people and learning about how they live, think, behave etc. Designers can then bring business ethos, brand values and product values together with core values from the life of the user, to define the spirit and substance of new and better products." TANGERINE

« En ce début de 21ᵉᵐᵉ siècle, il se passe des choses vraiment positives dans le domaine des marques et du design multimédia. Les compagnies commencent à comprendre que leur marque a une valeur immense, exprimant bien plus que l'identité d'une entreprise ; dans de nombreux cas, elle caractérise même l'attitude et le comportement de la compagnie. La croissance du secteur du multimédia connectera les consommateurs aux compagnies de manières riches et variées, permettant des formes de dialogue plus diverses et étendues. J'ai bon espoir qu'à l'avenir les compagnies prendront conscience que les consommateurs ne sont jamais dupes très longtemps (j'en ai rencontré de nombreux exemples récemment). Les meilleurs produits ne viennent pas de plannings basés sur la production des concurrents ni de gadgets pondus par les départements de recherche et développement. On conçoit les meilleurs produits en observant les gens et en apprenant comment ils vivent, pensent, se comportent, etc ... Les designers peuvent ensuite conjuguer leur philosophie, les marques et les produits avec les valeurs de base de l'utilisateur afin de définir l'esprit et la substance d'articles nouveaux et meilleurs. » TANGERINE

»Zu Beginn des 21. Jahrhunderts ereignen sich wirklich positive Dinge in den Bereichen Marken- und Multimedia-Design. Unternehmen erkennen, dass ihre Markenartikel von enormem Wert sind, da sie weit mehr als nur die Firmenidentität ausdrücken und in einigen Fällen sogar Einstellung und Verhalten des Unternehmens verkörpern. Der Wachstumsschub auf dem Multimedia-Sektor wird auf fruchtbare und vielfältige Weise Kunden mit Unternehmen in Verbindung bringen und damit mannigfaltigere und erweiterte Formen des Dialogs ermöglichen. Die Hoffnung, die ich für die Zukunft hege (und für die wir in letzter Zeit viele Beispiele erlebt haben), ist die, dass Firmen sich der Tatsache bewusst werden, dass man die Kunden nicht allzu lange für dumm verkaufen kann. Die besten Produkte entstehen nicht aus einer auf Wettbewerbsorientierung basierenden Planung oder aus irgendwelchen Spielereien, die sich die Forschungs- und Entwicklungsabteilungen ausgedacht haben. Die besten Produkte sind vielmehr darauf zurückzuführen, dass man die Menschen beobachtet und erfährt, wie sie leben, denken und handeln. Dann nämlich können die Designer Unternehmensethos, Marken- und Produktwerte mit den essentiellen Werten aus dem Leben des Benutzers kombinieren, um Geist und Gehalt neuer und besserer Produkte zu definieren.« TANGERINE

3. ← **Activ** walking frame (prototype)/Gehhilfe (Prototyp)/déambulateur (prototype), 1998 (co-designed with Benchmark modelmaking for Central St Martin's Design for Ability)
4.-6. **Oil candle** concepts/Entwürfe für Kerzenhalter/concepts de bougie à l'huile for Waterford Wedgwood, 1998

7. **Chaplet** e/web videophone/Internet-Videophone/
vidéophone électronique for Chaplet Information Systems,
1997

TANGERINE

FOUNDED	1989	London by Martin Darbyshire (b. 1961 Preston, Lancashire) and Clive Grinyer (who left Tangerine in 1993)
STUDIED		MARTIN DARBYSHIRE
	1983	BA (Hons) Product Design, Central St Martin's College of Art and Design, London
AWARDS	1987	Appliance Manufacturers USA Award
	1994	Shinanogawa Award, Technopolis, Japan
	1995 & 2001	Good Design Award, Chicago Athenaeum
	1995 & 2000	iF Design Award, Hanover
	1995	Presidents Award, Korea
	1997 & 2000	*I. D. Magazine Annual Design Review* Award, New York
	2000	D&AD Award Silver nomination, London; International CES Award
EXHIBITIONS	1990, 92, 94, 96, 97 & 98	The Design Museum, London
	1998	*High Definition*, British Council, Hong Kong
	1998	*Britain Online*, China
	1999	Glasgow Art Fair, Glasgow; *Creative Britain*, Stilwerk, Berlin
	2000	*Ideal Home* Exhibition, London; Expo 2000, Hanover

CLIENTS

Acco
Alcatel
Apple Computer
Bell Northern Research
British Airways
Cambridge Systems
DecaView
ElanVital
Fostex
GCS
Hitachi
Ideal Standard
LG Electronics
Maxon Cellular
Novamedix
Pace Micro Technology
Procter & Gamble
Samsung
Surgicraft
Unilever
Virgin Our Price
Waterford Wedgwood

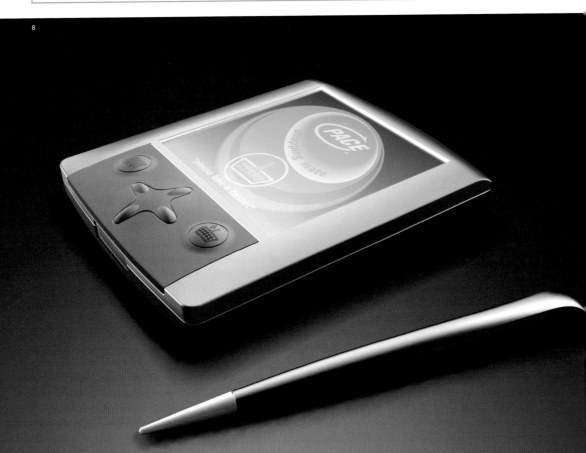

9

10

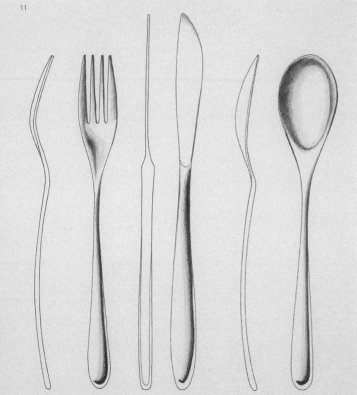

11

12

8. **Pace** home shopping tablet/Homeshopping-Schreib-
tafel/terminal de commandes à domicile for Pace Micro
Technology, 2000
9. **Blink** concept digital camera/Digitalkamera (Entwurf)/
appareil photo numérique (concept) for Shinanogawa
Technopolis, 1994
10. **Home facsimile** (concept)/Faxgerät (Entwurf)/
télécopieur (concept), 1990
11. **Cutlery** (design concept)/Besteck (Entwurf)/couverts
(concept) 1999
12. **GCS DECT** phone (concept)/Telefon (Entwurf)/
téléphone (concept) for Global Cellular Systems, 1997

"The Milan system is our power:
involved in fashion currents, design
and architecture, we are ready
every day to renew our creativity."

Matteo Thun

Mattheo Thun, Studio Thun, Via Appiani 9, 20 121 Milan, Italy
T +39 02 655 691 202   F +39 02 657 0646   info@matteothun.com   www.matteothun.com

*»Das Mailand-System ist unsere Macht:
Aktiv beteiligt an Modeströmungen, Design und Architektur sind wir jeden Tag
bereit, unsere Kreativität zu erneuern.«*

« Le système milanais fait notre force :
avec un pied dans les courants de la
mode, du design et de l'architecture,
nous sommes prêts chaque jour à
renouveler notre créativité. »

1. **A-Roma** bowls/Schalen/bols for Koziol, 1999
2. ↓ **Supersassi** sofa/Sofa/canapé for Rossi di Albizzate, 2000

»In meinem Zugang zu Design geht es um einfache Verfahren, einfache Materialien, schnelles Erkennen des Designobjekts, schnelle Fertigungstechnik und natürlich einen zügigen Gestaltungsprozess, der auf praktischen Erfahrungen in einer Vielzahl von Disziplinen beruht ..., sowie, last but not least, eine ästhetische und materielle Dauerhaftigkeit. Als ein in Mailand lebender Architekt arbeite ich – im Einklang mit den Traditionen unserer Lehrer – gleichzeitig in kleinen und in großen Dimensionen: ›Vom Löffel zur Stadt‹ (Ernesto Rogers, Charta von 1952, Athen). Ohne Interaktion und wechselseitige Befruchtung mit dem großen Maßstab kann es im kleinen Maßstab keine Fortschritte geben und natürlich umgekehrt ... Ich ziehe die Heterogenität der Homogenität vor, weil es nicht nur die eine ›beste Methode‹ gibt, mit der das beste Ergebnis zu erzielen ist.« MATTEO THUN

"My approach to design involves simple processes, simple materials, fast recognition of the designed object, a fast manufacturing process and naturally a fast design process, drawing on a multiplicity of disciplinary experiences ... and last but not least, aesthetic and material durability. As an architect living in Milan, I am engaged simultaneously – in line with the traditions of our teachers – with the small and large scale: 'From the spoon to the city' (Ernesto Rogers, Charter of 1952, Athens). Without interaction and cross-fertilization with the large scale, there can be no advance in the small scale, and of course vice versa ... I prefer heterogeneity to homogeneity because there is not only one discernible 'best way' to obtain the best results." MATTEO THUN

« Ma démarche consiste à utiliser des procédés simples, des matériaux simples, une reconnaissance rapide de l'objet de design, des processus de fabrication rapides ainsi que, naturellement, un processus de design rapide, puisant dans une multiplicité d'expériences disciplinaires ... et enfin, le plus important, une longévité esthétique et physique. En tant qu'architecte vivant à Milan, je travaille simultanément – conformément à la tradition de nos maîtres – sur la grande et la petite échelle : " de la cuillère à la cité " (Ernesto Rogers, Charte de 1952, Athènes). Sans interaction et hybridation avec la grande échelle, il ne peut y avoir de progrès de la petite échelle, et, bien sûr, vice versa ... Je préfère l'hétérogénéité à l'homogénéité car il n'existe pas qu'un seul " meilleur moyen " discernable d'obtenir les meilleurs résultats. » MATTEO THUN

3. **Balance** cutlery/Besteck/couverts for WMF, 1993
4. **Calore** cups/Tassen/tasses for Stil Lavazza, 1999
5. **Sphera** table lamp/Tischlampe/lampe for Leucos, 2000

"Never over-design a product. The form will be dictated by its function and the way it is made."

Arnout Visser

Arnout Visser, Alexanderstraat 31-33, 6812 BC Arnhem, The Netherlands
T +31 26 442 9046 F +31 26 351 4812 arnout.visser@planet.nl

»Man sollte ein Produkt niemals über-designen. Die Form eines Produkts wird von seiner Funktion und Produktions-methode diktiert.«

« Il ne faut jamais " sur-dessiner " un pro-duit. Sa forme doit être dictée par sa fonction et la façon dont il est conçu. »

1. **Archimedes** letterscale/Briefwaage/pèse-lettres
for DMD, 1990
2. ↓ **Glassdrop** floor tiles/Bodenfliesen/dalles pour le
sol for DMD, 1997 – co-designed with Erik Jan Kwakkel

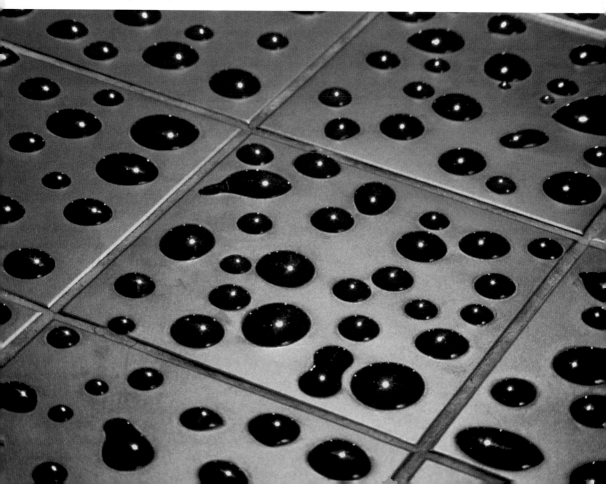

« A l'heure actuelle, la production de masse contrôle complètement le marché alors que nous (les consommateurs) cherchons des produits uniques. La beauté du produit à elle seule ne suffit pas, nous voulons connaître son histoire et voir les traces de sa fabrication manuelle plutôt que l'influence d'un "styliste". L'idéal serait que le designer regarde le produit par-dessus l'épaule du consommateur et lui fasse partager son enthousiasme sur la manière dont il fonctionne. Ce produit deviendrait alors un ami pour la vie. » ARNOUT VISSER

3. ← **Milk & Sugar containers/**Milch- und Zuckergefäße/ récipients de lait et sucre for DMD, 1998
4. **Optic Glass** decanter/Karaffe/carafe for DMD, 1998

"At the moment, mass production is completely in control of the market, while we (the consumers) are looking for one-of-a-kind products. A beautiful product alone is not enough, we like to hear the story and see the marks of craftsmanship and not the influence of a 'styling' designer. The ideal situation would be the designer looking over the shoulder of the consumer at the product and sharing his or her enthusiastic wonder about how it works. The product should be a life-long friend." ARNOUT VISSER

»Zur Zeit wird der Markt vollkommen von der Massenproduktion beherrscht, während wir – die Konsumenten – nach individuell gefertigten Produkten suchen. Ein schönes Produkt allein genügt nicht. Wir wollen seine Geschichte kennen und ihm die Spuren von Künstlertum und nicht von ›Styling‹ durch einen Designer ansehen. Im Idealfall würde der Designer über die Schulter des Konsumenten hinweg sein Produkt betrachten und sein oder ihr begeistertes Staunen über die Art und Weise teilen, wie es funktioniert. Das Produkt sollte ein lebenslanger Freund sein.« ARNOUT VISSER

ARNOUT VISSER

BORN	1962	Middelburg, The Netherlands
STUDIED	1984-89	degree in Design, Arnhem School of Art
	1990	MA Industrial Design, Domus Academy, Milan
PRACTICE	1983-	working as independent designer and collaborating with Droog Design
AWARDS	1998	co-winner (with Erik Jan Kwakkel and Peter van de Jagt), Public Design Prize, Rotterdam
EXHIBITIONS	1997	*Mutant Materials in Contemporary Design*, Groningen
	late 1990s-	present Droog Design exhibitions, Milan, Paris, New York
	2000	*Droog and Dutch Design*, Park Tower Hall Living Design Center, Tokyo

CLIENTS

Droog Design
Habitat
Poll's Potten
Provincie Gelderland local
government
Silvania Lighting

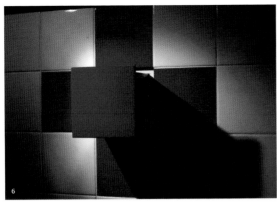

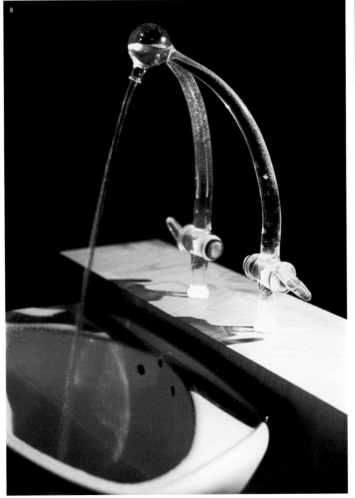

5. **Soft Toilet and bidet** project (prototype)/Toiletten- und Bidet-Projekt (Prototyp)/projet w.-c. et bidet (prototype), 2000 – co-designed with Erik Jan Kwakkel
6. **Red Cross** function tile (prototype)/Funktionsfliese (Prototyp)/carrelage (prototype) for DMD, 1997 – co-designed with Erik Jan Kwakkel and Peter van der Jagt
7. **Double walled tumblers**/zweiwandige Trinkbecher/ gobelet (self-production), 1997 – co-designed with Erik Jan Kwakkel
8. **Glass tap** (prototype)/Glashahn (Prototyp)/robinet en verre (prototype), 1997
9. **Microwave plates** (prototypes)/Teller für die Mikrowelle (Prototyp)/assiettes pour micro-ondes (prototypes) (self-production), 1997

"My role as a designer is to provoke change."

Jean-Pierre Vitrac

Jean-Pierre Vitrac, Vitrac (Pool) Design Consultance, 98, Rue de l'Ouest, 75014 Paris, France
T +33 1 40 44 09 50 F +33 1 40 44 7980 vitrac@design-pool.com www.design-pool.com

»Meine Rolle als Designer besteht darin, Veränderung zu provozieren.«

« Mon rôle de designer est de provoquer le changement. »

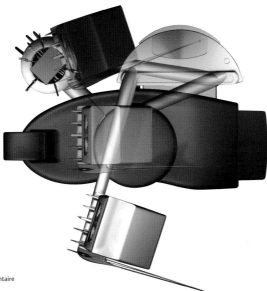

1. **Carisma** dental unit/Zahnarztstuhl/unit dentaire
for Fedesa, 1999
2. ↓ **Urban furniture**/Stadtmöbel (Haltestelle)/mobilier
urbain for Giraudy, 2000

« Le design a un avenir ! Oui, mais lequel ?
Ce qui est sûr, c'est que la création – la créativité – aura de plus en plus de place dans nos
sociétés. La tendance la plus forte de ces dernières années, c'est l'éclatement des genres.
La diversité des modes d'expression, la facilité
et une plus grande liberté de communication
favorisent l'accès, de la part des individus et
des entreprises, à une conscience nouvelle :
l'innovation, comme une composante normale
de toute entreprise (dans le sens d'entre-
prendre).
Peu importe que les motivations soient la
plupart du temps économiques. Peu importe
que l'on agisse dans des contextes de plus en
plus complexes – ce qui fait par ailleurs l'intérêt du métier de designer. La réalité est que
les besoins d'évolution amènent plus de ré-
flexion, plus de sens à nos productions. Beaucoup plus de gens se sentent concernés et
s'impliquent dans des démarches créatives.
Plutôt que d'être entraînés dans une sur-con-
sommation de produits identiques, je pense
que ce mouvement sera sélectif et générera,
dans l'avenir, plus de diversité, plus de qualité.
Et, en ce qui concerne le design, tout est
ouvert. » JEAN-PIERRE VITRAC

3. ← **Information meeting point**/Informationsstelle
und Treffpunkt/point d'information et de rencontre
for Arcomat Mobilier Urbain, 1999
4. **Venet-Sea** lagoon boat (project)/Faltboot (Projekt)/
bateau (projet) for Venice, 2000

"Design has a future! Yes, but what
kind? What is certain is that creativity is going to play an increasingly
important role in our societies. The
most obvious trend during the last
few years has been an increasing
break-up of the different genres or
disciplines. Increasing diversity of
expression as well as greater ease
and freedom of communication allow both individuals and enterprises
to attain a new kind of awareness:
innovation as a normal component
of any undertaking. It is not so important for the motivation to be
an economic one. Nor is it so important to be moving towards an
ever more complex context – which
is what makes the design profession
so interesting. The reality is that the
necessities of evolution bring more
reflection, more sense into our 'productions'. More and more people
are beginning to feel concerned
about design and are therefore entering into the creative process.
Instead of continuing the process
of simply consuming identical products, I think that there will be a
movement towards greater selectiv-
ity which will result in greater
diversity and better quality in the
future. And so far as design is concerned, everything is open."
JEAN-PIERRE VITRAC

»Design hat eine Zukunft! Ja, aber was für
eine? Sicher ist, dass die Kreativität in unseren
Gesellschaften eine zunehmend wichtige Rolle
spielen wird. Der eindeutigste Trend der letzten Jahre war ein beschleunigtes Aufbrechen
der unterschiedlichen Genres oder Disziplinen.
Wachsende Vielgestaltigkeit der Ausdrucksformen sowie größere Ungezwungenheit und
Freiheit der Kommunikation erlauben sowohl
Individuen als auch Unternehmen, zu einem
neuen Bewusstsein zu gelangen: Innovation
als normaler Bestandteil jeder Art von Unter-
nehmung. Dabei muss die Motivation nicht
unbedingt eine ökonomische sein. Und es ist
auch nicht so wichtig, dass wir uns auf einen
immer komplexer werdenden Kontext zu bewegen – was den Designberuf so interessant
macht. In der Realität bringen die evolutionären Notwendigkeiten mehr Reflexion und
mehr Sinn in unsere ›Produktionen‹ ein. Immer mehr Menschen fangen an, sich Gedanken über Design zu machen und treten folglich in den kreativen Prozess ein. Anstelle einer
Entwicklung, in der der Konsum identischer
Produkte einfach fortgesetzt wird, glaube ich,
dass es eine Bewegung hin zu einer strengeren
Auslese geben wird, die sich zukünftig in grö-
ßerer Vielfalt und besserer Qualität auswirken
wird. Und was das Design betrifft, so ist alles
offen.« JEAN-PIERRE VITRAC

		JEAN-PIERRE VITRAC	CLIENTS
BORN	1944	Bergerac, France	Alcatel
STUDIED	1967	graduated sculpture, Ecole des Arts Appliqués, Paris	Allibert
PRACTICE	1968	began designing packaging for Lancôme	Alpha Cubic
	1970	established product design office	ATT & Barphone
	1974	established Vitrac Design, Paris	Baby Relax
	1978-84	operated Vitrac & C., Milan	Bridgestone
	1983-93	operated Vitrac Japan-Pro Inter, Tokyo	Camping Gaz
	1991-95	partnership with Design Strategy and network with Minale Tattersfield (London) and Windy Winderlich (Hamburg)	Carrefour
			Daewoo Electronic
	1998	established Vitrac (Pool); established professional design network Design (Pool) in collaboration with Jeremy Morgan	Delsey
			Descamps
	2000	established Dézidés Production	Esselte Dymo
AWARDS	1984	Clio Award, USA	Honda
	1987	G-Mark/Good Design Award, JIDPO, Tokyo	JCDecaux
	1988	Prix du Nouvel Economiste, France	Kansai Yamamoto
	1993	Grand Prix National du Design, Ministry of Culture, France	Kerastase
	1997	Janus De l'Industrie Award, France	Kodak
	1998 & 2001	iF Design Award, Hanover	Kyocera
EXHIBITIONS	1989	*International Exposition of Universal Design*, Nagoya; solo exhibition, Seibu Yurakucho, Tokyo; solo exhibition, Galerie Binnen, Amsterdam	Lancôme
			Le Creuset
			Louis Vuitton
	1991	*Capitales Européennes du Nouveau Design*, Paris	Mobilier International
	1992	solo exhibition, Institut d'Arts Visuels, Orléans	National Panasonic
	1993	*Decorative Art and Design in France*, Cooper-Hewitt National Design Museum, New York; *Design, miroir du siècle*, Grand Palais, Paris	Philips
			Sabatier au Lion
	2000	*Pavilion of the 21st Century*, Expo 2000, Hanover	Shell Butagaz
			Sony
			Subaru

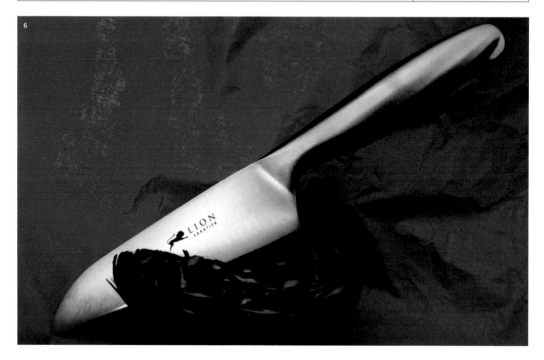

6

6. **Fuso** knife/Messer/couteau for 32 Dumas Sabatier au Lion, 1998
7. **Baby Move** child traveller/Kinderwagen/poussette de voyage for Marco Skates, 1999
8. **U.Bik** exterior lighting/Außenbeleuchtung/luminaire d'extérieur for Noral, 1999
9. **Flash Vote** everday democracy/tägliche Demokratie/démocratie permanente for Expo 2000
10. **Crossing Radio**/Radio/poste de radio for Arco Impex, 2001

7

8

9

10

"Continuity between tradition and
the present is important."

Pia Wallén

Pia Wallén AB, Nybrogatan 25, 11429 Stockholm, Sweden
T +46 8 665 3329 F +46 8 663 3801 info@piawallen.com

*»Die Kontinuität zwischen Tradition und
Gegenwart ist wichtig.«*

« La continuité entre la tradition et le
présent est importante. »

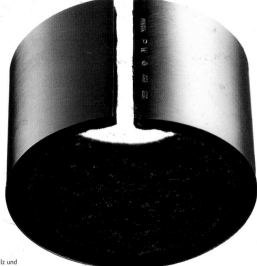

1. **Felt & silver sterling bracelet**/Armreif aus Filz und
Silber/bracelet en argent et feutre (self-production), 1998
2. ↓ **Crux blanket**/Decke/couverture for Element Design,
1991

»Ich arbeite im Hier und Jetzt. Materialien – deren Merkmale, Oberflächen, skulpturalen Eigenschaften sowie die Methoden ihrer Bearbeitung – wecken mein Interesse und dienen als Ansatzpunkt für meine Arbeit. Meine früheren Produkte spielen eine wichtige Rolle bei der Entwicklung neuer Designs. Ich bin bestrebt, das Maximum aus einzelnen Techniken herauszuholen und interessiere mich sehr für die konstruktionsspezifischen Aspekte von Design. Häufig braucht meine Arbeit Zeit, um zu ›reifen‹, und gelegentlich dauert es lange, bis ein neues Design ausgearbeitet ist. Das wechselseitige Spiel von Ideen ist sehr wichtig, damit ich sie zu einem fertigen Produkt ausbauen und dabei gleichzeitig für alle Möglichkeiten offen bleiben kann. Was die Werkstoffe betrifft, so mag ich besonders den Filz und habe mich seit 1983 intensiv mit den Techniken seiner Verarbeitung beschäftigt. Filz stellt die älteste Form textiler Materialien dar und hat eine faszinierende Geschichte. Jahrhunderte lang war Filz ein Überlebensmittel. In meiner Arbeit lasse ich diese alte Tradition wieder aufleben, um daraus etwas Neues zu schaffen. Aus globaler Perspektive gesehen ist es interessant, Design wieder mit nationalen Traditionen, Verwendungsarten, Klimaverhältnissen und Bedürfnissen zu verknüpfen. Es ist wichtig, dass wir auch weiterhin Materialien und Techniken aus unseren natürlichen Ressourcen entwickeln.« PIA WALLÉN

"I work in the here and now. Materials – their properties, texture, sculptural qualities and the methods of working them – awaken my interest and serve as a point of departure for my work. My earlier products play an important role in the development of new ones. I aim to get the most out of techniques and have a real interest in the constructional aspects of design. My work often needs time to 'ripen' and occasionally it takes a long time for a new design to be developed. The interplay of ideas is very important in order to develop them into a finished product, while at the same time remaining open to all possibilities. As far as materials are concerned, I am especially fond of felt and, since 1983, I have delved deeply into the techniques of working with it. It has a fascinating history and represents the oldest form of textile material. For centuries felt has been a material of survival. In my work I revive this old tradition so as to create something new. From a global perspective, it is interesting to link design once again to a national tradition, usage, climate and need. It is important to continue to develop materials and techniques from our natural sources." PIA WALLÉN

« Je travaille dans le " ici et maintenant ". Les matières – leurs propriétés, textures, qualités sculpturales et les techniques pour les travailler – éveillent mon intérêt et servent de point de départ à mon travail. Mes premiers produits jouent un rôle important dans le développement des nouveaux. Je cherche à tirer le meilleur profit des techniques et suis très intéressée par les aspects architecturaux du design. Mon travail a souvent besoin de " mûrir " et il faut parfois attendre longtemps avant qu'un nouveau design soit au point. L'interaction entre les idées est très importante afin de les faire déboucher sur un produit fini tout en restant ouvert à toutes les possibilités. Pour ce qui est des matériaux, j'affectionne particulièrement le feutre et, depuis 1983, me suis plongée dans différentes techniques pour le travailler. Il a une histoire fascinante et représente la plus ancienne forme de textile. Pendant des siècles, il a été une matière de survie. Dans mon travail, je ranime cette tradition ancienne de sorte à en faire quelque chose de nouveau. D'un point de vue mondial, il est intéressant de relier le design à une tradition, un usage, un climat et des besoins nationaux. Il est important de continuer à développer des matières et des techniques à partir de nos ressources naturelles. » PIA WALLÉN

3. **Felt bowl**/Filzschale/coupe en feutre (self-production), 1992
4. **Felt bag**/Filztasche/sac en feutre (self-production), 2000
5. **Hooded sweater**/Kapuzen-Pullover/pull-over à capuche (self-production), 1997
6. **Felt slippers**/Filzpantoffel/pantoufle en feutre for Cappellini Progetto/Ogetto, 1992

4

5

6

"We are here to create an environment of love, live with passion and make our most exciting dreams come true."

Marcel Wanders

Marcel Wanders, Jacob Catskade 35, 1052 BT Amsterdam, The Netherlands
T +31 20 422 1339 F +31 20 422 7519 marcel@marcelwanders.nl www.marcelwanders.com

»Wir sind hier, um eine Umgebung der Liebe zu schaffen, mit Leidenschaft zu leben und unsere aufregendsten Träume wahr werden zu lassen.«

« Nous sommes ici pour créer un environnement d'amour, vivre avec passion et concrétiser nos rêves les plus excitants. »

1. **VIP** chair/Sessel/fauteuil for Moooi, 2000
2. ↓ **Textile wall for a Lunch Lounge**/textile Wandinstallation für eine Kantine/mur en tissu pour salle de restaurant for Co van der Horst, 1999

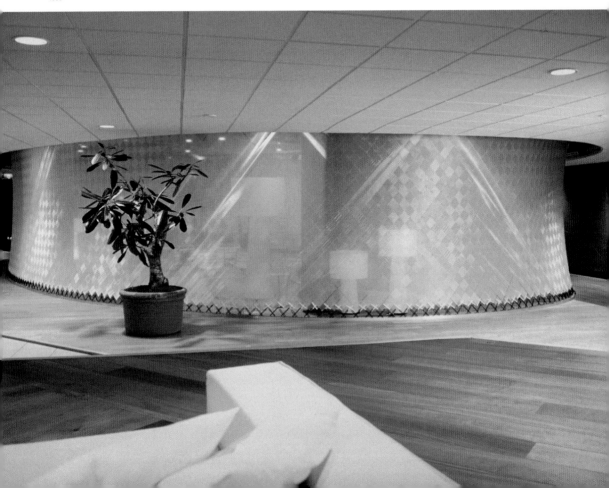

« Notre culture manque de respect pour le passé. Nous préférons le nouveau à l'ancien. Tout ce qui est récent est considéré comme meilleur. Les nouvelles d'hier n'ont plus rien de nouveau. Les produits doivent être lisses, tendus et sans défauts. Hélas, il semblerait que cette obsession du neuf et de la jeunesse soit encore plus répandue chez les designers (moi y compris). Je les soupçonne d'avoir encore moins de respect pour le vieux que mes autres, car créer du nouveau est leur métier. Nous souffrons de ce que j'ai appelé " la fixation sur la peau de bébé ".

L'espérance de vie des designs à peau de bébé est très brève. Cela en fait des amis provisoires sur lesquels les utilisateurs ne peuvent vraiment compter et qui ne feront jamais vraiment partie de leur vie. La fixation sur la peau de bébé est un problème dans un monde où l'on attache de l'importance à la durabilité d'un produit et à son lien unique avec l'utilisateur.

Comme j'aimerais que beaucoup de mes produits aient une relation à long terme avec leur utilisateur, j'utilise un mélange de métaphores nouvelles et anciennes dans les matières et les expressions matérielles que j'applique. En utilisant de vieilles métaphores dans mes produits, je communique un respect pour la vieillesse en général. Cela entraîne un vieillissement plus respectueux, plus acceptable et plus naturel de mes produits (ils vieillissent dignement). Ils ont la possibilité de gagner en qualité au cours de leur existence, ils sont plus durables et il est possible d'avoir avec eux une relation à long terme.

La longévité dans le domaine des idées, des relations, des objets, etc. permet non seulement de créer un monde où l'on gaspille moins, mais également des relations plus profondes et constructives avec notre environnement. » MARCEL WANDERS

"Our culture lacks respect for the old. We prefer the new to the old. New things are considered better, old news is no news. Products have to be smooth, taut and flawless. Sadly, it appears that this fixation on the new and the young is even stronger among designers than other people. I suspect that they (including myself) have even less respect than others for the old, as it is their profession to create new things. We suffer from what I call 'baby-face fixation'.

The life expectancy of baby-face designs is very short. This makes them temporary friends on which users cannot truly rely and which will never become a real part of their lives. Baby-face fixation is a problem in a world in which lasting quality and a unique bond between product and user is important. Since I would like many of my products to enter into a long-term relationship with the user, I use both old and new metaphors in the materials and material expressions that I apply. By using old metaphors in my products, I communicate a respect for old age in general. This leads to a more respectful, more acceptable and more natural ageing of my products (age with dignity). These products have the possibility of gaining quality during their life, they are more durable and it is possible to have a long-lasting relationship with them.

Durability in the field of ideas, relationships, objects, and so on, not only to create a world that is less wasteful but also to create deeper and more meaningful relationships with our environment." MARCEL WANDERS

»Unserer Kultur mangelt es an Respekt für das Alte. Wir ziehen das Neue dem Alten vor. Neue Dinge werden als höherwertig betrachtet, die Neuigkeiten von gestern sind keine Neuigkeiten. Produkte müssen glatt, sauber und fehlerfrei sein. Leider scheint diese Fixierung auf das Neue und Junge unter Designern noch stärker ausgeprägt zu sein als unter anderen Leuten. Ich habe den Verdacht, dass Designer – mich selbst eingeschlossen – das Alte so wenig achten, weil es ihr Beruf ist, neue Dinge hervorzubringen. Damit leiden wir unter etwas, was ich ›Babyface-Fixierung‹ nenne.

Die Lebenserwartung von ›Babyface-Design‹ ist sehr kurz. Das macht solche Objekte zu flüchtigen Bekannten, auf die sich die Benutzer nicht wirklich verlassen können, und die niemals zu einem realen Teil ihres Lebens werden. Die Babyface-Fixierung stellt ein Problem dar in einer Welt, in der dauerhafte Qualität und eine individuelle Bindung zwischen Produkt und Benutzer wichtig sind.

Da ich möchte, dass möglichst viele meiner Produkte eine langfristige Beziehung mit ihren Benutzern eingehen, verwende ich sowohl alte als auch neue Metaphern in meinen Materialien und Ausdrucksformen. Indem ich alte Metaphern in meine Produkte einbeziehe, vermittle ich meinen Respekt für das Alter im Allgemeinen. Das führt zu einer würdevolleren, angenehmeren und natürlicheren Alterung meiner Produkte – sie altern also in Würde. Diese Produkte haben die Möglichkeit, im Laufe ihres Lebens an Qualität zu gewinnen, sie sind dauerhafter, und man kann eine langfristige Beziehung mit ihnen haben. Dauerhaftigkeit auf dem Gebiet der Ideen, Beziehungen und Objekte ermöglicht nicht nur, eine weniger verschwenderische Welt zu schaffen, sondern auch eine tiefere und sinnvollere Beziehung zu unserer Umwelt.« MARCEL WANDERS

MARCEL WANDERS		CLIENTS
BORN	1963 Boxtel, The Netherlands	acme
STUDIED	1981-82 Academie voor Industriële Vormgeving, Eindhoven	Air UK
	1982-85 Academie voor Toegepaste kunsten, Maastricht	Boffi
	1983-85 Academie voor Schone kunsten, Hasselt, Belgium	British Airways
	1985-88 Hogeschool voor de Kunsten, Arnhem (1988 Cum Laude Certificate)	Cacharel
PRACTICE	1986 trained at Artifort	Cappellini
	1987 trained at BRS Premsela Vonk, Gijs Bakker, Amsterdam	Conran Shop
	1988-90 independent product designer	Droog Design
	1990-92 designer for Landmark Design & Consult b.v., Rotterdam	Floriade
	1992-95 partner of WAAC's Design & Consults, Rotterdam	Flos
	1995-2001 director of Wanders Wonders, Amsterdam	Habitat
	2001- director of Marcel Wanders Studio	KLM
AWARDS	1986 First Prize *Café Modern (Nescafé)*	Mandarina Duck
	1986 First Prize *Olympic Design 1992*	Magis
	1989 First Prize *Verzamelband*, Rotterdam	Randstad
	1996 Kho Liang Lee consolation prize	Rosenthal
	1997 winner of Rotterdam Design Award	Royal Leerdam
	1998 winner of *Woonbeurspin* Award; honorable mention for Compasso d'Oro, Milan	Salviati
	2000 Alterpoint Design Award, Milan	Swatch
EXHIBITIONS	1993 *Made in Holland*, Museum für Angewandte Kunst, Cologne	Virgin Atlantic Airlines
	1995 *Mentalitäten*, Securitas Gallery, Bremen & Design Center Stuttgart; *Droog Design*, Taideteolisuusmuseo, Helsinki; Centraal Museum, Utrecht; Stilwerk Design Center, Hamburg	WMF
	1995 & 97 *Mutant Materials in Contemporary Design*, Museum of Modern Art, New York and Groninger Museum, Groningen	also self-production
	1999 *Wanders Wonders – Design for a New Age*, Museum het Kruithuis, Den Bosch	
	2000 *Wanders Wanted*, Gallery Material Connection, New York; *Droog Design*, touring exhibition, USA	

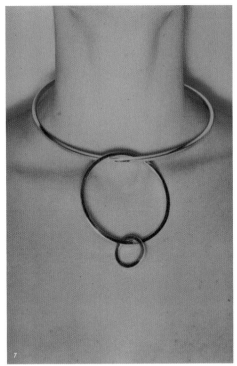

5. **Willow chair**/Korbsessel/fauteuil en osier for Oranien-baum, 1999
6. **Sponge vase**/Vase for Moooi, 1997
7. **Trinity necklace**/Kette/collier for Chi ha paura, 1998
8. **Henna table**/Tisch for Cappellini, 2000
9. **Nomad carpet**/Teppich/tapis for Cappellini, 1999

"My pieces are the essence of the time,
of abilities and of dreams."

Robert Wettstein

Robert Wettstein, Structure Design, Josefstrasse 188, 8005 Zürich, Switzerland
T +41 1 272 9725 F +41 1 272 0717 robert.wettstein@gmx.ch www.wettstein.ws

»Meine Arbeiten sind die Essenz von Zeit,
Fähigkeiten und Träumen.«

« Mes pièces sont l'essence du temps,
des facultés et des rêves. »

1. **Art. 003S** chair/Sessel/fauteuil for ctc, 2000
2. ↓ **Cement lamp** with mirrored bulb (prototype)/
Zementlampe mit verspiegelter Glühbirne/lampe en
ciment avec ampoule miroir (prototype), 1998

»Für mich liegt die Zukunft des Designs in einer Analyse der Konzepte zeitgenössischer Kunst. Die verblüffendste Kombination von Materialien ist möglich, wodurch sich ständig verändernde Wahrnehmungen und neue Arten des Begreifens von Materialien ergeben. Die Zukunft des Designs liegt in der Fähigkeit, die Zeiten widerzuspiegeln und die Grenzen des Vertrauten zu überschreiten. Design stellt die älteste Form der Abbildung gesellschaftlicher Konzepte und Einstellungen dar. Die Produkte der Zukunft werden die Bedeutung immaterieller Werte wie Ethik, Dienstleistung und geistige Haltung anerkennen. Das Design der Zukunft wird durch die Miniaturisierung der Technologie, den Verkaufspreis, die Interpretation von Kulturen und durch die Vergangenheit geprägt sein, denn die Zeit verleiht dem existierenden Design seine Wertschätzung. Design wird die Worte bilden, um ein Produkt zu beschreiben. Markenzeichen des Designs werden die Technologie und die Natur sein.«
ROBERT WETTSTEIN

"For me, the future of design lies in an analysis of concepts from contemporary art. The most surprising combination of materials is possible, providing ever-changing perceptions and new ways of understanding materials. The future of design lies in reflecting the times and in crossing the boundaries of the familiar. Design presents the earliest recognition of society's concepts and attitudes. The products of the future will acknowledge the importance of such non-material values as ethics, service and attitudes. The future of design lies in the miniaturization of technology, in the selling price, in the interpretation of cultures and in the past, for time gives esteem to existing designs. Design will become the words to describe a product. Technology and nature will be the hallmarks of design." ROBERT WETTSTEIN

« Pour moi, l'avenir du design repose sur une analyse des concepts de l'art contemporain. Les combinaisons de matériaux les plus surprenantes sont possibles, à condition que les perceptions changent constamment et qu'apparaissent de nouvelles manières de comprendre les matières. L'avenir du design réside dans notre capacité à refléter le temps et à franchir les frontières du connu. Le design représente la plus ancienne reconnaissance des concepts et des attitudes de la société. Les produits du futur reconnaîtront l'importance de valeurs non matérielles telles que l'éthique, le service et les attitudes. L'avenir du design dépend de la miniaturisation de la technologie, des prix de vente, de l'interprétation des cultures et du passé car, avec le temps, on accorde de l'estime aux designs existants. Le design deviendra les mots pour décrire un produit. La technologie et la nature seront les caractéristiques du design. »
ROBERT WETTSTEIN

3.-4. **Art. 002T.** club table/Tisch mit zweiseitig verwendbarer Platte/table de jeux for ctc, 1999
5. **Art. 001G** wardrobe/Garderobe/garde-robe for ctc, 1999
6. **Europalette** tray/Serviertablett/plateau for ctc, 2000
7. **Putzer** broom/Handfeger/balai for Die Imaginäre Manufaktur (DIM), 1998

	ROBERT WETTSTEIN		CLIENTS
BORN	1960	Zurich, Switzerland	Anthologie Quartett
STUDIED		self-taught (trained in orthopaedic technology)	Authentics
PRACTICE	1985	established own office and workshop	ctc (change.to/comfort)
	1986	established Structure Design	Die Imaginäre Manufaktur
AWARDS	1992	Design Plus Award, Frankfurt/Main	(DIM)
	1993	honourable mention, Design-Preis Schweiz, Switzerland	Noto/Zeus
	2000	honourable mention, Design for Europe Award, Interieur Biennial, Kortrijk	also self-production
EXHIBITIONS	1986	*Wohnen von Sinnen*, Kunstmuseum, Düsseldorf	
	1990	*Geordnete Arbeiten*, Galerie Hiltrud Jordan, Cologne; *Oggetti Inattesi*, Studio Scalise, Naples	
	1991	*Mehrwerte Schweiz und Design der 80iger*, Museum für Gestaltung, Zurich	
	1992	*Kreaturen*, Galerie Papenheim, Zurich	
	1993	*The Minimal Animal Interior*, Galerie Dilmos, Milan; *Design-Preis Schweiz*, Kunstmuseum, Solothurn	
	1994	*Polstermöbel und Schaukelleuchten*, Preussisch Oldendorf, Germany	
	1996	*Design im Wandel*, Übersee-Museum, Bremen	
	1997	*Dea Design Europeo Anteprima*, Milan	
	1999	*Black Schwarz*, Musée des Arts Decoratifs, Lausanne	
	2000	*Europalette*, Swiss Center, Milan	

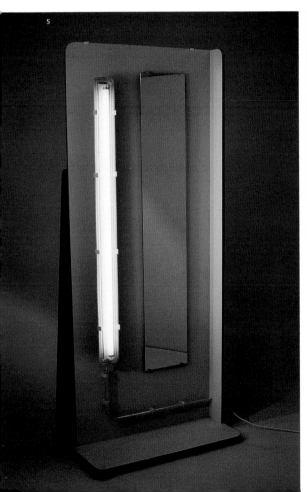

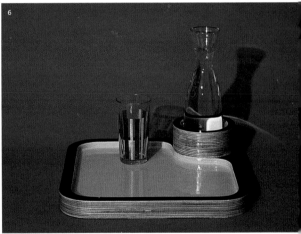

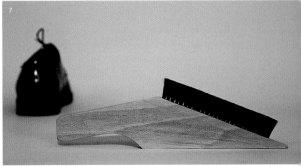

"All my designs are essentially paintings about colour, shape and space."

Helen Yardley

Helen Yardley, A-Z Studios, 3-5, Hardwidge Street, London SE1 3SY, England
T +44 20 7403 7114 F +44 20 7403 8906

»Alle meine Designs sind im Wesent-
lichen Gemälde über das Thema Farbe,
Form und Raum.«

« Toutes mes créations sont essentiellement des peintures sur la couleur, la
forme et l'espace. »

1. **Arc Nero** rug/Teppich/tapis for
Toulemond Bochart, 1998

»Alle meine Designs sind im Wesentlichen Gemälde über das Thema Farbe, Form und Raum. Es kommt vor, dass sich ein bestimmter Malstil leichter in eine Stickerei oder einen Druck übertragen lässt, aber immer kommt die ›Malerei‹ zuerst. Mit meinen Bildern, Teppichen und Wandbehängen strebe ich an, ein Objekt mit einer visuellen Wirkung zu schaffen, das aber gleichzeitig auch eine vielschichtige Bedeutung enthält. Für mich muss es im Design etwas Dauerhafteres geben als reine Dekoration.

Teppiche sind zweidimensional. In vielerlei Hinsicht kann man sie als Zeichnungen für den Boden sehen. Man muss sie jedoch von jedem Blickwinkel aus betrachten, um ein Unten und ein Oben zu vermeiden. Das macht die Gestaltung von Dynamik innerhalb der vorgegebenen Parameter zu einer größeren Herausforderung, als wenn man etwas für die Wand entwirft.

Wenn ich meine Arbeit in ihrer Gesamtheit analysiere, dann lässt sie sich in drei Kategorien aufgliedern: Die erste Gruppe von Entwürfen ist das Resultat einer direkten visuellen Stimulation – ich sehe etwas, das mir eine zündende Idee eingibt. Der zweite Zugang ist weniger unmittelbar, und ich würde ihn als sensualistisch beschreiben. Dieser Prozess beginnt mit einer Idee, die ausschließlich auf Farbe und der Wahrnehmung eines ›Gefühls‹ basiert. Die dritte Gruppe von Entwürfen entsteht aus meiner Reaktion auf die äußere, räumliche Umgebung des Objekts, wie es häufig bei Auftragsarbeiten der Fall ist. Diese Kategorisierung ist jedoch rein theoretisch. Wirklich wichtig ist für mich, etwas herzustellen, das gut aussieht, gleichzeitig aber auch eine Funktion erfüllt.« HELEN YARDLEY

"All my designs are essentially paintings about colour, shape and space. A certain style of painting may more readily be translated into a needlepoint or a printed piece but the 'painting' always comes first. What I aim for with these paintings/rugs/wall-hangings is to make something that works visually but also carries layers of meaning. There must be something rather more lasting than pure decoration.

Rugs are two-dimensional. In many ways they are like drawings for floors but one does need to consider them from every angle, so as to avoid an up and a down. This makes creating a dynamic within the parameters rather more of a challenge than when one is designing for the wall.

When I analyse the work as a whole it seems to break down into three categories. The first group of designs are the result of direct visual stimulation – I literally see something that sparks me off. The second route is less direct and is what I would describe as sensational. This process starts with an idea based purely in colour and the notion of a 'feeling'. The third group of designs come about as a response to the physical space, as is often the case with commissioned work. These delineations are purely theoretical. What is really important to me is to make something that looks good but also performs a function."

HELEN YARDLEY

« Toutes mes créations sont essentiellement des peintures sur la couleur, la forme et l'espace. Il arrive qu'un certain style de peinture soit plus facilement transposable au point de croix ou sur un imprimé, mais la "peinture" vient toujours en premier. Mon objectif, par ces tableaux / tapis / tapisseries, est d'aboutir à une création qui fonctionne visuellement tout en portant différents niveaux de sens. Elle doit offrir quelque chose de plus durable que le simplement décoratif. Les tapis sont bidimensionnels. A de nombreux égards, ils sont comme des dessins pour le sol sauf qu'on doit pouvoir les regarder sous tous les angles, ce qui évite d'avoir un haut et un bas. En ce sens, créer une dynamique au sein de paramètres établis est plus excitant que de dessiner simplement pour les murs.

Lorsque j'analyse mon travail dans son ensemble, il semble se diviser en trois catégories. La première est le résultat d'une stimulation visuelle directe, je vois littéralement quelque chose qui m'inspire. La seconde est moins directe et repose davantage sur les sens. Ce processus démarre sur une idée basée uniquement sur la couleur et la notion d'une "émotion". La troisième catégorie est le fruit d'une réaction à un espace physique, comme c'est souvent le cas avec les commandes. Ces classifications sont purement théoriques. Ce qui compte réellement pour moi, c'est de créer un objet qui soit beau tout en servant à quelque chose. » HELEN YARDLEY

2. **Spice No. 2** rug (drawing)/Teppich (Zeichnung)/tapis (dessin) (one-off), 1999
3. **Roma** rug/Teppich/tapis for Toulemond Bochart, 1998
4. **Pampas** rug/Teppich/tapis (one-off), 1999
5. **Cafe** rug/Teppich/tapis (one-off), 1999

HELEN YARDLEY

BORN	1954	Plymouth, England
STUDIED	1972-73	Plymouth College of Art (Foundation Studies)
	1973-76	BA Hons (1st Class) Printed & Woven Textiles, Manchester Polytechnic
	1976-78	MA Textiles, Royal College of Art, London
EXHIBITIONS	1985	*Wall Hung Textiles*, British Crafts Centre, London
	1987	*New Spirit in Craft and Design*, Crafts Council, London
	1990	*Great British Design*, Tokyo
	1993	*Visions of Craft*, Crafts Council, London
	1995	*Out of This World*, Crafts Council, London
	1998	Cambridge Contemporary Art, Cambridge

CLIENTS

Arthur Andersen
British Airways
British Rail
British Telecom
Cathay Pacific
Coca-Cola
Harrods
Lewis Moberley
Sony
Thames Television
Toulemond Borchart
Walt Disney

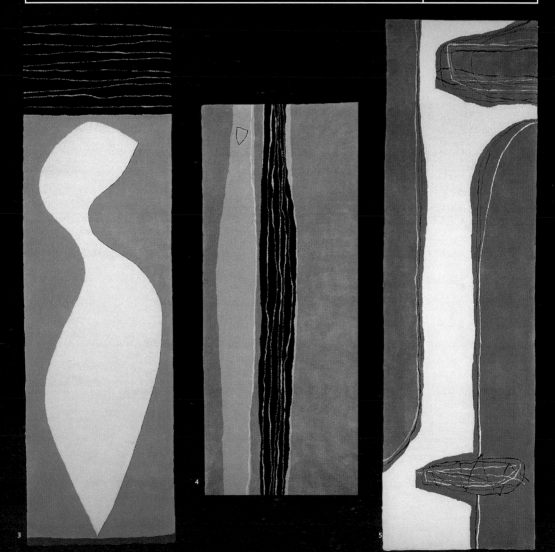

3

4

5

"I'm just looking at new yet rational
ways of realizing objects."

Michael Young

Michael Young, MY Studio, PO Box 498, 121 Reykjavik, Iceland
T +354 561 2327 F +354 561 2315 michaelyoung@simnet.is www.michael-young.com

*»Ich halte einfach nur Ausschau nach
neuen und dennoch rationalen Möglichkeiten, Objekte zu realisieren.«*

« Je cherche simplement des manières
nouvelles mais néanmoins rationnelles
de réaliser des objets. »

1. **MY 083** table/Tisch for Magis, 2001
2. ↓ **Armed chair**/Sessel/fauteuil for Cappellini, 1999

« A l'heure actuelle, les objets de designers ne constituent qu'un infime pourcentage du marché mondial. La majorité des produits sont des copies fabriquées en termes réels. La technologie d'aujourd'hui signifie qu'un objet conçu par un designer peut être copié par les concurrents travaillant sur le marché de masse en moins d'un an. A l'avenir, protéger une idée ou une innovation dans les techniques de fabrication devrait être de première importance, surtout dans la mesure où les programmes informatiques pourront bientôt "morpher" de manière aléatoire des objets d'une beauté surprenante sans l'aide de designers, tout en fournissant toutes les indications nécessaires à leur production. Sur le plan positif, le design se retrouvera ainsi dans une situation où l'aspect humain se situera dans l'innovation plutôt que dans le style. »
MICHAEL YOUNG

3. ← **Sticklight**/Stableuchte/luminaire for Eurolounge, 1999
4. **MY 082** table/Tisch for Magis, 2001
5. **MY 080** bedtray/Tablett für das Bett/plateau petit-déjeuner for Magis, 2001
6. **Magis Pens**/Stifte/crayons for Magis, 2001

"Currently, 'designed' objects challenge only a tiny percentage of the world market. The majority of products are in real terms engineered copies. Present-day technology means that a designed product may be copied by mass-market competitors in less than one year. Protecting an innovation in either manufacturing technique or idea would seem to be of utmost importance to design in the future. Especially so when computer programmes will soon be able to morph surprisingly beautiful objects at random without designers and provide all the necessary production data as well. On a positive note, this would leave design in a position where innovation will become the human aspect rather than style." MICHAEL YOUNG

»Gegenwärtig beanspruchen ›designte‹ Objekte nur einen winzigen Prozentsatz des Weltmarkts. Bei der Mehrzahl der Produkte handelt es sich genau genommen um maschinell gefertigte Kopien. Die moderne Technologie bedeutet, dass ein Designprodukt von der Konkurrenz des Massenmarkts in weniger als einem Jahr kopiert werden kann. Für das Design der Zukunft scheint der Schutz einer Innovation, entweder im fertigungstechnischen oder im ideellen Bereich, von äußerster Wichtigkeit zu sein. Besonders dann, wenn Computerprogramme bald imstande sein werden, verblüffend schöne Objekte aufs Geratewohl und ohne Beteiligung von Designern ›morphogenetisch‹ herzustellen und außerdem alle erforderlichen Produktionsdaten zu liefern. Das Positive an dieser Entwicklung könnte sein, dass sie dem Design eine Position überlässt, in der Innovation mehr den menschlichen Aspekt als den Stil betrifft.«
MICHAEL YOUNG

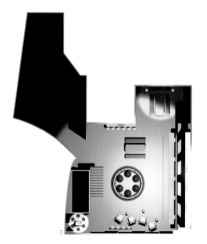

7.-14. **Astro Bar** nightclub (interiors), Reykjavik/Nachtclub (Innenansichten)/night-club (intérieurs), Reykjavik, 2000

MICHAEL YOUNG			CLIENTS
BORN	1966	Sunderland, England	Cappellini
STUDIED	1988-89	Art Foundation Course, Sunderland Polytechnic	E&Y
	1989-92	BA (Hons) Furniture and Product Design, Kingston University, London	Eurolounge
PRACTICE	1990-94	worked in Tom Dixon's studio, Space	Idée
	1994	established MY 022 design studio in London (also in Reykjavik)	Laurent Perrier
AWARDS	1995	Winner of Talente '95 design competition, Munich	Magis
EXHIBITIONS	1994	solo exhibition, Galerie Gladys Mougin, Paris; group shows in Paris, London, Tokyo and Hong Kong	Sawaya & Moroni
			MY O22
	1995	E&Y co., solo exhibition, Tokyo	Rosenthal
	1996	Salon du Meuble, Paris; E&Y/MY 022 presentation, Paris, Kyoto	S. M. A. K. Iceland
	1997	Salon du Meuble, Paris; Internos, Milan; Synapse, Fukuoka	
	1998	Oikos, Athens; Totem, New York, group shows in London, Cologne, Milan	
	1999	Jasper Morrison, Marc Newson, Michael Young, Reykjavik Art Museum	
	2000	designed and co-curated Design in Iceland, Reykjavik Art Museum	

15

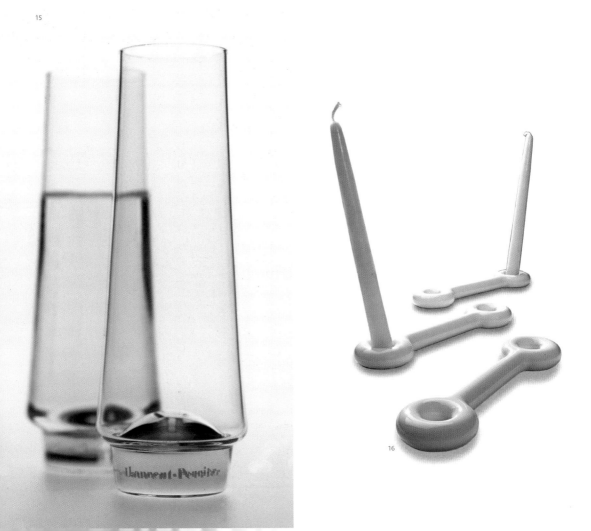

16

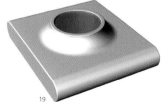

15. **Champagne glass**/Sektglas/flûte à champagne
for Laurent Perrier, 1999
16. **Candlestick**/Kerzenhalter/bougeoir for Sawaya &
Moroni, 1999
17. **Slit** chairs/Sessel/sièges for Sawaya & Moroni, 1999
18. **Wood table**/Holztisch/table en bois for Sawaya &
Moroni, 1999
19. **MY 086** light/Leuchte/luminaire for Idée, 2000
20. **MY 068** chairs/Stühle/chaises for Sawaya & Moroni,
1998

We are immensely grateful to those designers, design groups, photographers and manufacturers who have allowed us to reproduce images from their archives. The publisher has endeavoured to respect the rights of third parties and if any rights have been overlooked in individual cases, the mistake will be correspondingly amended where possible.

L = left/links/à gauche
R = right/rechts/à droite
T = top/oben/ci-dessus
C = centre/Mitte
B = bottom/unten/ci-dessous

3 Azumi, photo: Kumi Saito
10 Dumoffice, photo: Matthijs van Roon
12 T Emmanuel Dietrich
12 B Sam Hecht
13 Philippe Starck, photo: Studio Bleu – Michel Lelièvre for GOOD GOODS/La Redoute
15 Japan Airlines, photo: Lee Funnell for *Domus* magazine
17 Alberto Meda, photo: Vitra
19 Ford Motor Company
20 Dahlström Design
21 Sydney 612, photo: Jamie Gray
22-23 Büro für Form, photo: David Steets
24 Studio Aisslinger, photo: Steffen Jänicke
25 T Studio Aisslinger
25 B Studio Aisslinger, photo: Steffen Jänicke
26-27 Studio Aisslinger, photo: Steffen Jänicke
28 T L & T R Zanotta, photos: Adriano Brusaferri
28 B Studio Aisslinger, photo: Philip Radowitz
29 T R Studio Aisslinger
29 C & B Studio Aisslinger, photos: Steffen Jänicke
30-31 Studio Aisslinger, photos: Steffen Jänicke
32 Ron Arad Associates, photo: Perry Hagopian
33 T Ron Arad Associates, photo: Guido Pedron
33 B Ron Arad Associates, photo: Wilhelm Moser
34 Ron Arad Associates, photo: Wilhelm Moser
35-37 Ron Arad Associates
38-39 Moroso, photos: A. Paderni
40 Azumi, photo: Julian Hawkins
41 T Azumi, photo: Michael Tesmann
41 B Azumi, photo: Julian Hawkins
42 Azumi, photo: Brühl&Sippold
43 Azumi, photos: Julian Hawkins
44 T L Azumi, photo: Hiroyuki Hirai
44 T R Azumi, photo: Thomas Dobbie
44 B L Azumi, photo: Shin Azumi
44 B R Azumi
45 T Azumi, photo: Thomas Dobbie
45 B L Azumi, photo: Julian Hawkins
45 B R Azumi
46 Azumi, photo: Julian Hawkins
47 T L & T R Azumi, photos: Studio Synthesis
47 B L Azumi, photo: Julian Hawkins
47 B R Azumi, photo: Lapalma
48 Bartoli Design
49 T Bartoli Design – Di Palma
49 B Bartoli Design, photo: Segis

50-51 Bartoli Design, photos: Snr. Mascheroni/Obiettivo F
52 Bartoli Design, photo: Deltacalor
53 B R Bartoli Design, photo: Studio Uno
53 B L Bartoli Design – Di Palma
54-57 Jonas Bohlin Design
58-63 Ronan & Erwan Bouroullec, photos: M. Legall
64 Büro für Form
65 T Büro für Form, photo: Bjarne Geiges
65 B Büro für Form, photo: David Steets
66 Büro für Form, photo: David Steets
67 L Büro für Form, photo: Daniel Mayer
67 T R Büro für Form, photo: Bjarne Geiges
67 B R Büro für Form, photo: David Steets
68 Antonio Citterio, photo: Gitty Darugar
69 T Antonio Citterio, photo: Hackman
69 B Antonio Citterio, photo: B&B Italia – Fabrizio Bergamo
70 Antonio Citterio, photos: B&B Italia
71 Antonio Citterio, photo: Flos
72 Antonio Citterio, photos: B&B Italia
73 L Antonio Citterio, photo: Flos
73 R Antonio Citterio, photo: Hackman
74-79 Dyson
80-85 Elephant Design
86 Naoto Fukasawa, photo: IDEO-Japan
87-91 IDEO-Japan
92 Giovannoni Design
93 T Giovannoni Design, photo: Alessi
93 B Giovannoni Design, photo: Segno
94 Giovannoni Design, photo: Alessi
95 B L Alessi
95 C Giovannoni Design, photo: Magis
95 T R Giovannoni Design, photo: Alessi
96 Giovannoni Design, photo: Magis
97 Giovannoni Design, photo: Alba-Seiko
98 L Giovannoni Design, photo: Alba-Seiko
98 R Giovannoni Design, photo: Alessi
99 Giovannoni Design, photos: Alessi
100-105 IDEO-Europe
106 Hollington Associates
107 T Hollington Associates, photo: © Hollington
107 B Hollington Associates, photo: © Eastman Kodak Co, Rochester, NY, USA
108-109 Hollington Associates, photos: © Hollington
110-112 Inflate, photos: Jason Tozer
113 Inflate
114 Inflate, photo: Jason Tozer
115 T L Inflate, photo: Jason Tozer
115 T R & B Inflate
116 Iosa Ghini Srl
117 T Iosa Ghini Srl, photo: Bonaldo
117 B Iosa Ghini Srl, photo: Roche Bobois
118 Iosa Ghini Srl, photo: Bonaldo
119 T L Iosa Ghini Srl, photo: Dornbracht
119 T R Iosa Ghini Srl, photo: Bonaldo
119 B L Iosa Ghini Srl, photo: Massin Tuttoespresso
119 B C & B R Iosa Ghini Srl, photos: Bonaldo
120-122 James Irvine
123 James Irvine, photo: Magis
124-125 Arabia

126 T L James Irvine, photo: BRF
126 B L James Irvine, photo: Cappellini
126 R James Irvine, photo: BRF
127 T James Irvine, photo: CBI
127 B James Irvine, photo: B&B Italia
128 Apple Computer, photo: Catherine Ledman
129-133 Apple Computer
134-137 Jam, photos: Jason Tozer
135 B Jam, photo: Paul Musso
138-139 Jam
140-141 Jam, photos: Jason Tozer
142-145 Hella Jongerius
146-149 Ouzak Design Formation
150-153 Tom Kirk
154 Iittala
155 T Hackman
155 B Iittala, photo: Marco Melander
156 Harri Koskinen, photo: Teret Tolvanen Oy
157 Harri Koskinen, photo: Marva Helander
158 T Arabia
158 B L & B R Iittala
160-161 Iittala
162-165 Isabelle Leijn
166 Lissoni Associati
167 Lissoni Associati, photos: Living Divani
168-169 Lissoni Associati, photos: Porro
170-171 Ross Lovegrove/Studio X, photos: John Ross
172 Ross Lovegrove/Studio X
173 Ross Lovegrove/Studio X, photos: John Ross
174 T Ross Lovegrove, photo: John Ross
174 B Japan Airlines, photo: Lee Funnell for *Domus* magazine
175-177 Ross Lovegrove/Studio X, photo: John Ross
178-183 Lunar Design
184-187 Sharon Marston
188-191 Ingo Maurer GmbH
192 Alberto Meda
193 T Alberto Meda, photo: Alias
193 B Alberto Meda, photo: Luceplan
194 Alberto Meda, photo: Vitra
195 Alberto Meda
196 Alberto Meda, photo: Alias
197 L Alberto Meda, photo: Kartell
197 R Alberto Meda, photo: Ramak Fazel
198 Office for Design, photo: Emily Anderson
199-205 Office for Design
206 Pascal Mourgue
207 Pascal Mourgue, photos: Cinna-Ligne Roset
208 Pascal Mourgue, photo: Artelano
209 L Pascal Mourgue, photo: Fermob
209 T R & B R Pascal Mourgue, photos: Cinna-Ligne Roset
210 Marc Newson, photo: Karin Catt
211-215 Marc Newson
216-217 Ford Motor Company
218-219 Marc Newson
220 Vent Design, photo: Rick English Pictures
221-223 Vent Design
224 Jorge Pensi
225 T Jorge Pensi
225 B IDPA, Perobell